An Altitude SuperGuide

Southern Gulf Islands

An Altitude SuperGuide

Southern Gulf Islands

OF BRITISH COLUMBIA

●

by David and Andrea Spalding, Georgina Montgomery and Lawrence Pitt

●

Altitude Publishing Canada Ltd.
Canadian Rockies/Vancouver

Publication Information

Altitude Publishing Canada Ltd.
1500 Railway Avenue, PO Box 1410
Canmore, Alberta T0L 0M0

Copyright 1995 © Altitude
Text Copyright 1995 © David and Andrea Spalding,
Georgina Montgomery and Lawrence Pitt

Extreme care has been taken to ensure that all information presented in this book is accurate and up-to-date,
and neither the author nor the publisher can be held responsible for any errors.

Canadian Cataloguing in Publication Data
Montgomery, Georgina
 Gulf Islands superguide

(SuperGuide)
ISBN 1-55153-067-8

1. Gulf Islands (B.C.)--Guidebooks. I. Spalding,
Andrea. II. Spalding, David A.E., 1937- III. Title.
IV. Series.
FC3845.G8A3 1995   917.11'2
C94-910965-7   F1089.G8M66 1995

Made in Western Canada
Printed and bound in Canada
by Friesen Printers, Altona, Manitoba.

Altitude GreenTree Program
Altitude Publishing will plant in Western Canada twice as
many trees as were used in the manufacturing of this
product.

Front cover photo:
   Thetis Island
Inset front cover:
   Karon Wallace
Frontispiece:
   Old Orchard Farm, Pender Island
Back cover photo top:
   Pender Island sailboat race
Back cover photo bottom:
   Pacific killer whale

Project Development

Concept/Art Direction	Stephen Hutchings
Design	Stephen Hutchings
Editing/Proofreading	Georgina Montgomery
Index/Proofreading	Noeline Bridge
Maps	Catherine Burgess
Scanning	Debra Symes
Electronic Page Layout	Sandra Davis
	Nancy Green
Financial Management	Laurie Smith

A Note from the Publisher
The world described in Altitude SuperGuides is a
unique and fascinating place. It is a world filled with
surprise and discovery, beauty and enjoyment, questions and answers. It is a world of people, cities, landscape, animals and wilderness as seen through the eyes
of those who live in, work with, and care for this world.
The process of describing this world is also a means of
defining ourselves.

It is also a world of relationship, where people de-
rive their meaning from a deep and abiding contact
with the land – as well as from each other. And it is this
sense of relationship that guides all of us at Altitude to
ensure that these places continue to survive and evolve
in the decades ahead.

Altitude SuperGuides include *Altitude CityGuides*
and *Altitude NatureBooks.* They are books intended to
be used, as much as read. Like the world they describe,
Altitude SuperGuides are evolving, adapting and growing. Please write to us with your comments and obser-
vations, and we will do our best to incorporate your
ideas into future editions of these books.

Stephen Hutchings
Publisher

Contents

1. Introduction	6
How to Use the SuperGuide	11
2. The Wild Islands	13
3. Time and the Islands	26
4. Life of the Islands	32
5. Calendar of Events	40
6. Galiano	43
7. Mayne	58
8. Saturna	73
9. Pender	81
10. Salt Spring	99
11. Thetis	121
12. Gabriola	129
13. Other Islands	143
Reference	152
Recommended Reading	152
Index	157
Photographic Credits	160
Acknowledgements	160
About the Authors	160

The **Southern Gulf Islands SuperGuide** is organized according to the following colour scheme:

Information and introductory sections.........

Galiano ....

Mayne ....

Saturna ....

Pender ....

Salt Spring ....

Thetis ....

Gabriola ....

Other Islands ....

1. Introduction

Trees, rocks and water—Pilkey Point, Thetis Island

The Robinson Crusoe in all of us makes our hearts beat faster at the thought of an island—a bite-sized chunk of the world which we can discover for ourselves. Who then can resist a whole bunch of islands? What's more, these have Canada's best climate, beaches where seals and otters splash in the shallows, and forests where eagles and ravens soar. British Columbia's southern Gulf Islands are rapidly growing in popularity both as a tourist destination and a place to live. When you add in the (relatively) efficient ferry service, a crime rate so negligible that some people never lock their doors, and the absence of any dangerous animals bigger than a wasp, it's hard to imagine why the entire population of Canada doesn't move in. It's perhaps fortunate for all of us that there aren't enough jobs or houses to go round.

The southern Gulf Islands are nestled in the rain shadow of southern Vancouver Island, have more sunshine and frost-free days than almost anywhere else in Canada, and receive most of their precipitation in the form of rain during the winter months. There are around 200 islands—locals say the number depends on the state of the tide—of which eight larger ones are served by a regular ferry service. One of these, Kuper, is predominantly an Indian Reserve and is not open to the uninvited public. Of the smaller islands, three are currently accessible by scheduled water taxi, and the others by private boat.

The attractive features of the southern Gulf Islands are continued in the more isolated northern Gulf Islands, and in Washington State's San Juan Islands (often in sight to the south). For this guide, we define the southern islands as the archipelago that stretches from Gabriola, south as far as D'Arcy. Galiano, Mayne and Saturna—the three most distant from Vancouver Island—are sometimes referred to as the Outer Gulf Islands.

Landscapes in Miniature

Islands are by definition surrounded by water—in our case

Sailing soon?

ture." They explore on foot, by cycle or car, kayak or yacht; or they just hang out on a beach or at a quiet cottage. They find each island a landscape in miniature, combining many of the most attractive features of British Columbia within a small space, from rocky shores to the summits of small mountains. On rocks and beaches, farms and villages, the islands preserve remnants of a fascinating prehistory and history. They provide opportunities for visitors to play golf and other outdoor games, visit studios of potters and painters, and encounter music, drama and writing of quality at festivals and other events.

Many visitors return to the islands repeatedly, and some are tempted to move their place of work to a cottage on one of the islands, or retire to a condo in urban Ganges. In such ways the writers of this guide came to live on the islands, and we hope that being on the spot has helped us to share some of our enthusiasm.

Even with the lightest hand, visitors and residents alike cannot help affecting the islands. The more popular places are already being loved to death. In interpreting the islands through this book, we have tried to encourage an appreciation of the true character of the islands and to suggest ways in which all of us can lighten our impact on them. The beauty loved by all islanders and visitors is vulnerable and must be protected. Like modern Robinson Crusoes, let us enjoy our discoveries with a necessary minimum of shelter and support, for unlike the original hero, we can

a complex of relatively narrow channels and the wider (and sometimes rougher) Strait of Georgia. The "Gulf" Islands are named from the days when only one end of the supposed "Gulf of Georgia" was known. Although Captain Vancouver knew a couple of centuries ago that he was sailing a strait open at both ends, "gulf" has stuck. The channels, passages and sounds surrounding the islands form a favourite cruising ground of skilled sailors and weekend anglers who enjoy the Orcas, water birds, and

(when they catch them) the salmon and other fish that frequent the area. Although often calm and sunny, these sheltered waters are sometimes rough enough to challenge the expert.

Ferries thread the waterways, giving millions of people a fascinating glimpse of another landscape and lifestyle. The smaller numbers who actually visit the islands every year may be exploring solo or in groups, getting married, honeymooning, or bringing their kids to "get back to na-

Recipe for happiness: children, beach and sunshine

Thetis, get cash from the bank machine on Pender, go for a leisurely dinner with wine on a Sunday evening on…well, you get the picture. If you don't want to add your sad story to the list, read and heed the following awful warnings carefully. With a little awareness and forethought, your island trip can be as relaxed and trouble free as your best dream holiday anywhere.

Getting There Really Is Half the Fun

To us, our vacation always started when we stepped on the ferry. Though not every Gulf Islander agrees, the islands are generally well served by BC Ferries. Just remember that no system is perfect, and that because there was a ferry

return to the amenities of the city whenever we want to.

Enjoying Your Visit

Having a Gulf Island good time seems so easy. You hop on a ferry to the island of your choice and have fun at the other end till it's time to go home! Well, it can be like that of course, but (unless you have previous experience or can pick someone's brains), it's not always quite so simple. The assumptions you can reasonably make when you go to a city or even a national park are not always appropriate in an area as diverse as the southern Gulf Islands. Only in downtown Ganges can you expect to find most city services available.

Certainly the ferries will take you there…but not every day or in every direction, and they may not have room to take you back. Certainly you can get local information…but the map may be out of date or print, or the tourist information centre closed. Certainly there are places to stay and eat…but they may be full,

closed on the night you arrive, or not have a vegetarian dish on the menu. Certainly there are places to get money or gas, or amuse yourself when it rains… but not always on the island you are on. Every Gulf Islander has stories about the people who plan to camp on

Water Water Everywhere?

ALL THE GULF ISLANDS struggle with the availability of fresh water. On the small islands particularly it is a very limited resource. Many island B&Bs are on wells and have their own septic fields. In the hot dry summers, water can run out and use of the septic system by visitors who are not familiar with them can result in costly problems.

Favoured Gulf Island visitors are the ones who carefully observe the following few rules:

• Please ask your hosts what the water situation is when you arrive.
• Conserve water by taking short showers or small baths.
• Don't leave taps running while cleaning your teeth.

• Don't flush anything other than toilet paper down the toilets. Use the waste basket for everything else, including hair, tissues and personal products (even if the label assures you they can go down a toilet system, don't do it!)
• Many island accommodations have little notes in the bathrooms reminding visitors of the water or septic field situation. Please don't be offended by them; water and septic treatment is a major concern and an expensive nightmare when it goes wrong.
• As the Mayne Island visitor's brochure suggests, forego a late afternoon glass of water in favour of a gin and tonic.

Leaving the ferry

at that time yesterday, not necessarily will there be one today. The weather also has a habit of intervening from time to time: on fine days everyone decides to leave Vancouver, on wet weekends it seems everyone decides to go home early, and during storms the ferries may be delayed.

For much of the year ferries run half empty, but you are still expected to book (and pay) in advance on the Tsawwassen-Gulf Islands run. Credit card service is gradually extending through the system, but don't assume your terminals or ferry will take them unless you know for sure. In the summer, and any time of the year on Friday nights from Tsawwassen and Sunday nights from the islands, you may find yourself left behind, even as a foot passenger. Plan your journey out and back before you leave. Get the current

ferry timetables, and study them carefully, phone BC Ferries and ask lots of questions, or get advice from residents of the island you are going to.

Staying Over

Some of the islands have regular hotels or motels, if you want the sort of accommodation you can find in a city. But don't forget there are other choices more in keeping with the islands' character. Each island has a different mix of cabins, cottage resorts, and bed and breakfasts (B&Bs); hostels and camping on some islands provide budget alternatives. Widely travelled B&B guests tell us that operations on the islands are a cut above B&Bs in most urban and many other resort areas. Generally, the operators know each other and try to match up, so the overall standard is high, with great breakfasts that will keep you

going all day. Don't forget that in the peak seasons and at weekends the total number of rooms on any island doesn't always match the number of visitors; the wise visitor has a booking before arrival.

To get a booking, you have basically three options. The provincial government's Discover BC number, 1-800-663-6000, gives you (eventually) access to helpful staff, but the information in their database is limited to the *British Columbia Accommodations Guide.* Absurdly, in 1995 this only includes a selection of island B&Bs, though the situation is improving.

More useful for the first timer is the Canadian Gulf Islands B&B Reservation Service (604-539-5390), which can book you into more than 100 B&Bs on the Gulf Islands and will do their best to match your needs to suitable accommodation.

The visitor with more time can send off for information from the island of choice, read the various published guides, ask friends for recommendations, and set up an individual booking. If you find yourself heading out without a booking, look for the brochures that can be picked up on the ferries, and phone around as soon as you arrive.

For longer stays, you can sometimes rent rooms or even a cottage or house. Most islands have one or more agencies that handle rentals; look in the local phone book or ask at a real estate office. Local bulletin boards and newspapers often carry offers or requests for rentals.

Wherever you are living or

staying, be prepared to burn, compost and recycle at island depots, and, if necessary, to take any remaining garbage off island with you.

Eating Out

Eating out can be fun on the islands and sometimes offers gourmet delights of the highest order (and not necessarily the highest price). Look in the local paper or phone book or ask your hosts for recommendations. Depending on the size and popularity of the island, you can assume that facilities will be open longer hours on more days in summer and shorter hours in winter, when some may close altogether. Spring and fall hours are between these extremes. Restaurants often close on Sunday and sometimes other days. Even if open, they usually close early by city standards, and may be a long way from your campsite or accommodation. Motels don't always have restaurants, and most B&Bs aren't allowed to serve meals other than breakfast. If you expect to arrive early, late, or off season, either eat on the ferry or ask your host before you set out if you can get food. If you are travelling by foot or bicycle, or have special needs (for instance, as a vegetarian or diabetic), get information in advance, arrange for a ride to the nearest restaurant if you can, or carry a minimum of emergency supplies.

Cash, Gas and Other Necessities

If you like to travel with a couple of credit cards and no cash, think again. Many small businesses don't take plastic, and few islands have cash machines. A supply of traveller's cheques or cash is usually the best solution, though some island businesses may take your personal cheque. U.S. currency will usually be accepted, but not everyone can figure out current exchange rates.

If you are taking a vehicle, check ahead that there is gas on the island. Even if there is, don't leave a fill-up to the last minute: island gas stations have been known to run out for a day or so when the demand is higher than anticipated.

Greek lunch, Bouzouki Café, Ganges

Getting Around

Most of the islands (but not all) have some sort of visitor information centre and publish a local map which you may find on the ferry or in marinas or stores. Such maps will supplement this book, and help keep you up to date with fast changing local information. If you have trouble, ask the real estate people or any passerby for assistance. If you are planning to visit several islands, maps covering the whole region are published by governments and other agencies. However, don't feel you have to visit several islands in a short time to get the best of them. Doing it that way means you spend most of your time on the ferries and have only time to find out what the islands have in common, not what makes each of them special.

Individually, most islanders welcome visitors and are likely to go out of their way to be helpful, but some may be more reserved. Remember, many islanders live where they do because they love peace and isolation.

Not all parks, beaches and other public places are signed. Be aware that beaches below high tide line are public, but that there may not be a public

Lunch on the deck, Springwater Lodge, Mayne Island

chapter 5 summarizes the main events that attract islanders and visitors alike.

We have laid out the rest of the book with the assumption that most visitors are coming from the mainland, so successive chapters cover the islands in the order they are reached by ferry from Tsawwassen, and then from Vancouver Island heading north.

Each island chapter is presented in a standard way. A general introduction gives a brief overview of the characteristics of the island, so that you have an idea of why you may want to visit it. Boxes provide basic statistics about the island, tell you how to get there, what facilities and services you will find, and what recreational opportunities it offers. Populations are growing fast, so we give the exact figure of the 1991 census first, then an estimate of current population (on most islands this number usually doubles in the summer, with cottagers). We have listed some of the key services on each island, with phone numbers (all have the area code 604), but if you are planning repeat visits to the same island we recommend you buy a copy of the local phone book on your first visit.

access to them. Check access with a map, and respect adjacent private property.

Last, but most important, go prepared to enjoy the features your island of choice can offer, rather than expecting urban amenities that are not likely to be available. If you can drive round a small island in half an hour and think you have "seen it"; if video games, night clubs or movie theatres are an essential part of your culture; if you can't enjoy a walk in the rain or curling up by the fire with a good book; if you're not prepared to slow down for a day or two…perhaps you would prefer a holiday elsewhere.

How to Use the Superguide

We have tried to make this book useful to all island residents and visitors, but have concentrated on those islands and places that are easiest to visit, and emphasized the features and facilities available to those travelling on land by their own transport (there is virtually no public transport on the islands). Altitude Publishing has a complementary guide to the ferry system, and books by other publishers emphasize the special needs of cyclists, kayakers and boaters.

Chapters 2 to 4 describe the history, nature and lifestyles of the islands in general, and

We have tried to provide enough information about the logistics of travel, accommodation and meals to facilitate visits, but have made no attempt to list all such facilities. These change rapidly from year to year, so there is no guarantee that a particular service we mention will be

Beach access is easy on some islands

available when you make your visit. Wherever possible, we have given names of central agencies which will provide further information, and strongly recommend that you obtain the most current information before visiting the islands. We have not listed opening hours or prices, which also vary from year to year. Inclusion of a business in this guide is merely an indication that it existed at the time the book was prepared; no warranty of safety or quality is offered, and no criticism is intended or implied of the many other businesses that are not listed.

The rest of the text for each island is structured to give you information about the most interesting features, in an order suitable for that island. We feature first the area you might want to tour if you only have a few hours, then the rest in a logical sequence. We recommend routes which take in the most interesting places, showing these as road logs, or occasionally as walking tours. Approximate distances give an indication of travel time, but bear in mind that speed limits are low and there are usually many twists and turns in the road.

In each area we have focused on the features that make the islands interesting and enjoyable—the history and natural features that define their character—and that allow a visitor to make the best use of any stay. We have only included publicly accessible places, but be warned that even in parks there are cliffs, trails and other areas that can be hazardous. Visitors should

View from Hope Bay, across Plumper Sound

exercise due caution, especially when accompanied by children. Furthermore, no one should venture onto the sea without proper equipment and some experience of small craft safety.

Chapter 13 gives information about a few of the smaller southern Gulf Islands, including the three with a regular water taxi service and others with particularly interesting stories. General services and recommended reading are listed in the reference section at the end.

Use this guide to enhance your Gulf Island living and visiting, and please write to us via the publisher to let us know of significant changes needed or anything special we have missed.

2. The Wild Islands

Bigleaf Maple leaves glow in the fall

Sparkling seas, rocky shores, striking trees, a Mediterranean climate, and a wealth of wildlife in the sea and on the land combine to create a unique natural paradise. Amazingly, it sits as a central parkland in the middle of a single conurbation—Greater Vancouver, Greater Victoria

and Greater Seattle—that has a regional population of around 5 million and an even greater number of visitors each year. This area is predicted to double its population in the next 25 years.

A geological pattern initiated more than 370 million years ago determines the basic characteristics of the region, superficially modified by the heavy impact of the great glaciers of the last ice age. Connected to the Pacific, the Strait of Georgia has one of the richest mixtures of underwater life to be found anywhere in the world. This creates a paradise for fish (including incredible

hordes of several salmon species) and supports seals and sea lions, small and great whales, and a spectacle of seabirds.

Within the Strait, more than 200 islands are scattered, ranging from barely emergent rocks to baby mountain ranges. The islands intersect with the water in many ways, with points and bays, canals and coves, narrows and harbours constantly providing fresh views of the land and the water. Wherever the shore is low, beaches of sand, gravel and shell have built up, and spits spread into the sea and connect small islands.

Since the Ice Age glaciers melted, the larger islands have become clothed in rich forest, though there are occasional grassy slopes, and the relatively few low-lying areas are occupied by swamps, ponds and lakes. Beneath the trees, deadfall combines with a dense growth of shrubs, ferns and other ground cover to make travelling difficult. Orchids, lilies and violets bloom in spring, and colorful fungi star the ground, especially after rain begins in the fall. Spiders decorate the spaces between rocks and trees with spectacular orb webs, and colourful banana slugs

Regular ridges on Mayne

astonish visitors from drier regions.

Animal life is a patchwork; each island seems to have its own mix of mammals, reptiles and amphibians. A rich bird life is resident year round, and the bays and woods are lively with migrant species rushing north in spring and south in the fall. The waters are winter quarters for many birds, gathering from summers inland or in the Arctic.

For probably all the 10,000 years since the ice retreated, First Nations people have made their home at least part of the year in this landscape. Some 5,500 years ago they began building middens of shells on the most favoured beaches; even older deposits are now being found below the waters, drowned by a rising sea level. Somewhat more than a century ago, hardy pioneers from Eastern Canada, Europe, the western States, and even Hawaii and Australia began to hack a living from quarry and mine, farm, fishery and forest.

In the last couple of decades mainstream society has discovered the islands, and already the more popular ones are being rapidly

Erratics were carried by the ice

changed by development. Old and new residents alike are finding the peace and beauty that first attracted them is beginning to disappear. The emergence of conservancy movements and the establishment of parks and nature reserves show that it is not too late to save some of the beauty for future generations.

Cuestas and Conglomerates

Most silhouettes of the southern Gulf Islands show a simple, repetitive, stepped pattern. Geologists call these asymmetrical ridges "cuestas" (from the Spanish for "hills"). Each long, gentle slope is underlain by a gently dipping bed of hard sandstone; the steep slope is formed by a joint or fault fracture breaking across the same bed.

The uniformity of structure reflects the geological history of the area, for most of the rocks of these islands were formed within the Nanaimo Sedimentary Basin. This shallow coastal marine trough was confined between older rocks on both sides: the spine of Vancouver Island to the west and the mainland Coast Range to the east. Rivers roared down these mountain slopes bringing sand and clay into the sea, which happens today into the Strait of Georgia.

Part of the boundary of the basin can be seen on the southern parts of Salt Spring Island, where the oldest rocks in the Gulf Islands (some 370 million years old) are found. Here, igneous rocks (formed by cooling of molten rock) and metamorphic rocks (changed by intense heat and pressure from other kinds of rock) were part of the ancestral mountains and volcanoes that were weathered to form the new rocks of the Nanaimo Basin.

Deposition in the Nanaimo Basin took place some 70 million years ago, at a time in geological history when mountain building and volcanoes were active along the Pacific margin of the North American continent. At that time, further east in what are now the Prairies, deltas associated with another sea were inhabited by many kinds of dinosaurs. In the Courtenay area of the Nanaimo Basin, fossils of marine reptiles have been found, and a dinosaur fragment was recently discovered there.

The basin floor subsided as debris piled up. The sediments were buried and compacted, became partially cemented, and hardened into layers of sedimentary rocks, with hard sandstones and conglomerates often alternating with soft shale beds. The crunch between the colliding North American and Pacific plates, which led to the building of the Western Cordillera of North America, only slightly compressed the rock layers of the Nanaimo Basin, creating gentle folding and minor fault displacements, and leaving rocks lying at every angle from horizontal to vertical. Occasional mild earthquakes remind us that this process still

continues. Areas above sea level were eroded by the weather, which sculpted an early form of the landscape we see around us.

Starting around 2 million years ago, ice sheets built up and flowed off the mountains. They coalesced in the Strait of Georgia, developing to a great thickness over the Gulf Islands. Erosion by these glaciers deepened valleys in the soft shales, and rounded and smoothed the sandstone uplands. Deposits of loose glacial melt debris can be seen in some cliffs, and glacial erratic boulders dot the Gulf Island shorelines. Erratics look out of place: as granites or dark crystalline boulders originating in

Viewpoints and Mountains

Viewpoints
Good viewpoints are found on a number of the islands, though some of the highest points are covered in forest so that you can't see out very well.

The highest points on the Gulf Islands include, in metres (m):

- 703 m Mount Bruce (Salt Spring)
- 609 m Mount Tuam (Salt Spring)
- 602 m Mount Maxwell (Salt Spring)
- 602 m Mount Sullivan (Salt Spring)
- 497 m Mount Warburton Pike (Saturna)
- 311 m Mount Galiano (Galiano)
- 271 m Mount Norman (Pender)
- 271 m Mount Parke

Mount Baker from Saturna's East Point

(Mayne)
- 265 m Brickyard Hill (Gabriola)
- 240 m Bodega Hill (Gabriola)

Mountains in Every Direction
Across the water, all around the islands, there are ranges of mountains, and it can be confusing to viewers trying to work out where they are when they see snow-capped peaks in unexpected places. North, beyond the

Strait and the skyscrapers of Vancouver, are the Coast Ranges. West, on Vancouver Island, the rounded mountains are not a lot higher than the Gulf Island hilltops, so it is sometimes difficult to see where the Gulf Islands stop. South, beyond Saanich and Victoria, the Olympic Range forms a jagged wall, sometimes seeming to be supported only by a base of fog. East and southeast the Cascade Range stretches from near the border down into the U.S. On clear days the Cascade's most spectacular peak, Mount Baker (3,285 m), a perfect volcanic cone, looks like Fujiyama in Japanese prints. It's always peeking round the corner of the next island, providing a point that invariably draws the eye.

Breezy day on South Pender

the Coast Ranges, they stand out among the local sandstones.

The lowland ice melted some 12,000 years ago, though glaciers still survive in all the surrounding mountain ranges. Freed from the ice, erosion of the islands continued, especially where high-energy

Honeycomb Weathering

ALONG GULF ISLAND shores, the partly cemented porous sandstones can be penetrated by sea water, which then dries and leaves salt crystals in the pores. The growing crystals loosen and pry out sand grains, creating some of the most spectacular examples of honeycomb weathering to be seen anywhere in the world. The sand created by erosion of the bare sandstone is recycled into beaches, sand spits, and bars.

storm waves have battered and reshaped rocks in the tidal zone. Indented shorelines of rocky headlands alternating with sandy bays show the underlying bands of hard and soft rocks. The harder rocks form headlands, which are sculpted into cliffs, sea caves, and sometimes overhanging ledges, which occasionally break off to form piles of angular talus rubble.

Summer Sun and Winter Rain

The Gulf Islands are sheltered by the mountains of Vancouver Island and the Olympic Peninsula in Washington State, but within reach of the westerly flow of air from the North Pacific. This results in a cool Mediterranean-type climate. Annual rainfall is less than 840 millimetres—about a third of the amount on the west coast of Vancouver Island. There are frequent

droughts in the summer; most precipitation falls from November to January. Usually there are few snowfalls. When they do occur, however, road travel is typically disrupted for a day or two. (A century ago, winters with two-metre drifts were recorded, so severe

Honeycomb weathering: a Gulf Island treat

storms are not impossible.)

Temperatures are pleasantly cool and comfortable in summer (typically 20—25°C for highs) and mild in winter (with highs ranging from 6 to 9°C and lows infrequently falling below freezing). In fact the Gulf Islands enjoy Canada's longest frost-free season, more than eight months. Sunshine is over 2,000 hours a year—more than in the Okanagan. Sea fog from Juan de Fuca Strait can invade the southerly Gulf Islands in late summer, usually in the mornings. Typically it is burned off by the sun later in the day.

From October to April, winds over the islands are generally northerly. Low pressure areas, which sometimes develop into storms, can occur roughly every three days. Islanders are very aware of severe wind storms, which frequently cause power outages lasting from a few minutes to several hours. From May through to September, the dominating North Pacific High generates a northwesterly flow over the coast, but winds are often light and variable—a matter of ongoing interest to the many sailors who explore these waters. Recorded weather forecasts are available by phoning 604-656-3978; marine forecasts, 604-656-2714.

The Open Sea

To reach the islands, we must cross the sea, and almost the first thing we do after settling in is to head for a beach or cliff and gaze out to sea again. Such a view convinces us we are indeed on an island, orients us to where we came from, and provides a wonderful opportunity to look for the more conspicuous marine life.

So bring your binoculars (or even better, a small telescope on a tripod), and scan for jumping salmon, soaring gulls or eagles, rafts of cormorants, ducks or murres, or the black backs and fins of a pod of Orcas.

Close to the shore you might see a family of River Otters, swimming through the sinuous strands of Bull Kelp, or the round head of a curious seal.

On the Shore

On the beach itself, a mink or raccoon may forage among the logs, but their interest (and often ours) is usually on the smaller marine life. Most fascinating is the world of tide pools, natural aquariums that can be studied at low tide. Each provides a selection of the life of the adjacent sea, which can be best watched by the patient observer

equipped with knee pads. The best tides are those of greatest extent, known confusingly as the spring tides though they occur at intervals round the year. These retreat to the lowest levels, providing access to life not otherwise seen above water.

Caution: Don't forget that the tide may rise around you while you are gazing into a pool. Consult tide tables, check your escape routes, and always keep an eye on the sea. Passing ships create large waves which may not strike the shore until the vessel is out of sight. The unwary can easily get a soaking.

Every kind of seashore offers some fascinating natural history. Between the pools, different zones of rocky shores have barnacles, limpets, and a variety of seaweeds. Higher up, Rocky Mountain Juniper trees may grow on isolated points. On cliffs, gulls pause to feed, leaving a litter of crab and mollusc fragments among their droppings. On muddy shores, burrowing shellfish reveal their presence by sudden squirts of water and the abundance of broken shells that mingles with the other beach material. A flowering plant, Sea Asparagus, grows just above and even below the tide line.

Island beaches may be gravel or sand, or a mixture of the two. Along the line of debris left by high tides, you may see lengthy strands of Bull Kelp, scraps of Eel Grass (intriguing as one of the few flowering plants that has adapted to living under the sea), and occasionally a dead fish, bird, seal, or even a sea lion. Wasps

Great Blue Heron

Sea and Shore Birds to Watch For

THIS LIST provides a quick guide to some of the more common birds you may see on or over the water. Species included are listed as common or fairly common on at least one Gulf Island checklist, but are not necessarily present on all islands. Not all species occur year-round, and you should check your field guide for information on identifying the species in the appropriate season. Some species of ducks are more often seen on inland waters.

- Loons: Pacific, Common
- Grebes: Pied-billed, Horned, Red-necked, Western
- Cormorants: Double-crested, Brandt's, Pelagic
- Herons: Great Blue
- Swans: Trumpeter, Mute
- Geese: Brant, Canada
- Dabbling ducks: Green-winged Teal, Mallard, Northern Pintail, Northern Shoveler, American Wigeon
- Diving ducks: Ring-necked Duck, Greater and Lesser Scaup; Harlequin; Oldsquaw; Surf, and White-winged Scoters; Common and Barrow's Goldeneyes; Bufflehead
- Sawbills: Hooded, Common and Red-breasted Mergansers
- Stifftails: Ruddy
- Birds of prey: Osprey, Bald Eagle
- Plovers: Black-bellied Plover, Greater Yellowlegs, Black Turnstone
- Sandpipers: Western and Least Sandpiper; Dunlin; Short- and Long-billed Dowitcher
- Jaegers: Parasitic
- Gulls: Bonaparte's, Heermann's, Mew, California, Thayer's, Glaucous-winged
- Terns: Common
- Murres: Common, Pigeon Guillemot, Marbled Murrelet, Rhinoceros Auklet
- Kingfisher: Belted

"Why Is There No Beach, Daddy?"

SOMETIMES A VISIT to the beach can be disappointing because most of it is under water, hiding beach sand, rock formations, tide pools and treasures. Fortunately, Gulf Island tides have a very simple pattern in the summer that is easy to remember: the highest tide generally occurs at night, and the lowest tide occurs in the morning or later that day. For beachcombing in the summer, Mother Nature has blessed us with one more reason to be in the Gulf Islands. For more sophisticated information, you need to learn to understand the tide tables.

The amount of rise and fall of the sea level is called the range of the tide and this can be as much as 3 metres at various Gulf Island locations. The tides in this region have two highs and two lows a day, with a cycle from Higher High Water to Higher Low Water, then Lower High Water and finally Lower Low Water. This cycle repeats itself every 24 hours and 50 minutes—the length of the lunar day. The beachcomber should determine the time of Lower Low Water, when the maximum amount of shoreline is exposed. The easiest way is to obtain a copy of the current year's *Canadian Tide & Current Tables, Volume 5,* published by the Canadian Hydrographic Service and available in many stores throughout the Gulf Islands and elsewhere. Extracts are also published in the local bi-weekly *Island Tides* newspaper.

For all southern Gulf Island locations we use the listing for the tides at Fulford Harbour, Salt Spring Island, in the tide and current tables. Locate the month and day that you want to know the time of lowest tide. Look at the numbers in the third column (in bold type) under the heading Ht/ft, which means "height in feet," or the fourth column Ht/m for "height in metres." Locate the smallest number in that group of numbers for that day. Read from the adjacent column on the left giving the time this smallest value occurs. You have now determined the time of lowest tide for that date. If it is the summer, add one hour to the time to get Pacific Daylight Savings Time (the listings in the tables are in Pacific Standard Time).

Life in a Tide Pool

Tide pool: a natural aquarium

ANY TIDE POOL is likely to contain representatives of a greater number of different groups of animals than does the adjacent land area. This checklist gives you an idea of some of the different things you may commonly see, but every pool is different from the next and may change with the tide. Don't forget that some animals appear to be something else, like a hermit crab hiding its soft body in a snail shell.

Plants
• Seaweeds (Algae): Bladder Wrack, Sea Lettuce

Invertebrates (animals without backbones)
• Ascidians: Sea squirts
• Coelenterates: Sea anemones, jellyfish
• Crustaceans: Barnacles, crabs, shrimps
• Other Arthropods: Rock louse, sandhoppers
• Echinoderms: Sea cucumbers, sea urchins, starfish
• Molluscs: Chitons, clams, limpets, mussels, oysters, snails
• Sponges: Bread Crumb Sponge
• Worms: Plume worms, tube worms

Vertebrates (animals with backbones)
• Fish: Gunnels, shiner perch, sculpins

hunt zealously along the debris line looking for food.

Most beaches are decorated by drift logs, formerly trees which have been undermined by erosion or felled and included in log booms, from which they have escaped. As logs are increasingly carried by ship today, these may not be replaced as they decay. Among the tree trunks, advancing waves chase flurries of sand hoppers. In growing trees behind the shore you may hear the raucous rattle of a kingfisher taking a short cut across a bay, or see a Bald Eagle or Great Blue Heron digesting the last meal.

Lake habitat on Pender Island

Marshes, Lakes and Streams

Some ocean bays provide shelter for winter ducks, which gather and then perhaps move inland to freshwater lakes.

Shellfish Warning

TEMPTING AS IT may be to eat the shellfish you've just gathered from a southern Gulf Island beach, it may not be safe. Contamination by human pollution, plus the occurrence of the natural phenomenon known as "red tide," combine to make imprudent shellfish consumption a gastronomic Russian roulette.

Clams, mussels, oysters, and scallops are filter feeders, and contaminated water does not damage them, but can affect the eater. Areas closed to the harvesting of scallops, mussels, oysters and all clams include Boot Cove on Saturna Island, Village Bay and Horton Bay on Mayne Island, Montague Harbour on Galiano Island, and Hope Bay, Bedwell Harbour, and Thieves Bay to Oak Bluffs on Pender Island. Butter

A government warning

clams have been permanently banned from harvesting everywhere in the area.

Red tide is caused by a toxic one-celled sea organism (*Gonyaulax catenella*) that can proliferate in coastal waters during the summer. Where and when it occurs, the affected waters take on a reddish tinge. The shellfish that feed in red tide water become toxic themselves. Anyone consuming an affected clam, oyster, scallop, or mussel runs the risk of paralysis and death by paralytic shellfish poisoning. Cooking shellfish does not rid them of their toxicity.

At most anchorages and public beaches, red tide warnings and notices of possible shellfish contamination are posted on the information boards by the Department of Fisheries and Oceans.

Before you give up eating local shellfish altogether, note that the commercial harvest of shellfish is strictly regulated. Enjoy those fresh clams or oysters in the restaurant or grocery store.

Some Common Land Birds

THIS SELECTIVE LIST indicates some of the more common birds that can be seen by the inexperienced birder who wants to know "what is that?" Not all species are present (or as common) on all the islands. More experienced bird-watchers should consult park naturalists or local groups to find some of the rarer species.

California Quail

- Birds of prey: Turkey Vulture; Sharp-shinned, Coopers and Red-tailed Hawk; Merlin
- Game birds: Ring-necked Pheasant, Blue Grouse, California Quail
- Rails: Virginia, Sora
- Coots: American Coot
- Plovers: Killdeer
- Sandpipers: Common Snipe
- Pigeons: Rock Dove, Band-tailed Pigeon
- Owls: Western Screech
- Nighthawks: Common Nighthawk
- Hummingbirds: Rufous
- Woodpecker: Downy, Hairy and Pileated Woodpeckers; Northern Flicker
- Flycatchers: Olive-sided, Willow, Western
- Swallows: Tree, Violet-Green, Northern Rough-winged, Cliff, Barn
- Jays and crows: Steller's Jay, Northwestern Crow, Common Raven
- Chickadees and tits: Chestnut-backed Chickadee; Bushtit
- Creepers: Brown
- Nuthatch: Red-breasted
- Wren: Bewick's, House, Winter
- Kinglets: Golden-crowned, Ruby-crowned
- Thrushes: Swainson's, Hermit & Varied Thrush; American Robin
- Pipits: Water
- Waxwings: Cedar
- Starlings: European
- Vireos: Hutton's, Warbling
- Warblers: Orange-crowned, Yellow, Yellow-rumped, Black-throated Gray, Townsend's, MacGillivray's and Wilson's Warblers; Common Yellowthroat
- Towhee: Rufous-sided
- Sparrows: Chipping, Savannah, Fox, Song, Golden-crowned, White-crowned
- Juncos: Dark-eyed
- Blackbirds: Red-winged and Brewer's Blackbirds; Brown-headed Cowbird
- Finches: Purple and House Finch, Red Crossbill, Pine Siskin, American Goldfinch
- Weaver finches: House Sparrow

Behind middens and sand spits, a few salt marshes have survived the pressure of marina development. One of the biggest, beside Sidney Spit on Sidney Island, is part of a provincial marine park. Medicine Beach on Pender Island provides a home for unusual plants and attracts such birds as the Red-winged Blackbird and Virginia Rail.

Freshwater wetlands are relatively uncommon on the Gulf Islands. Only the larger islands have streams of any size and, except on Salt Spring, there are few lakes. Those that are relatively undisturbed attract an abundance of birds, including cormorants as well the anticipated ducks and geese. Marshy areas have often been drained for agriculture, but those that remain show the spectacular Skunk Cabbage.

Forests

Before settlement, the natural vegetation of the islands was largely forest, and although most original growth has been logged and often burned, most of the islands are still wooded.

Dominant coniferous trees are Douglas Fir, Grand Fir, and Western Red Cedar. Broadleaf Maple gives welcome colour in fall, the striking red-barked Arbutus is common on sunny slopes and hilltops, and the Garry Oak is an important species in some areas. In the lower and wetter areas, stands of relatively short-lived Red Alder develop, and there are occasional willows, including large trees of the Scouler Willow.

Beneath the trees, the understory may be dominated by

swordferns, Salal and Oregon Grape, and thick carpets of mosses and lichens. Among many delightful wild flowers which may be found growing in limited areas for a short period are Blue Camas, Chocolate Lilies, and Calypso and Rattlesnake Orchids. You may even find Brittle Prickly Pear cactus on sunny bluffs. Serendipity will provide interesting finds during the right season, but the help of a local naturalist who knows where and when to go will greatly increase your chances of seeing flowers. The same is true of fall, when mushrooms attract mycophagists (eaters of mushrooms) and mycologists (students of mushrooms). If you want to be the former, you'd better also be the latter.

Gardens are rarely safe from island deer

Wildlife and People

People have changed the Gulf Islands by introducing some plants and animals and removing others, by building industrial sites, by logging and burning, by clearing forest for farmland, and by developing many residential and some commercial areas.

The first pioneers extirpated the large predators that once lived on some of the islands and preyed on domestic stock-(and occasionally on children). Salt Spring, for instance, has lost bears, cougars and wolves. Wapiti (elk) were also formerly present on some of the islands. Early industry such as quarrying and fish packing has largely ceased, but some logging continues, and aquaculture affects various offshore areas. The islands have extensive cleared areas of farmland which encourage foraging by Turkey Vultures. Historic orchards attract crows and other birds to gorge on the ripe fruit. Accidentally imported European weeds such as thistles and Chicory flourish on farmland and along roadsides. Deliberately imported yellow-flowering Broom and its prickly relative, Gorse, have taken over large areas of open ground, resisting any less-than-determined efforts to remove them. Imported game birds such as Ring-necked Pheasants and California Quail add a decorative if unnecessary element to the bird life, and game fish are stocked in some of the larger lakes.

In the few dense residential developments and those where trees are largely felled, the landscape and its residential species changes, losing forest flowers and birds and encouraging those species more tolerant of the presence of people. Where acreages are larger, little forest has to be destroyed, and wildlife in effect continues to live in a woodland enhanced by pockets of additional food and shelter. Clearing of old trees discriminates against native woodpeckers and other hole nesters.

Any householder with a garden either builds a huge

Mature trees survive on some islands

23

fence or wages an unending war against the abundant little Black-tailed Deer. Without disturbance by predators, the deer drop their fawns beneath windows, and walk up steps onto decks to chew fuchsias as if they owned the place. Some islanders have also inadvertently introduced black slugs which are even fiercer on garden plants than the spectacular native banana slugs.

Residents who take delight in feeding wildlife increase populations of such people-tolerant species as Rufous Hummingbirds, Rufous-sided Towhees, and Juncos, and some people successfully feed Band-tailed Pigeons and even put up bat houses. Some people are thrilled to have a nesting pair of Bald Eagles on their property, but others try to get rid of them.

Protecting the Islands

The islands' diverse natural landscapes and their wild inhabitants are under threat from many pressures, including competition for habitat from the rapidly growing human population, effects of residential and commercial development, legal and illegal harvesting of food species, and air and water pollution. The scope of the problem is underlined by examples: some salmon stocks using the Strait have declined disastrously; Humpback Whales (numerous enough to support a fishery in the early years of this century) have disappeared; dioxins are being found in Bald Eagle eggs. On the other hand, there have been some successes: Bald Eagle and seal stocks do not seem to be declining; and pesticide levels in cormorants have declined since pesticide use was banned.

The effects of these threats are partly cushioned by the development of a network of protected areas. Although the

Fire: Gulf Island Scourge

NATURAL FIRES, started by lightning, used to open up the forest periodically and clear the fallen branches and dead needles that accumulate on the ground. The great Gabriola fire of 1938, which destroyed 800 hectares (2,000 acres) of forest, was the last major conflagration. In the last half century, fires have largely been controlled, so that inflammable material builds up in the woods, making them increasingly vulnerable. With ever more houses scattered throughout the forest, the potential for a devastating burn increases from year to year.

Take careful note of the fire hazard warnings on all the islands. The summer climate is dry, water is at a premium, and the islands rely on fire services run by volunteers. Do not butt out cigarettes on a woodland trail or toss them into the bush or out of a car window: the whole island could go up in flames behind you. No open fires are allowed in summer without a fire permit, and in the dry periods the woods may be closed for everyone's protection. Please check at the local stores for the current status of burning permits.

Many older trees show scars from forest fires

Gulf Islands region is recognized as being worthy of its own national park, only rumours suggest that progress on this is being made in delicate negotiations. However, a network of provincial and regional parks, ecological reserves, and locally purchased lands is protecting some significant sites and species. Many of these areas are open to the public, but their special purposes should be respected.

On the Gulf Islands, there is often far too little information available to make proper conservation plans possible. For instance, the rare Sharp-tailed Snake survives on Pender Island but its population and distribution are almost unknown. Planning agencies also face many dilemmas, trying to solve conservation problems while respecting the rights of existing landowners and visitors. Island lands are largely in the hands of individuals and corporations, and not all of these are sympathetic to what they may see as unreasonable attempts to change planning directions. On both Gabriola and Galiano, large forestry companies have been in conflict with local interests. Smaller scale disagreements are apparent on some of the other islands.

However, individuals and corporate islanders have also made determined efforts to set aside important areas, and this work continues. As island populations continue to increase, only determination by all those interested will provide systematic protection of an adequate sample of significant natural features and species for the future.

Some Protected Areas in the Gulf Islands

Cormorants nesting in the Ballingall Islets

THIS SELECTION of the Gulf Islands' protected areas gives an idea of the diversity of sites available. New parks are in various stages of planning and establishment.

Provincial Parks
- Bellhouse Park (Galiano)
- Dionisio Point (Galiano)
- Drumbeg Park (Gabriola)
- Gabriola Sands Provincial Park (Gabriola)
- Mouat Provincial Park (Salt Spring)
- Mount Bruce Provincial Park (Salt Spring)
- Mount Maxwell Provincial Park (Salt Spring)
- Prior Centennial Park (North Pender)
- Ruckle Park (Salt Spring)

Marine Parks
- Ballingall Islets (near Galiano)
- Beaumont Marine Park (South Pender)
- Cabbage Island Marine Park (off Tumbo Island)
- D'Arcy Island Marine Park
- Discovery Island Marine Park
- Isle-de-Lis Marine Park (Rum Island)
- Montague Harbour Marine Park (Galiano)
- Newcastle Island Marine Park
- Pirates Cove Marine Park (De Courcy Island)
- Princess Margaret Marine Park (Portland Island)
- Sidney Spit Marine Park (Sidney Island)
- Whaleboat Island Marine Park (off Ruxton Island)
- Winter Cove Marine Park (Saturna)

Regional Parks
- Mount Norman Regional Park (South Pender)
- Mount Parke Regional Park (Mayne)

Ecological Reserves
- Brackman Island - ungrazed vegetation (near Portland)
- Canoe Islets - seabird colony (near Valdes)
- Galiano Island - peat bog
- Mount Maxwell - Garry Oaks (Salt Spring)
- Mount Tuam - Arbutus-Douglas Fir Forest (Salt Spring)
- Oak Bay Islands - rare plants and seabirds (off Oak Bay)
- Rose Islets - seabird colony (north of Reid Island)
- Satellite Channel - marine life (off Salt Spring)
- Saturna Island - Douglas Fir forest
- Trial Islands - rare and endangered plants (south of Oak Bay)

3. Time and the Islands

Tom Collison's home at Miners Bay, about 1895

The islands bear traces of geological events of more than 370 million years ago, and people have been in the area for at least 12,000 years. For the last 5,000 there has been a fairly continuous record on the islands of a culture similar to that of the historic Coast Salish. By contrast, contact between First Nations and newcomers on the islands—the start here of what modern society calls "history"—took place only about 200 years ago. Serious settlement has taken place mainly in the present century. In recent decades the pace of change increases ever faster. *(abbreviations: my = million years; BP = before present.)*

The Geological Past

(all dates BP)

370 my – Formation of Devonian igneous and metamorphic rocks now exposed on Salt Spring.

70 my – Upper Cretaceous Sandstones laid down in Nanaimo Sedimentary Basin.
2 my – Ice Age began.
12,000 – Coast ice-free after last ice age.
9,000 – Sea level much lower than present.

Human Prehistory

(all dates BP)

12,000 – Mastodon hunters in nearby Washington State.
5,500-1,500 – Middle Period represented in Gulf Islands sites, with a Salish-type culture.
5,170 – Oldest dated bone in Pender archeological excavation.

3,070-2,790 – Dated charcoal from human site at Georgeson Bay, Galiano.
1,500 – Late Period represented in Gulf Islands sites.

18th Century

1774 – Spanish Hernandez Expedition sights the Queen Charlotte Islands.
1778 – English navigator Cook landed at Nootka Sound.
1791 – Spanish Don Juan Pantoja reached Pender Island. Captain Jose Maria Narvaez explored other islands in Strait of Georgia.
1792 – Spanish commanders Galiano and Valdez, and English Captain Vancouver

explore Strait of Georgia.

19th Century

1843 – Fort Victoria established by Hudson's Bay Factor, James Douglas.

1846 – Boundaries of British and American mainland territories defined by Oregon Boundary Treaty, leaving Vancouver Island British, but other islands unclear.

1849 – Coal discovered on Newcastle.

1854 – William and David Hoggan, coal miners, farmed on Gabriola and brought their mother from Glasgow round the Horn.

1858 – Fraser River gold miners passed through Active Pass, establishing Miners Bay on Mayne. Crown colony of British Columbia established.

1858-9 – Survey of islands carried out by Captain Richards on H.M.S. *Plumper*.

1859 – Kanakas (from Hawaii) settled on Portland Island, given to them by Hudson's Bay Company.

1859 – First settlers to Salt Spring, including Australians, English, Scots, Irish and Blacks.

1859 – Jonathan Begg opened a store and post office on Salt Spring.

1860 – Eight Bella Bella natives killed by Cowichans in the last battle on Salt Spring.

1860 – Vesuvius Bay Sandstone Quarry opened on Salt Spring, later providing flagstones for Victoria and building stone for the Esquimalt Graving Dock and San Francisco Mint.

1861 – Christian Mayers and James Greavy each preempted 100 acres on Mayne.

Petroglyphs: Images from the Past

SPIRIT FACES...hypnotic eyes...geometric shapes...fantastic mythological creatures...these and many other figures are carved into the sandstone of the Gulf Islands. Such petroglyph images are still much of a mystery; little is known about who carved them, when and for what purposes.

The Pacific Northwest coast is one of the outstanding rock art regions of the world, and the Gulf Islands are a rich petroglyph area. Most islands have some petroglyphs, but they are most abundant and diverse on Gabriola Island and the nearby Nanaimo area of Vancouver Island. They are usually found near ancient aboriginal villages or freshwater streams, often within view of the ocean and occasionally below high tide mark.

Rock art styles in this area represent a simpler version of the Classic West Coast aboriginal art tradition. The figures are drawn in a curvilinear style (with curving rather than angular lines), with inner structural detail (such as an "X-ray" view of the skeleton) and emphasized heads. Figures are geometric human-like or animal-like forms, varying in length from a few centimetres across to over 2.5 metres. Some figures are crudely carved; other works have great aesthetic appeal and display the precision of a master carver.

The figures on the Gulf Islands were probably carved by ancestors of the Coast Salish people as far back as 3,500 years ago. Oral histories and archeology provide a few clues as to why the petroglyphs may have been carved. Some may be evidence of puberty rites—images carved by adolescents on a spirit quest. Others may have been carved by hunters seeking the aid of spirit powers in the hunt. Still others may record the dreams, rituals or spirit aids of shamans, or may record personal experiences of symbolic value only to the carver.

These mysterious images, frozen in time, give us a tantalizing glimpse into another world, one that recognized a close link between the spirit world and the day-to-day activities of human beings. They represent an extremely valuable link with the past, and as such are protected by law. Please do not trace, mark or deface them in any way. If you wish to make a copy of a petroglyph image, take a photograph, or make a rubbing from the casts outside the Nanaimo museum.

1861 – Ebenezer Robson held the first church service on Salt Spring.
1861 – John Jones, a black

teacher, opened the first school on Salt Spring.
1861-2 – Severe winter killed 100 cattle on Salt Spring.

1862 – Smallpox spread through First Nations population, killing at least one-third.
1863 – Henry and Sophie

The S.S. *Iroquois*

STR IROQUOIS AS SHE APPEARED ON OCT. 27TH 1908 AFTER THE WRECK.

The Iroquois *after an earlier wreck*

THE 195 TON S.S. *Iroquois* was launched in 1900, and carried mail between Sidney and the Gulf Islands. It was partly owned by Thomas W. Paterson, a Victoria politician, who was accused of some shady electioneering when he cancelled a regular run and sent the *Iroquois* into Vancouver to bring questionable voters to Galiano. Although his associate was fined and sent to jail, Paterson was not charged.

Co-owner of the *Iroquois* was its captain, A.A. Sears, who made himself unpopular by shooting at ducks from the pilot house window—whether or not there was anyone in the way. His purser, Munroe, was more popular, sup-

plying the islanders with bottles of whisky at 75 cents.

Paterson successfully pressured the Dominion government into dredging the canal between North and South Pender to save time for the *Iroquois*. He purchased Moresby Island in 1906 and, after becoming Lieutenant Governor of the province, used his influence to get a government dock built there, from which he was able to ship produce from the farm he developed.

The *Iroquois* was always unstable in heavy seas, yet Paterson added three feet to the width of her upper deck. In 1911, the ship sank in a gale near Sidney, soon after leaving the wharf. Six crew-

men (including the popular purser) and 15 passengers died. The captain was one of the 11 who managed to get in the only lifeboat to be launched.

Among the dead was Fanny Hooson, aged 38, who had come to Pender from the Maritimes as the island's first teacher. She had married Evan Hooson, a Yorkshire stonemason, bricklayer and blacksmith, who had built his own house along what became Hooson Road. Fanny and their three-year-old son Evan were both drowned. On their tombstone in the Pender Cemetery are the sad words "the child lies here," implying that the mother's body was never found.

Georgina Point Lighthouse, Mayne Island

Georgeson settled on Galiano.

1863 – First Nations village on Kuper shelled in retaliation for a murder of two white settlers on Saturna.

1864 – American-owned *Fideliter* began first commercial steamship service to Salt Spring.

1868 – Southern Gulf Islands became part of the Cowichan Electoral District. Salt Spring islander John Booth was elected in 1871, and later became Speaker of the BC Legislature.

1871 – British Columbia entered confederation.

1872 – William Elford was the first settler at Winter Cove on Saturna.

1872 – Boundary between the U.S. and Canada is settled, with Gulf Islands in Canada and San Juans in the U.S. Smuggling begins.

1872 – Abraham Copeland

built Vesuvius Bay wharf on Salt Spring.

1873 – Robert Foster became the first landowner on Thetis.

1873 – First school on Gabriola; the teacher had 16 students.

1874 – Hugh Munroe was one of the first settlers to farm James Island.

1877 – Indian Reserve established on Mayne.

1878 – First dock built at Miners Bay, Mayne, so that settlers no longer had to row out and intercept steamers to send and receive mail.

1878 – Noah Buckley and David Hope started to farm 2,500 acres on North Pender.

1880 – Pender surveyed into quarter sections.

1880s – Indian fishing settlement on South Pender had up to 80 people.

1882 – Washington Grimmer became Pender's first post-

master, rowing to Miners Bay to get the mail.

1884 – Warburton Pike and Charles Payne bought part of Saturna.

1885 – Henry Georgeson became the first keeper of Georgina Point lighthouse, Mayne.

1885 – St. Paul's, Salt Spring's first Catholic church, consecrated.

1886 – Barque *John Rosenfeld* wrecked off Saturna.

1886 – Arthur Spalding bought 800 acres of South Pender.

1887 – Stevens' Boarding House opened on Salt Spring.

1889 – Canon Beanlands of Victoria became the first minister to visit Mayne regularly.

1889 – Neptune Grimmer was born in a boat on Navy Channel.

1889 – Chinese servants escaped by raft from Horatio

29

A steam dredger digs the Pender Canal

Robertson of Moresby, causing a scandal.

1890s – A group of Victoria businessman stocked James Island with a wide variety of game as a hunting preserve.

1891 – William Scott started development of an orchard with 1,200 fruit trees at Fruitvale on Salt Spring.

1892 – D'Arcy became a leper colony with a single inhabitant, later increasing to as many as six.

1892 – First schoolhouse on Galiano.

1893 – Three-story, 35-room Point Comfort Hotel opened on Mayne to cater for summer visitors.

1893 – Coal mine sunk on Tumbo by Charles Gabriel and Japanese Kisuki Mikuni.

1894 – Edward Wilson arrived on Salt Spring and became its first resident minister.

c. 1895 – Brickyard started on Gabriola.

1896 – Jail built on Mayne.

1896 – Minister and naturalist G.W. Taylor moved to Gabriola.

1897 – First phone line on Salt Spring.

20th Century

1900 – Georgeson Bay wharf built on Galiano.

Magic Lake Estates

Houses in Magic Lake Estates

THIS 1,200-LOT subdivision was started in 1963, when Pender's total population was around 700. Concern that high-density, suburban developments such as this could spring up across the Gulf Islands sounded the alarm for what many people began to see as a threat to the islands' unique character. By raising this concern, Magic Lake Estates helped prompt the creation of the Islands Trust in 1974.

Originally called the Gulf Garden Estates and then Magic Lake Estates (most locals today have dropped the "estates" part), the development had the dubious distinction of being the largest planned subdivision in Canada at the time. It was heavily marketed in the Vancouver, Calgary and Edmonton areas as "A Superbly Planned Private Estate of Gracious Living." Like every good subdivision, it also had the requisite themed street names, in this case, terribly nautical: Sailor Road, Jolly Roger Crescent, Yawl Lane, Galleon Way, Cutlass Court, Buccaneers, Privateers, Foc'sle, Frigate, Doubloon, Harpoon—and on and on. Back in 1965, lots with water views started at $995; waterfront properties along Schooner Way ranged from $2,625 to $4,550. It wasn't long before most of the lots had been sold and building began in earnest.

Today, much of North Pender's population is concentrated in this area. Although the density of homes is greater here than in many other parts of the island, the Magic Lake area still retains a somewhat rural character.

1901 – *Tilikum* readied on Galiano for its round-the-world voyage.

1902 – Pender canal dug, separating the island into two parts.

1902 – Harris brothers brought the first powerboat, a 30-foot steam launch *Pearl*, to Pender.

1903 – First creamery built on Salt Spring, with funding by Henry Bullock, the Mouats and Scotts.

1904-1905 – H.M.S. *Egeria* surveyed tidal waters around Mayne and Pender.

1905 – Canal dug between Thetis and Kuper.

1907 – Sir Richard McBride, then Premier of the province, established James Island Club.

1908 – Japanese started two herring salteries on Reid, with up to 300 workers.

1910 – Hunter family built a 30-foot gasboat, the *Thetis*, on Thetis.

1910 – Richard Hall came to Mayne and built the first commercial greenhouses for growing tomatoes.

1911 – John Hepburn started a regular barge service from Fulford on Salt Spring, making it possible to carry cars.

1912 – First car brought to Gabriola by John Rollo. First church built on Gabriola.

1913 – James Island sold to Canadian Explosives Co. for manufacturing dynamite and TNT.

1913 – Jeannie Hamilton ran for school board on Pender— the first woman candidate for public office on the islands. She lost.

1920 – Japanese family, the Okanos, moved to Salt Spring.

1925 – Lady Constance Fawkes and others organized the first Fall Fair on Mayne.

1927 – Shingle Bay fish plant opened on Pender to produce lubricating oil and fertilizer.

1929 – CPR's first diesel ship, and the first modern car ferry in the area, the *Motor Princess* began Gulf Islands service, carrying seven cars at a time.

1932 – Millstone working began on Gabriola, for pulp mills in Canada and Europe.

1933 – Brother XII of De Courcy sued by his followers.

1941 – First Japanese moved from Mayne.

1949 – Galiano Light & Power Company, a cooperative, switched on.

1955 – Pender bridge built connecting North and South.

1959 – Montague Harbour Marine Park on Galiano established, the first in BC.

1961 – BC Ferry Corporation began operation with takeover of the Gulf Islands Ferry Company.

1962 – James Island town dismantled.

1963 – Magic Lake Estates established on North Pender Island, with 1,200 lots.

1969 – Government placed a "ten acre freeze" on development on the islands.

1974 – *Islands Trust Act* passed, establishing the trust with a mandate "to preserve, and protect…the environment and the peculiar nature of the islands…"

Island Time

SOMETIME IN THE 19th century, the Gulf Islanders' notoriously relaxed approach to time must have developed, to the ongoing frustration of visitors and ferry people attempting to keep schedules.

The only totally reliable timekeeper on the islands is the tide, which goes in and out more or less as the tide tables say. The next most realistic time on the Gulf Islands is ferry time, and those time tables can be more than a little loose some days. It's part of the charm here that everyone stops to chat at the store checkout, while passing at the pumps in the gas station, and sometimes with cars idling in the middle of the road. In fact, we once overheard someone call out to a friend, "Hey Pete, do you have the time?" "Yes," replied Pete, "I think it's Monday."

Some retirees really lose track, and we did hear of one couple who complained for six weeks that the hockey games weren't being broadcast on time, before they realized they should have turned their clocks back.

Those who take island time really seriously can go after the "Living on Gabriola Time" clock, offered as a prize by the Gabriola *Sounder* for its gumboot contest (with categories such as the prettiest, sexiest, and most used). This custom-designed clock can (sometimes) be relied on to run consistently four hours and 20 minutes late.

A retired horologist keeps track of island time

4. Island Life

A busy day at Hope Bay, Pender Island

The islands have a vigorous and diverse life of their own, and visitors can find plenty of opportunities to participate. You can find out how other people make a living, look for special foods or snap up a bargain, rub shoulders with eccentrics at home or celebrities off duty, learn a new word or a new song, or find a new way to have a good time in the outdoors.

First Nations

In the late 18th century the southern Gulf Islands and adjacent areas of Vancouver Island and the Fraser Valley were occupied by a number of Coast Salish nations, including the Halkomelem (around Nanaimo), the Penelakuts (Kuper), and several Saanich bands. Some of the islands seem to have been occupied year round, while others were used seasonally, though it is not easy to assess the effects of the epidemics which devastated whole areas. A number of reserves were set aside, including almost the whole of Kuper Island, but not all the smaller ones are occupied at present, because many groups were consolidated on reserves on Vancouver Island. Some of the early settlers married First Nations women, so that native traditions live on in long-established pioneer families as well as among the aboriginal people.

A Living from the Sea

The economy of the Gulf Islands residents has always depended on both the sea and the land, and many early settlers exploited both to make a living, perhaps fishing one week and logging the next. Later people were able to specialize in farming, logging or quarrying, but many still worked off-island for part of each year or part of their lives. Commercial whaling started a century ago, but a network of fish reduction plants was a more viable business. Increasing water traffic around the islands led to development of a network of lighthouses, staffed by families who devoted their lives to the service of the sea. It is not surprising the islands have always been attractive to seamen, whether their preferred vessels were fish boats, freighters, ferryboats or recreational sailboats. Many early residents were seamen who retired to a farm within sight of the sea.

Rocks and Trees

The islands' industries have often disappeared leaving little trace, but a cluster of pilings or a beach covered with broken bricks can lead to an exploration of a little unexpected history.

Island sandstones, attractive to many architects, have been quarried and exported for paving stones, building and grindstones in neighbouring cities and farther afield. More recently, brick making was carried out on Gabriola and

Lamb and mum

Pender, and aggregate mined on Saturna.

Trees had to be cut down and the stumps dynamited before land could be planted, but gradually off-island markets emerged for lumber. Large trees were used for building houses and ships, and as pit props in nearby coal mines.

Wood also attracted Japanese from Steveston who came to make charcoal for the salmon canneries, and sometimes stayed to grow vegetables. Most of the islands still have a small sawmill somewhere, and commercial logging is an active industry on the larger islands. Logs may be trucked off

Shingle Bay Fish Plant

THE VESTIGES OF a pier are the only remains on the ground of one of Pender's first significant industries: a fish reduction plant typical of many on the islands. Established in 1927, the plant operated for more than 12 years, employing about 15 men during the summer. The plant processed herring and dogfish and turned out lubricating oil and fertilizer. Fire destroyed the plant in 1940. It was rebuilt in 1947, but again burned down 12 years later, this time not to be replaced.

Fruit at Old Orchard Farm, Pender Island

Apples
Beitigheimer, Golden Russet, Gravenstein, Greening, King (of Tomkin County), Melba, Pippins, Snow (Fameuse), Transparents, Wagner, Wealthy, Yellow Bell Flower

Pears
Anjou, Bartlett, Clapp's Favourite, Louise Bonne de Jersey, Vicar of Winkfield, Willard, Winter Bartlett

Plums
Cherry Plum, Golden, Italian Prune

Island bounty

Karon Wallace and Good Earth Farm

IN THE CENTRE of Good Earth Farm on Hooson Road, Pender Island, is a vine-covered arbour surrounded by prolific beds of organic vegetables. Here one can sometimes find Karon Wallace as she sits serenely among her herbs and vegetables and gives tarot readings. Along with her spiritual approach to life and down-to-earth gardening is a talent for art and business, for

Karon wears many hats, as successful Gulf Islanders do. She was once a buyer for a major chain of fashion stores in Western Canada. Karon now makes pottery masks, several of which grace her garden, and dries and arranges the many flowers she grows. She sells both flowers and vegetables from the stand at her gate. Karon was a founder of Galloping Moon Gallery at Hope Bay, where her combination of artistic eye and business acumen helped to make the store thrive. Her garden is enjoyed by visitors at the annual Tapestry of Words Festival, where it is one of the most beautiful festival sites. It is open to visitors by donation. To contact Karon, phone 604-629-6413.

Some Famous Gulf Islanders

SOME OF THE more famous current and former, full- and part-time Gulf Islanders:

Broadcasters
• James Barber (Pender)
• Jack Webster (Salt Spring)

Film Makers
• Ann Wheeler (Salt Spring)

Musicians
• Bob Bossin (Gabriola)
• David Essig (Thetis)
• Robert Minden (Pender)
• Shari Ulrich (Salt Spring)
• Valdy (Salt Spring)

Playwrights
• Frank Moher (Gabriola)

Politicians
• Bill Bennett senior (Salt Spring)
• Andrew Brewin (Pender)
• Senator Pat Carney (Saturna)
• Premier Mike Harcourt (Pender)

Sailors
• Miles and Beryl Smeeton (Salt Spring)

Storytellers
• Ted Stone (Salt Spring)

Visual Artists
• Peter Aspell (Pender)
• Robert Bateman (Salt Spring)
• Carol Evans (Salt Spring)
• H.G. Glyde (Pender)
• Keith Holmes (Galiano)
• Elizabeth Hopkins (Galiano)
• Ronaldo Norden (Galiano)
• Anne Popperwell (Saturna)
• Bill Reid (Thetis)

Writers
• William Deverell (Pender)
• Jean Howarth (Saturna)
• Stephen Hume (Saturna)
• Dorothy Livesay (Galiano)
• Susan Mayse (Saturna)
• Jane Rule (Galiano)
• Audrey Thomas (Galiano)

Gulf Islands Culture

IN ADDITION TO the hundreds of visual artists who have taken the islands as their subject matter, many musicians and writers have also been inspired by them. A few samples include:

Classical Music
• Jean Coulthard's ballet *Excursion* details a visit to the Gulf Islands as remembered in 1940.
• Derek Healey has written *Gabriola Suite*.

Folk Music
• Many songs and instrumental pieces refer to the islands.
• Bob Bossin's 1994 CD is called *Gabriola V0R 1X0*, which may be the first time a postal code has been used in an album title.

Literature
• Jean Howarth's *Treasure Island* first appeared in columns in the Toronto *Globe and Mail*, and gives a picturesque view of life on Saturna.
• Malcolm Lowry's novel *October Ferry to Gabriola* describes a journey to that island, though the protagonists never actually get there.
• CBC broadcaster Bill Richardson's Leacock award-winning *Bachelor Brothers' Bed & Breakfast* is set in an imaginary B&B on an unspecified Gulf Island.
• Many other writers have written vividly of the islands; see for instance some of Audrey Thomas's short stories.
• A number of children's stories set in the islands provide entertaining reading for young visitors. See list in the reference section.

by ferry, or sorted and prepared for towing in booming grounds. However, traditional jobs gradually evolve, and the one-time lumberman may now specialize in putting up TV aerials on tall Douglas Firs, or pruning trees that block the view.

Farming and Fruit

Early farmers tried a number of ways to make the islands productive. Mixed farming, with an emphasis on sheep raising, proved the first recipe for success. Next, apples and other orchard fruit were profitable before the railways and irrigation made the Okanagan a viable rival. In spring, many settled parts of the islands are gay with blossom. They reveal fragments of old orchards, bearing many varieties of fruit which are now rare, their names forming a poetry of their own.

A Variety of Islanders

As well as farmers and fishers, typical occupants of the southern Gulf Islands include re-

THE COMBINATION OF surplus garden produce and a blind faith in the honesty of neighbours and visitors makes the "honesty stand" an attractive feature of island life.

Often simple tables or trestles beside the road, honesty stands offer freshly picked surplus fruit, flowers and vegetables produced in bountiful island gardens, and fresh eggs. Choose your produce, work out how much you owe from the price list and drop your money in the prominently displayed "honesty box." In some places, we've even seen honesty stands for pottery—a charming custom we hope will stay around. Unfortunately the numbers of stands sporting flowers alarmed one

Pottery honesty stand, Gabriola

well travelled island visitor, who mistook them for memorials to people killed in road accidents.

tirees, back-to-the-landers, aging hippies, professors, consultants and other business people, occasional millionaires, artists and musicians, and a fair number of just plain working folks— in fact, a fair cross section of society.

Some of the earliest settlers were remittance men or other Brits who were at least partly dependent on money from elsewhere and tried to maintain some form of gracious living with tennis and croquet. In the '60s, what were often

Springboards and Swede Fiddles

WHEN WALKING ISLAND trails or travelling a road through the forest, watch for large tree stumps with notches cut in their sides — a reminder of old logging methods. The bases of old growth trees were often too wide for a cross-cut saw — nicknamed a "Swede fiddle" — as well as being buried in dense shrubs and deadfall. Loggers cut notches in the trunk and inserted metal-tipped springboards so that they could stand on the boards and cut the tree higher up where the trunk was narrower. A notch was chopped in one side with axes, and then the tree was sawed from the other side until it began to fall. At that point the springboard was more of a diving board, as the loggers

Felling on Pender Island

had to scramble to get out of the way.

35

Our Favourite Gulf Island Lunch for Two

- From an honesty stand pick up a fresh lettuce and some herbs.
- From the dock buy two live crabs.
- From the store buy a lemon.
- Take a large pot, a Coleman stove, a bowl, two forks and a sharp knife to a secluded beach.
- Set up the stove on a flat rock (not a log—watch out for fire hazards).
- Fill the pot with sea water and bring to a boil.
- Add crabs and boil for 15 minutes. (No, they do not scream.)
- While crabs are boiling, wash lettuce in sea water, shake it well, and tear it up into the bowl.
- Chop herbs and toss with lettuce, drizzle with a squeezed lemon slice. Eat this salad while cooking the crabs or have it with the crabs as desired.
- When the crabs are done, dunk them in the sea to stop the cooking, rip off their backs and scrape out the soft parts. Swill again with sea water.
- Crack open the legs and claws, and pull out the sweet meat, adding a squeeze of lemon if desired.
- Consign the shattered shell pieces to the deep (where the nutrients will be recycled) and swill your hands in the surf.
- Sleep in the sun.

Some Island Bumper Stickers

- He's dead, Jim. You grab his tricorder, I'll get his wallet.
- I Brake For Dinosaurs
- Islands in Trust, yours to protect and preserve
- It will be a great day when our schools get all the money they need and the air force has to hold a bake sale to buy a bomber
- Love Your Ocean
- Protect Me From The Islands Trust
- Real Fish Don't Eat Pellets
- Real Islands Don't Have Bridges
- The Rat Race Is Over—the Rats Have Won
- Visualize Whirled Peas
- You otter be on Galiano

Gulf Islands Words

ANY AREA WITH its own character develops its own vocabulary. These words were formerly or are currently heard on the Gulf Islands. (A few are used elsewhere on the BC coast, but are included for the benefit of inlanders.)

- Bush Salmon - illegally hunted deer.
- Canal - A natural deep narrow inlet, which may sometimes have been deepened by human action. (From the Spanish.)
- Chuck (saltchuck) - the sea, a surviving word from the Chinook "pidgin" language once commonly used on the coast.
- Ferry's in - this expression may be used when you meet more than three cars driving in the same direction.
- Flying Shingle - nickname for a former Gabriola ferry, remembered in the name of one of its community newspapers.
- The Gulf - the Strait of Georgia.
- The Island - Although residents of Vancouver Island suffer from the illusion that this term always refers to their island, Gulf Islanders know that it refers to whichever one they live on. Compare "the lake" on the Prairies.
- Island Beater - an old car kept on the island so that regular visitors and commuters can travel the ferries as foot passengers.
- James Island Spinner - stick of dynamite thrown in the water to stun fish.
- Kanaka - Hawaiian word for "man." Many were employed by the Hudson's Bay Company in the mid-nineteenth century, and some settled on Portland and Salt Spring islands.
- Midden - debris of a long-continuing First Nations settlement, which on the Gulf Islands is normally behind a beach, made up largely of shell debris and often including important archeological remains.
- Pender Lender - Pender Island's public library.
- Salish - Aboriginal language spoken by numerous First Nations groups on and around the Gulf Islands.
- Springboard - Plank inserted into a notch cut into the base of a tree, in preparation for chopping down the tree.
- Swede fiddle - Old-fashioned slang for a crosscut saw.
- Trust - The Island's Trust, a government body established to manage some of the affairs of the islands.

called "hippie drop-outs" came back to the land, where they lived what in the sophisticated nineties is more likely to be called an ecologically sound alternative lifestyle. In the '70s, many retirees discovered the islands as a congenial place to settle down. Some work at productive hobbies, some scratch out a living on a limited pension, and some spend the winter in California or Costa Rica, or pop off for the occasional cruise. Since the '80s, young families and urban professionals have begun making the islands their home, bringing yet another dimension to island life.

Many full-time residents work on the islands, some in construction,

schools, stores, or services, or for the ferries. As there are not enough on-island regular jobs to go around, other islanders work just as hard at several part-time jobs. Some people live on the islands and commute daily to work elsewhere. A few leave the island each week, and weekend visitors returning home may rub shoulders in the ferry line-up with a computer specialist or a university professor heading to work. Telecommuting is making an island lifestyle increasingly possible for professionals such as lawyers, consultants, engineers and other specialists.

The islands attract more than their share of those creative people (such as writers, painters and musicians) who can work at a distance from their clients. Some of these are well-known, and if added to the business people and politicians who like to retreat to the islands, provide a good list of the relatively famous who are at least part-time at home in ferryland. Although the truly famous tend to hide out, you may well buy your ticket from Senator Carney at the Saturna Lamb Barbecue or catch a lift with Premier Mike Harcourt on Pender.

Living on the Islands

Many people on the islands try to be self sufficient. This may involve growing a garden (usually organic), which in turn involves devising elaborate watering methods. The gentle climate provides wonderful flower growing, and one elderly lady confidently told us that she had the best garden in Canada. Serious gardening is impossible without a high fence to keep out the deer, who can be Olympian high jumpers if the prize is right. The giant banana slugs are a bit harder to keep at bay, and more than one tender-hearted person lobbing them into the distance rather than seeking more fatal remedies. Islanders tend to be equally gentle on themselves, practising a wide variety of alternative medicines on each other.

If island residents tend to be health conscious, the low crime rate can make them somewhat casual about locking vehicles. However, one Salt Spring minister always used to lock his car. "Otherwise," he complained, "someone would always stick a couple of zucchinis in it."

Compared with their urban neighbours, islanders have been relatively slow to protect their historic buildings and develop museums interpreting their history. That is simply because most heritage buildings (even those dating from the 1860s) are still lived in. With the increasing pace of development, a study of *Island Heritage Buildings* has been

Original sign on Salt Spring

made and published, and a number of private and public museums now exist or are in development.

Despite the variety of "normal" people living on the islands, there is some justification for the stereotypical image of the eccentric and outspoken Gulf Islander. In a small society, the non-con-

Galleries Galore

MANY ISLAND ARTISTS, fabric artists, potters, craft persons and photographers operate home studios with public visiting hours. Watch for roadside signs, then turn in for a visit. Many of the artists are well known and ship their work across Canada. Enjoy the chance to meet some of them on their home ground.

formists stand out, and we do perhaps have a higher proportion of people who have chosen to pursue alternatives to the mainstream life style. Their fashion statement may be rubber boots and a politically correct T-shirt, and their food choices often organic, but they do not have their heads in the sand. Many have brought a rich experience with them, and many are widely travelled. Conversations therefore tend to be intelligent and vocal about politics, policies, and world issues. At the same time, the sense of community is so strong and vibrant that everyone's opinion is loudly and forcibly expressed, often in the ferry line where the real island issues are dealt with.

Favourite topics of conversation include the iniquities of

the ferry system and the islander's own private fight, for or against, the Islands Trust. Its mandate to preserve and protect the islands is strongly supported by some islanders; while others resent any kind of actual or implied interference in their freedom of action. It's perhaps not surprising that island politics are polarized, with recent MPs chosen alternately from the New Democratic Party and the Reform Party. Bumper stickers supporting many different points of view decorate vehicles in the ferry line-up and give a sample of island opinion, propaganda and whimsy.

Guest Houses and Tourists

Since boat service to the islands became regular, tourism

Paul Wood

ASK MOST CYCLISTS what they think of the Gulf Island terrain for pedalling and they'll admit it provides a strenuous workout. Ask Paul Wood, a 35-year-old Pender Island resident, and he'll say it's a gold-medal training ground.

Since 1990, when he moved to Pender from Banff, Alberta, Paul and his trike "Mike" have been a common sight on Pender's roads. As a result of two near-fatal accidents he suffered in the 1980s (the first, a 12-metre fall to cement; the second, a car accident that left him in a coma for five weeks and partially paralyzed for months), Paul is unable to drive. For those hundreds of little errands and trips that most of us do by car, he uses his trike, year-round, regardless of the weather.

Paul Wood shows off his travel books

All that cycling gave Paul the nerve to enter the BC Summer Games for the Physically Disabled in 1992. He received financial assistance from two local service

groups to modify his trike, and took himself quietly to the competition, without trainers, without fanfare. The dark horse, he nabbed two gold medals, "leaving the provincial coach, the former Olympic champion, and myself utterly stunned."

Now Paul has moved on to a new challenge: long distance cycle touring. His different trips have taken him through the Rockies from Banff to Pender, along the Sunshine Coast, across Vancouver Island to Long Beach, and up to the Queen Charlotte Islands. In addition to tackling ever more ambitious routes and writing accounts of them, Paul plans to spend more time in future visiting with young hospital patients. The 90s circuit rider, inspiring us all.

has gradually increased in importance in the economy of some of the islands. Early guest houses and hotels were followed by the development of cottage resorts on lakes and shores. Now a network of small hotels, marinas and B&Bs cater to the many visitors. Associated with the tourist trade is an ever-growing network of shops, studios, restaurants and special events designed to serve and attract the visitor. Salt Spring's summer-long arts festival, the Gulf Islands Poetry Festival and Saturna's Lamb Barbecue are among the events that attract great interest. (Chapter 5 lists some of the main events.)

Casual tourism has led to a related industry in real estate development and construction. Many Victoria and Vancouver families have a "cottage" some-where on the islands, which may be anything from a shack to a large and elegant house. It sometimes seems that every casual visitor ends up in the real estate office, and certainly good builders are booked up with work, sometimes for years ahead.

Outdoor Recreation

The skiing is not great and skating is a rare treat, but for just about every other sea, land, and air sport you can think of, the Gulf Islands are a true playground for islanders and visitors.

The inter-island waterways are undisputedly among the best in the world for cruising, fishing, kayaking, canoeing and scuba diving. Charters, rentals, lessons, and other support services (such as air fills for dive tanks) are available on most of the islands. Swimming, wind surfing and water skiing, while somewhat more limited by the chilly temperatures of the water year-round, are nevertheless popular in a number of shallow bays on hot summer days, and at the warmer freshwater lakes on several of the islands.

The topography of the islands makes for a terrain that is anything but monotonous. Cyclists will find the islands to be good, and in some cases chal-lenging, riding, with hills well interspersed by long level stretches for recovery. Though the highest peak in the southern Gulf Islands does not exceed 703 m, hikers will find lots of opportunity to climb local hills or "mounts" to gain panoramic views. On Salt Spring Island, the same peaks provide hang-gliders with the perfect launch sites. Added to these activities are ample opportunity for bird and mammal watching, beachcombing, and kite flying.

Camping is popular in the islands, too. Several provincial parks provide excellent camp facilities for vehicle or walk-in campers, and a number of marine parks—some accessible only by water—offer boaters mooring buoys and dock facilities. On many of the larger islands there are also private campgrounds, as well as marinas that cater to a boater's every need.

For those interested in more organized sports, you'll find four nine-hole golf courses located on the islands (Salt Spring, Pender, Galiano and Gabriola), an 18-pole "disc golf" course located on Pender for the frisbee enthusiast, and on several of the islands, public tennis courts and horseback riding opportunities.

Does the baby scarecrow keep young birds away?

5. Calendar of Events

Nail hammering contest, Saturna Lamb Barbecue

Many of the islands have regularly occurring events, some of which are aimed mainly at visitors; others are organized more for islanders, but visitors are welcome. The list provided here will help you plan your visits if are interested in a particular kind of event; fuller details are given on individual islands. Bear in mind that organizing groups are small and usually do not have staff or a permanent office, and locations, dates, programs and phone numbers may change from year to year. In addition to regular events, many smaller events of high quality— readings, concerts, art shows, theatre presentations, workshops and nature walks— occur frequently; check local papers and bulletin boards for listings and current information if you want to get the best out of the cultural scene.

January
- Polar Bear Swim (New Year's Day) Pender, Salt Spring

February
- Cedar Beach Resort Annual Trout Derby, Salt Spring

May
- Farmers' Market (Saturdays to Thanksgiving), Pender
- Pender Islands International Disc Tournament, Pender
- Sheep to Shawl Competition, Salt Spring
- Around the Island Sailboat Race, Salt Spring
- Mountain Bike Festival, Salt Spring
- Open Golf Tournament, Salt Spring
- Artists' Studio Tours (Sundays to September), Salt Spring
- Salt Spring Island Painters' Guild Annual May Show, Salt Spring
- Outdoor markets (to October), Salt Spring

Saturna Lamb Barbecue

Enough lamb to feed a thousand

WE CAUGHT THE open deck water taxi from Hope Bay, Pender Island, and sped across wet and windy Plumper Sound to Winter Cove, Saturna. There the exhilarating progress became a crawl as we hit the yearly boaters' traffic jam. We carefully edged between hundreds of boats anchored in the cove, for the fame of the yearly Canada Day Lamb Barbecue has reached epic proportions in West Coast boating circles. By the time we had docked and walked to the grounds the sun was out and we were wishing we had remembered our sun hats.

The sight of the roasting lamb was both spectacular and stomach turning. The smell was incredibly delicious as Head Chef Jon Guy basted and turned meat using a secret Saturna marinade and a large switch of rosemary, mint and other herbs. But the sight of 27 whole lambs (enough to feed 1,400 people), split down the middle and skewered to metal crosses around a massive bonfire was awfully reminiscent of a mass crucifixion scene. (Jon assured us all the lambs were vegetarian!)

The event started out modestly enough in 1949 when Mr. Cruikshank, a Saturna rancher, decided to give up ranching and, as a treat for his friends and neighbours, slaughtered and barbecued the last couple of lambs, Argentinian style. This was such an enjoyable event it was repeated. Eventually someone had the brilliant idea of using it as a money maker to benefit the whole community.

"We are unabashed anarchists," laughed water taxi skipper Al Sewell. "We use outsiders' money to run our community hall for a year." This seems like a very practical solution to a small island's problem. Besides, as outsiders we get a great meal (an enormous plateful of lamb, coleslaw and Spanish rice), the chance to visit another Gulf Island, as well as live music, competitions and races for the kids, clowns, a craft booth and a beer tent. In fact, everything for a wonderful day out. However, learn by our experience, and take a survival kit: rain gear, sun block, sun hat, sweaters and cash for tickets, beer tent and handicraft stores.

Having fun at Solstice Festival, Pender Island

June
- Market and Café (to August), Saturna
- Summer Solstice Festival, Pender
- Sea Capers Festival, Salt Spring
- Artcraft Show and Sale (to August), Salt Spring

July
- Jamboree (1st), Galiano
- Canada Day Celebration Community Picnic (1st), Mayne
- Garden Party, Pender
- Lamb Barbecue (1st), Saturna
- Canada Day Celebrations (1st), Salt Spring
- Art Show, Galiano
- Lions Fiesta, Galiano
- Country Fair, Mayne
- Summer Festival of the Arts (month long), Salt Spring

August
- Springwater Salmon Derby (3rd weekend), Mayne
- Mayne Mast Salmon Derby, (3rd Saturday), Mayne
- Mayne Island Fall Fair, (3rd Saturday), Mayne
- Tapestry of Words, Pender
- Fall Fair, Pender
- Fulford Days, Salt Spring
- Music Festival, Salt Spring
- Salmon Barbecue, Gabriola

September
- Gulf Islands Poetry Festival, Galiano and other Gulf Islands
- Lions Club Salmon Bake (Labour Day Sunday), Mayne
- Fall Fair and Sheepdog Trials, Salt Spring
- Terry Fox Run, Salt Spring
- Fall Fair, Gabriola
- Gabriola Islander Days, Gabriola

October
- Halloween Fireworks, Gabriola, Pender

November
- Christmas Craft Fair, Mayne, Pender, Saturna, Salt Spring
- Studio Tours, Salt Spring
- Light Up Parade, Salt Spring

December
- Santa Ship, Mayne, Pender, Salt Spring, Saturna
- Otter Bay Symphony Orchestra and Choral Society (Christmas Eve), Pender
- First Night (31st), Gabriola

6. Galiano Island

Enjoying the view from Bellhouse Park

L ong, lean Galiano is shaped like a cudgel, with a handle reaching to the north and a blunt, knobby bottom end bounded by Active Pass. At the south end, Sturdies Bay is the first stop for travellers from Tsawwassen, and so Galiano has long been a favourite haunt of Vancouverites seeking a short break.

A cudgel is perhaps an appropriate image, for Galiano is the fighting island, as islanders and forestry giant MacMillan-Bloedel have locked horns in the woods and in the courts on issues of protection versus development. This controversy follows a history of greater cooperation, when both business and community contributed to the development of fine parklands on this interesting island.

Ongoing conflicts can affect the visitor; at the time of writing for instance, there is no public road access to Dionisio Point Provincial Park. No doubt this dispute will be resolved by the time these words are in print, but others may be expected.

Galiano was named after Commander Dionisio Alcala Galiano, the Spanish naval captain who explored this area in the survey ship *Sutil* in 1792. Other geographic features that bear his name: Dionisio Point at the upper end of the island and Alcala Point on the east side of the island. The Spanish influence remains elsewhere in place names such as Salamanca Point, Quadra Hill and Bodega Ridge.

Galiano is divided jurisdictionally into two parts, north and south, mainly out of practicality for servicing the 25-kilometre long island. Most of the population lives in the southern part of the island, where early farming, commerce and residential development began along Active Pass in the 1860s. The ferry terminal in Montague Harbour was used for some years, and it still serves occasionally because it is more sheltered

Facilities and Services

Emergency Services

- Ambulance, Doctor, Fire, Police: 911
- Doctor: Galiano Health Care Centre, 604-539-9900
- Pharmacy: Drugstore section at the Corner Store, 604-539-2986
- Police: 604-539-2309

Accommodation

- Inns/Resorts: Eight, in various parts of the island, ranging from the log cabins of up-island Bodega Lodge Resort (604-539-2677), to the classy Woodstone Country Inn (604-539-2022) on Georgeson Bay Rd and Galiano Lodge by the ferry (604-539-3388).
- B&Bs: At least 20 spread around the island, with diversity including La Berengerie with its restaurant (604-539-5392), the views of Cliff Pagoda (604-539-2260), High Bluffs with its sauna (604-539-5779), north end's Seaward Getaway (604-539-5601), or historic Sutil Lodge (604-539-2930). Consult local listings, the Travel Info-Centre, the Canadian Gulf Islands B&B Reservation Service (604-539-2930), or Little Island Reservation Services (604-539-2442).
- Camping: Montague Harbour Provincial Parks. No trailer or RV hookups on the island.

Eating Places

Around 10 to suit various tastes and pockets. Most are in the south end: Chez Ferrie is the ferry fast food outlet; Eva's Place (604-539-2001) is in an old store; the Hummingbird Pub (604-539-5472) is well known for good pub food; La Berengerie (604-539-5392) is a gourmet restaurant; Galiano Lodge (604-539-3388) is close to the ferry and is noted for its Pacific Northwest cuisine.

Transportation

- Bus: Pub bus (604-539-5472) transports customers in summer to and from Montague Harbour Marine Park.
- Service: Repairs and gas at Sturdies Bay Gas and Groceries (604-539-5500); Sky's Paradise Garage (repairs, 604-539-2780); Paul Elliott (repairs, 604-539-5462).

Other

- Groceries: Five stores
- Liquor outlets: The Corner Store, off-sales at the Hummingbird Pub
- Post office: Next to the Daystar Market
- Public washrooms: Ferry terminal and parks

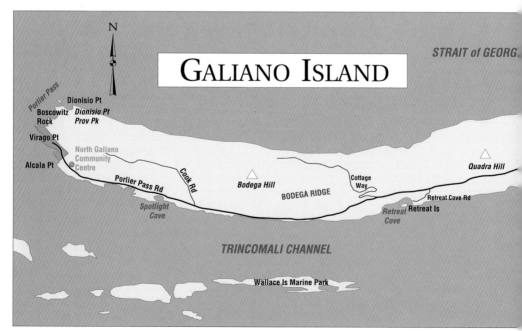

than Sturdies in rough weather. Today most of the retail businesses are concentrated near Sturdies Bay itself and at the junction of Sturdies Bay, Georgeson Bay and Porlier Pass roads.

By contrast, development of the upper end of the island has moved more slowly, and is mainly along the main road. There are fewer houses among the trees, and even in the summer, traffic is generally quieter than the bustle that descends on South Galiano.

Most of the rest of the island is relatively wild, and a wealth of public lands has been secured for everyone's pleasure—lands that range from high ridges and hill tops to serene seaside trails and brilliant white shell beaches. One of these, Montague Harbour Marine Park, is the largest park in the Gulf Islands. A special feature of Galiano is the availability of educational programs interpreting the environment, provided by Elderhostel and the Gulf Islands Institute. The less serious minded visitor can easily fill days with a diversity of outdoor attractions and recreational opportunities including golf, sailing, kayaking, and hiking.

Two provincial campgrounds, five country inns and resorts, and at least 20 B&Bs cater to all travel styles and

Galiano Information

Size: 57 square kilometres
Population: 952 in 1991, now over 1,000
Visitor Information: Write to the Galiano Island Travel Info-Centre, Box 73, Galiano Island, BC V0N 1P0, 604-539-2233. On the island check the unmanned tourist information booth on Sturdies Bay Road (100 m from the ferry dock).

Galiano Access

Ferry: From Tsawwassen (twice per day, takes about 1 hour); from Swartz Bay (three to four times per day, about 1.5 hours); both to Sturdies Bay. Connections to Mayne, Pender, Saturna and Salt Spring. Local information, 604-629-3215.
Float plane: By arrangement, Hanna Air (Salt Spring) offers four return flights a day between the islands and Vancouver International Airport and downtown, 1-800-665-2359. Harbour Air offers daily return service via float plane between Montague Harbour and downtown Vancouver, 1-800-665-0212.
Water taxi: By arrangement, Inter Island Launch, 604-656-8788.
Boat moorage: Montague Harbour Marina (604-539-5733); government docks at Montague Harbour, Retreat Cove, Sturdies Bay, Whaler Bay.

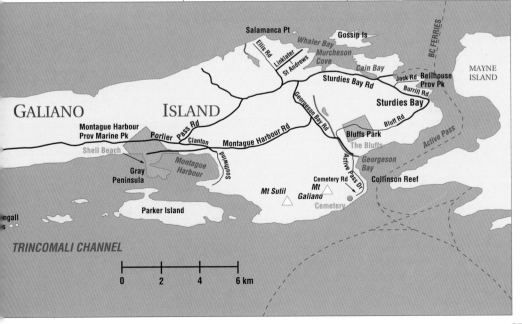

From Bluffs Park, a superferry in Active Pass

legs before heading off to see the rest of the island, make Sturdies Bay itself your first stop. Turn onto Madrona Drive, the first left just past the entrance to the ferry terminal. You'll find parking in front of the several businesses situated there, including a real estate office, the Dandelion Gallery, Sturdies Bay Gas and Groceries, and Gulf Islands Kayaking. For future reference, you might want to take note of the Chez Ferrie fast food stand located at the foot of the ferry terminal parking lot. Many a trip to Galiano has wound down with a Perrier and a muffin from this green and yellow caravan.

A government dock located adjacent to the ferry terminal offers boaters navigating Active Pass a handy temporary moorage and easy access to groceries.

Across Sturdies Bay Road from Madrona is a bus-shelter-like self-serve tourist information booth. It provides a good selection of maps and up-to-date brochures about the island. Particularly useful is the Galiano Visitor's Guide and Map, which is also available on the ferry. Down the short length of Madrona is

budgets. Along with these are the restaurants, cafés, pub and take-out operations which provide an assortment of dining fare, ambience and price to make any community proud. Several galleries, shops and studios offer shoppers many interesting temptations.

For a short stay there is plenty of interest around Sturdies Bay, and a side trip by Burrill Road leads to Bellhouse Park and the Bluffs, both with fine views of Active Pass. For those with more time, we recommend following the main road from Sturdies Bay, which passes a number of noteworthy features and leads to Galiano's biggest park at Montague Harbour. From there, an exploration takes you up the spine of the island to Dionisio Point Provincial Park at the northern tip.

Sturdies Bay

Scarcely off the ferry on Galiano and you'll find yourself promptly absorbed into the island's mainstream. Not only is Sturdies Bay Road one of the island's busiest thoroughfares, but there is much of interest within the first half kilometre.

If you'd like to stretch your

Some Galiano Highlights

- Bluffs Park
- Bodega Ridge
- Cruise on *Great White Cloud*
- Dandelion Gallery
- The Daystar Market - Corner Store - Ixchel shopping area
- Dionisio Point Provincial Park
- Montague Harbour Marine Park and the Gray Peninsula

Porlier Pass from Dionisio Point Park

Galiano Lodge, with its restaurant overlooking Sturdies Bay.

The Dandelion Gallery, a well-established artists' co-op, features the talent of island painters, sculptors, jewelers, writers and musicians. Among those whose work you can see are Keith Holmes, Ronaldo Norden, Sandra Froese, Win Stephen and Elizabeth Steward. A little farther along Sturdies Bay Road—a short stroll

from Madrona—is the Trincomali Bakery and Deli. It's a busy place and makes a good morning stop for coffee and a cinnamon bun. Just past the bakery on the left is what is known locally as the "old Burrill store." Though moved from its original site and restructured over the years (and currently housing Eva's Place), it remains a beloved landmark and reminder of Yorkshire

bachelor brothers Joe and Frank Burrill. Arriving on Galiano in the late 1890s, the two kept islanders stocked with groceries and other household needs for 40 years.

Side Trip to the Bluffs and Active Pass (4 km)

If you have limited time on Galiano, the area near Active Pass makes a good half-day trip. It can be completed as a circle tour via the shopping area on Sturdies Bay Road, or with more time makes a good starting point for exploration of the rest of the island.

The area still has the rural feeling of earlier times. Along Burrill Road, Georgeson Bay Road and Active Pass Drive some of the oldest properties on the island still look much as they must have done a century ago.

From the ferry terminal, follow Sturdies Bay Road for

Recreational Opportunities

- **Birding:** Active Pass, Ballingall Islets, Montague Harbour, Porlier Pass
- **Catamaran cruises:** Canadian Gulf Islands Catamaran Cruises (604-539-2930)
- **Cooking:** Peter's Cooking Retreats (604-539-5848)
- **Cycling:** Rental and repair at Galiano Bicycle (604-539-2806); Gulf Islands Kayaking (604-539-2442)
- **Diving:** Galiano Island Diving Service (604-539-3109)
- **Education:** Elderhostel and Therah Learning Centre (604-529-2127); Gulf Islands Institute for Environmental Studies (604-539-2930, fax 604-539-5390)

- **Fishing:** Charters, tackle and bait; Mel-N-I Charters (604-539-3171); Sea Devil Charter (604-539-2974)
- **Golf:** Galiano Island Golf and Country Club (9 holes), 24 St. Andrews, off Linklater Road (604-539-5533)
- **Hiking:** Bluffs Park, Bodega Ridge, Dionisio Point Provincial Park, Montague Harbour Provincial Marine Park, Mount Galiano
- **Horse riding:** Bodega Trail Rides, Manastee Road (604-539-2677)
- **Kayaking:** Kayak with the Institute (604-539-2930); Gulf Islands Kayaking for lessons, rentals, tours (604-539-2442)

- **Personal development:** Look for yoga and other courses in local information
- **Playgrounds:** Galiano Island School, 1290 Sturdies Bay Rd
- **Shopping:** Dandelion Gallery, Ixchel, Small World Gift Shop, and numerous home shops and studios around the island (look for pottery, fabric art including weaving and painted silk, knives, dried flowers, knitted goods, jewelry, and paintings)
- **Swimming:** Sea dips at Dionisio Point Provincial Park, Montague Harbour Provincial Park, Cain Bay

half a kilometre and turn left onto Burrill Road. Just beyond St. Margaret of Scotland Anglican Church, turn left onto Jack Drive and go down the short road to its end. Here is Bell-house Provincial Park, a two-hectare rocky shelf that slopes gently down to Active Pass. Bequeathed to the province by the Bellhouse family in 1964, this park is easily accessible by everyone. It's a delightful spot to picnic or simply lie back and enjoy the view and passing boat traffic. Across Active Pass (which at this eastern entrance is less than one kilometre wide) stands the lighthouse at Georgina Point on Mayne Island. When conditions are right, Mount Baker, located in Washington State, looms mirage-like to the left of the lighthouse. At this park there's never a shortage of front-row seats.

When you've had your fill, head up to Bluffs Park for an upper balcony perspective on the pass. From Jack Drive, return to Burrill Road and turn left. This route passes several old homes and farms; it also passes the island's new medical clinic on the right and a new community hall. Burrill Road turns into Bluff Road, which winds uphill from the seaside homes facing Active Pass. Along here, too, is the Driftwood Village Resort.

About a kilometre from the start of Bluff Road, the paved surface gives way to gravel and

Matthew Schoenfeld: Sharps and Flats

MASTER KNIFE MAKER and cycling enthusiast, Matthew Schoenfeld brings a Zen-like attitude and thoughtfulness to his work and life on Galiano—which is perhaps not so surprising for someone who did post-graduate work in philosophy, theology and psychology at Berkeley in the '60s. A resident of Galiano since 1979, Matthew has combined his two passions into a satisfying livelihood.

Through one entrance of his workshop is his knife making machinery. Here he cuts the stainless steel forms, shapes them, grinds them, and polishes them to a mirror finish. He then adds his trademark multi-coloured handles—laminated layers of birch. To describe these knives as works of art sounds too frivolous, yet to describe them as mere tools sounds too mundane. The fact is they are both beautiful and functional, and as a result are highly sought after by international collectors, as well as ordinary folk who want a perfectly designed knife for the job. The selection is wide: knives for hunting, camping, fishing; knives for carving; knives for every job in the kitchen; and knives meant only for display.

Through the other entrance of Matthew's workshop is his bicycle business. From here, he and business partner Pamela Taylor operate Galiano Bicycle, repairing sick bikes, renting new ones, and selling cycling accessories. Matthew began this enterprise about five years ago, partly out of need—in the great tradition of "multi-tasked" island living—and partly because he has the know-how. A serious, off-road technical rider himself, Matthew tackles the roads and trails of Galiano regularly, keeping in shape for the extended cycling tours he does abroad every few years. "Steep doesn't bother me, it just slows me down," he says. Not much, though.

The cutting edge

Galiano Events

June
- Strawberry Tea

July
- North Galiano July 1 Jamboree
- Art Show sponsored by the Artists Guild of Galiano
- Weavers' Show
- Gulf Islands Poetry Festival

August
- Lions Fiesta

October
- Blackberry Festival

November
- North Galiano Christmas Craft Show

a sign marks the park entrance. Even on a hot day, the forest forms a cool canopy overhead. About 200 metres from the entrance, a well-marked side road leads off to the left and up a short distance to the parking area at the bluffs. From here, follow the trail that winds along the 180-metre ridge. At your feet lie Active Pass and Helen Point on Mayne Island; beyond is a Gulf Islands vista: Saturna, Pender, Prevost, Salt Spring, and the waterways between. In the distance is southern Vancouver Island and beyond that the Olympic Mountains.

Returning from Bluffs Park, you can return to Sturdies Bay the way you came, or carry on through the park down Bluff Road to Georgeson Bay Road, picking up the Sturdies to

Déja Vu recycles clothes

Montague route.

Sturdies Bay to the Hummingbird Pub (3 km)

Half a kilometre from the ferry, Sturdies Bay Road winds up along the edge of Whaler Bay. Once an anchorage for small coastal whaling boats, the bay is now used as a log booming ground, a launching site for local boat-builders and a home for several commercial fish

Public Land on Galiano

SHORTLY AFTER World War II, a group of residents wanted to acquire the magnificent bluffs overlooking Active Pass. The group reached an agreement with the land owner, Max Enke, to purchase a 38-hectare strip of waterfront along Georgeson Bay for $1,000. In a pattern that was to be repeated in later years, a fundraising committee was struck. One popular source of funds was the donations made by the many weekly visitors who attended classical music concerts at the home of Galiano resident Paul Scoones (concerts made possible by his gramophone and extensive record collection). Soon the $1,000 was raised. Mr. Enke, meanwhile, decided it would be "too much trouble" to survey and subdivide his land, and instead donated the remainder of his

property to the community, more than tripling the size of the new park. The land is held in trust by the Galiano Club, a community service organization established in 1924. Club volunteers still maintain the park today.

The acquisition of Bluffs Park launched a tradition of preserving public land through community action, and the establishment of Montague Provincial Marine Park and Bellhouse Provincial Park followed in later years. In 1990 the Galiano Club mounted a campaign to raise $250,000 to acquire Mount Galiano; and another community group, the Galiano Conservancy Association, led the effort to obtain Mount Sutil. Both efforts succeeded. Dionisio Point Provincial Park has been the most recent park added to the growing list of public land on

the island.

Still, the community can't rest yet. The middle portion of the island, accounting for over 50% of the island area, is faced with development. MacMillan-Bloedel, which has owned and logged the land for many years, proposed a plan in the late 1980s to sell its holdings for residential development. In the opinion of many islanders, this threatens everything from future water supplies and the treasured Bodega Ridge trail, to the island's lifestyle and character. Court wrangles and lawsuits have followed.

Although development is proceeding on a portion of this land, the hope of preserving much of the area is still very much alive in the hearts and minds of many residents—a legacy of that same spirit that created Bluffs Park.

Murcheson Family Story

Finlay and Mary Murcheson

MURCHESON COVE was named after Finlay and Mary Murcheson, Scots who arrived on Galiano in 1882. Along with their two sons, Archibald and Finlay Alexander, they purchased 400 acres of land near Sturdies Bay. Archibald became a master mariner, but drowned on the Fraser River in 1901. At age 42,

Finlay Alexander went on to marry and have seven children (appropriately, thereafter he was referred to as "Father Finlay"). In addition to farming, he worked for many years as road foreman on the island—much of the road you travel on Galiano today was originally laid out under his supervision.

After Father Finlay died in 1931, the family moved to Victoria, all except the eldest daughter, Rosamund, who stayed on Galiano with her new husband, Kenny Hardy. They in turn had four children, the eldest of whom became known to Canadians as Liberal M.P., Iona Campagnola.

boats. Between the many homes perched above the bay you can glimpse the water below and the houses across the way on the Cain Peninsula. Another glimpse of the water is at Murcheson Cove.

Along this route is the Galiano School and the Galiano Home Building Centre and Small World Gift Shop. The eclecticism of the goods in the gift shop—from gumboots, tube socks and small appliances, to angora wool, Medici stationery and pewterware—almost guarantees that you'll discover something here you'd forgotten you needed.

Just up the hill from the gift shop is the Hummingbird Pub on the right. Galiano's neighbourhood pub, the Hummingbird is something of a legend among island visitors, especially those who arrive via

Keith Holmes: Landscape as Art and Inspiration

THE DAYSTAR MARKET mural features a larger-than-life tangle of sunflowers and poppies that has become an island landmark of sorts, and even on the greyest of January days it emanates the scent of sweet grass, the buzz of nectar-sodden insects and the sultriness of mid-summer heat.

Once the concept for the piece was set, it took Keith and his Calgary-based partner in murals, Stan Phelps, a week of painting. Many of their murals have been commissioned in Alberta, including one 80- X 20-foot project that they recently completed for the City of Calgary. Closer to home, in addition to the Daystar garden, is their heron mural on Saturna Island's general store, the Narvaez Bay Trading Company.

Keith came to Galiano 16 years ago, giving up the commercial arts career he had settled into following study at the Banff School of Fine Arts and the Alberta College of Art. Both he and his wife, artist Debbie Carpentier-Holmes, wanted a change of climate and lifestyle. Galiano gave them just that.

Murals are only a part of the work that Keith does. At a smaller, more conventional scale, his subject matter has ranged from portraiture and compositions reminiscent of Alex Colville, to landscape and still life. His colours are strong, but the moods he creates are soft and warm.

Keith's artistic sensibility extends beyond the canvas, and he remains an ardent supporter of what the community has achieved in securing public parkland on the island—areas that he calls "some of the most inspirational pieces of our landscape."

The work of Keith Holmes can be seen at the Dandelion Gallery, Madrona Drive.

Montague Harbour Marine Park. The 16-page menu is part of it, and so is the friendly atmosphere. Mostly, though, it's "The Bus." In July and August, the Hummingbird runs a red and white converted school bus back and forth every evening between Montague and the pub. The hourly shuttle service is inexpensive, Chuck Berry rocks over the sound system, and the driver makes everyone feel like a long-lost buddy.

The junction just beyond the pub is where Sturdies Bay Road meets Porlier Pass Road and Georgeson Bay Road. Bearing right onto Porlier Pass Road, you'll come to the nine-hole Galiano Island Golf and Country Club (604-539-5533) at 24 St. Andrews, off Ellis and then Linklater roads. Clubs and carts are available for rent, and the fully licensed restaurant is open for lunch and dinner. Continuing on Porlier Pass Road gives you a shortcut to the 22 kilometre up to the north end of the island, but if there is time we recommend a more leisurely route via Montague Harbour.

Hummingbird Pub to Montague Harbour (5 km)

Bear left at the junction onto Georgeson Bay which will take you to another polestar of island commerce. On the right is the Daystar Market with its eye-catching wall mural of a thriving garden. The Daystar sells fresh fruits and vegetables, bulk foods, fresh baked goods, and a sound variety of epicurean temptations. On the left of the Daystar is the Galiano post office; to the right

the Candlelite Café, open for lunch and dinner. Nearby is the Déja Vu Clothing Trailer.

Across the road is the Corner Store. In addition to selling "supermarket groceries," it also carries drugstore items and videos. Next door, its blue walls commanding attention, is the craft shop Ixchel. Named for the Mayan goddess of women's endeavours, it features goods from around the world (many from third-world co-ops), as well as local handmade items. Pottery, jewelry, clothing, books and music are among some of its wares.

Georgeson Bay Road heads across the southern part of the island, passing the Woodstone

Country Inn. About one kilometre from the Sturdies Bay turnoff, our main route heads up Montague Harbour Road, for the four-kilometre trip to the provincial marine park. Cyclists should be prepared for a steady climb along the first kilometre. In addition to stamina, they also need good brakes. After the upward grind, the road descends for more than a kilometre to the harbour.

However, before you leave Georgeson Bay Road you may want to take a side trip to see the other end of Active Pass from the foot of Mount Galiano.

Galiano Cemetery

SCREENED FROM THE bustle of Active Pass by a swaying curtain of fir and Arbutus, this secluded spot is the final resting place of many Galiano pioneers, including members of the Bellhouse, Burrill, Georgeson, Murcheson, New and Scoones families.

It was the Georgesons who donated the land to the community in 1927, setting two conditions: that there be no charge for burying a Galiano resident in the cemetery, and

that a plot be reserved for the Georgeson family. Visible through the trees just off-shore in Active Pass is the Collinson Reef marker. Here the ferry *Queen of Alberni* ran aground in 1979, fortunately with no loss of life but incurring over a million dollars in damage to the ship. Nearby, a collision in 1970 between the Russian freighter *Sergey Yesenin* and the ferry *Queen of Victoria* resulted in three deaths.

Island pioneers rest in Galiano's cemetery

Sutil Lodge

WHEN THE JACKSON FAMILY moved from Liverpool to Vancouver in 1912, they brought fond memories of holidays in Brighton, a seaside resort on England's south coast. Stanley, trained as a marine engineer, came to Canada first in 1910, and two years later was joined by his parents and two sisters. One sister, Margaret, became friends with a family named Egan, who then occupied the only house on Galiano's Montague Harbour.

In 1926, Margaret brought Stanley over to visit. So taken was he by the huge maples and sunset views of the southwest corner of the harbour that he purchased a large lot below Mount Sutil. Two years later, he built a guest house on the site, adopting the "British colonial bungalow style."

"Sutil Lodge" became the permanent home of the Jacksons and, from 1929, a thriving resort. Mrs. Jackson brought her piano and Victorian furniture to fill the house, and Margaret, free in the summers from her teaching job, came as cook and gardener. Stanley—in white flannels—rowed out to meet the CPR ferries in Active Pass with his converted fishing boat, the *Mary Jean*, and conveyed guests to the lodge. Ashore, he functioned as social director, encouraging play on the grass tennis court he had created, singing the songs popular in Brighton in his youth, and telling ghost stories about the ancient inhabitants of the island. Within a few years, 16 guest cabins were added along the waterfront, as well as a dining cabin which also provided space for games and dancing.

Tom and Ann Hennessy at Sutil Lodge

Margaret eventually moved full time to the lodge, which struggled on through the depression and World War II until its owners were too elderly to continue its operation. In 1948 it closed. By the 1960s Mr. and Mrs. Jackson and Margaret had died. As young artists and urban dropouts moved to Galiano in the 1970s, Stanley let them use his cabins, chauffeured them about the island, and once again entertained them by playing his electric organ.

When Stanley died in 1983, his neighbours included Ann and Tom Hennessy, an American couple who, like Stanley more than half a century before, had come to Galiano for a visit and been smitten. The Hennessys purchased the lodge and in 1986 carefully restored it to maintain its 1920s appeal. Today they run it as a bed and breakfast. A guest book dating from 1929 still remains at the lodge, full of poems contributed by generations of satisfied guests.

Strong proponents of ecotourism, the Hennessy family also leads kayaking and sailing expeditions, ranging in style from picnic outings to three-day excursions. Their 46-foot catamaran, *Great White Cloud*, is a common sight leaving and entering Montague Harbour throughout the summer, and Tom has initiated the Gulf Islands Institute for Environmental Studies. Together They have also created the Gulf Islands Bed & Breakfast registry, providing a focal point for bookings on all the islands.

Side Trip to Mount Galiano (2 km)

Continue left along Georgeson Bay Road to Active Pass Drive. Much of this area was originally owned and farmed by Henry Georgeson, one of the first white settlers to move to Galiano in 1858. His great-granddaughter, Joan Carolan, still lives part of the year on Georgeson Bay. If you stop by the Camas Shop at 90 Active Pass Road, you can see some of her woven goods, in addition to knitting, pottery, jewelry and sheepskin slippers made by island artists and crafts people.

Half a kilometre beyond the Camas Shop the road ends. A sign on the right marks the start of the trail up Mount Galiano. The climb is moderately steep and, at a relaxed pace, it takes about 50 minutes to reach the 311-metre summit. The views from the open grassy verges are worth every step.

Cemetery Road is a short dip down to the left off the end of Active Pass Drive. It passes a 3,000-year-old midden, and ends at the entrance to Galiano Cemetery.

Montague Harbour Provincial Marine Park

The sun sets on Montague Harbour

THE FIRST MARINE park established by the province of British Columbia, Montague Harbour Provincial Marine Park occupies the former site of an ancient Coast Salish settlement. The beauty, bounty and security of the harbour that made it attractive for several thousand years of occupation have endured. Archeologists (nicknamed the "Montague mudsuckers") have been undertaking underwater excavations in the harbour, successfully testing the idea that a rise in sea level may have submerged older deposits.

At the head of the harbour, an isthmus of sand and tidal lagoon connects Gray Peninsula to the rest of Galiano. Five kilometres of trail wind through the forested peninsula, spilling out here and there onto the white shell and sand beaches that encircle the point. On a hot summer day, the water is aqua and the sun on the fine crushed shell is dazzling.

The 97-hectare park was established in 1959. It remains the largest in the Gulf Islands, with 15 walk-in campsites (also popular for cycling or kayaking to), 25 drive-in sites, and 23 mooring buoys (plus a large natural anchorage). Facilities include hiking trails, a group campsite and shelter, outhouses, water, wood, picnic tables, fire pits and garbage disposal. A boat launch is located at the end of the road leading into the vehicle camping sites. Beside the warden's house are an information rack and pay phone.

It's not uncommon on some peak weekends in July and August to find more than a hundred boats sharing the harbour.

Shell Beach is a popular spot for swimming, boating and general playing. Along with the great peel of sunbathers that gravitate here are often various motorized sea, air and amphibious machines. If you're looking for a place to sit and contemplate the mesmerizing scenery, this is not usually the place to be on a summer weekend afternoon.

BC Parks runs an extensive summer schedule of free interpretive programs. These are held at the "meeting place"—an outdoor setting with rows of log benches—or at the Marine Park Nature House located on the dock. The nature house is also open during the day (see the information boards in the park for times).

Montague Harbour Area

As you head down the hill along Montague Harbour Road, you pass La Berengerie, a French restaurant and "auberge," immediately before the junction with Clanton Road. Each evening's table d'hôte menu is well worth considering at this indoor restaurant and outdoor café, both of which have all the flavour and colour of their Avignon-born proprietress.

Off Montague Harbour Road to the left is Southwind Road, at the end of which is Sutil Lodge, a resort B&B with a '20s atmosphere.

Montague Park Road leads directly to the head of the harbour's government dock. From this point you can get a good look over the large bay. Outside the harbour lies Parker Island; to the right, sweeping around in a wide arc, is Montague Provincial Marine Park. The waters here are always busy with sail and motor boats, working boats and float planes (including Harbour Air's scheduled Gulf Islands - Vancouver service).

Montague Harbour Store, beside the dock, caters mainly to the needs of boaters, selling fuel, groceries, ice and fishing tackle.

Harbour Seal

Harbour Seal

A ROUND HEAD with big eyes and no visible ears emerges gently from the harbour, watches you silently for a few minutes, then as quietly submerges. You are being given the "once over" by one of the most familiar marine animals, the harbour seal. Sail or paddle past a remote rock and you are likely to see a group of seals of varying shades of brown and grey perched in sometimes absurd positions, enjoying a break from their fishing activities.

Underwater the seal is a vigorous swimmer, taking shellfish from rocks and sea floor, and pursuing herring, rockfish, and the occasional salmon. Although they like fresh food, they are not averse to hanging round a fish cleaning station for debris from our catches. Adaptations to marine life include an ability to drink sea water and dive for up to 20 minutes at a time by slowing the heart rate and restricting blood circulation.

Baby seals are born in May and June, and left by their mothers on what they no doubt hope is a quiet beach while she gets food. Unfortunately, as the Gulf Islands become busier, the baby seals are often disturbed, and may be abandoned if they attract too much human attention.

Gulf Islands Poetry Festival

IF YOU WANT to see 50 or 60 real live poets all in one place, turn up at La Berengerie on Galiano for the annual Gulf Islands Poetry Festival held in July. Usually the weather can be counted on to provide a warm day, so the poets, apprentice poets and poetry appreciators are able to lounge on the grass under the trees and indulge in several enjoyable hours of listening to the readers. Not everyone's cup of tea, but this event has developed a loyal following. The "sound poetry," "poetry in action," "poetry and percussion," and a raft of other techniques displayed can be counted upon to stretch one's idea of poetry. This event is free and no one minds if you drop in for an hour as long as you time it between presentations to minimize disturbances. Some years, reading events are held on other islands as part of the Galiano Festival. As this event is a moveable feast, it is wise to read the local notice boards and papers for more precise information.

Porlier Pass Road to North Galiano (19 km)

Once you've explored the many corners of South Galiano, it's time to head up the spine of the island to the north end. You can begin from Clanton Road half a kilometre from Montague Harbour; it connects with Porlier Pass Road one kilometre along.

The 18-kilometre distance from this junction seems a long stretch after the close weave of roads, houses and businesses around South Galiano. The road profile, mildly undulating, is generally rated by cyclists as "intermediate"; the road surface is well maintained. In addition to several natural attractions along the route there are a number of studios and craft shops. Watch for roadside signs indicating when they're open.

About nine kilometres up Porlier Pass Road from the Clanton Bay Road junction, Retreat Cove Road leads down

Bodega Ridge

You can park in the turn-around at the end of Cottage Way, where the start of the trail is signed. The route itself is not a difficult ascent, but along the ridge are sections where less talking over one's shoulder and more paying attention to footing are recommended. Part way up from the start of the climb, the trail splits, one route for hikers, the other for mountain bikers. At its highest point, Bodega Hill is 240 metres. The view over Trincomali Channel is never the same twice.

View out over Trincomali Channel

to the left. At the end is the government dock at Retreat Cove and a small grassy point overlooking the water. In years past, this spot has served as a community hub, having had at different times a fish saltery, a grocery store and a school.

A further one and a half kilometres along Porlier Pass Road, is Cottage Way on the right. At the end of this road (not quite two kilometres up) is the Bodega Ridge trailhead.

Continue along Porlier Pass Road about two kilometres from Cottage Way, and you can enjoy a great view (with less effort than it takes to walk Bodega Ridge) by pulling into the lay-by on the left. Here you can look across Trincomali Channel to Wallace and Salt Spring islands.

The Elderhostel is located a little farther along Porlier Pass Road, and Galiano Dive Services and a boat launch are also here. Less than a kilometre farther along is Bodega Resort, just up Cook Road, to the right off the main road.

One of the nicest ways to spend at least an afternoon on this end of Galiano is to hike or drive into Dionisio Point Provincial Park. At the time of writing, the former road access via Cook Road is closed over disputes about easements across private land, and it is not clear whether it will be reopened or replaced by other access. Watch for signs directing you to the park.

From Cook Road you can continue north along Porlier Pass Road, along a stretch where the route winds close to the water

Trail sign for Bodega Ridge hikers

Dionisio Point Provincial Park

Walking the rocks at Dionisio Park

Arbutus on the rocks

Coon Bay at high tide

ALTHOUGH ONLY OFFICIALLY acquired from MacMillan-Bloedel and designated as a provincial park in 1993, Dionisio Point has been a favourite hiking and camping spot for years. In 1991, Mac-Blo made a gift to the province of the waterfront properties; the province bought more than 100 hectares of adjoining land. Provided in the park are 13 drive-in campsites and 12 walk-in sites. Facilities include water and outhouses.

Dionisio offers everything that the ultimate Gulf Island park should have: a sandy beach, sculpted sandstone with honeycomb weathering, rocky ledges and a surfeit of marine life all arranged around a sheltered retreat on the inside of the point. Coon Bay, facing Georgia Strait, looks out at a world of freighters, tugs and ferries in the distance, with the mainland as a distant backdrop. One trail winds out to the tip of the point itself, a short walk over a rocky promontory covered with small stands of Arbutus and Garry Oak. Along the water's edge are shelves of rock sculpture. From here, Valdes Island and the lighthouse on Boscowitz Rock are little more than a holler away. Other trails lead to outlooks toward the western end of the pass. Virago Point, with its lighthouse, is on Indian Reserve land and, although no one is living there full time any more, the "no trespassing" signs must be respected.

During tidal change, the current snorts through the pass between the two islands at up to nine knots. Any venturing out in small craft should be done at slack tide.

Kayakers in paradise

past several little coves. One of these, Spotlight Cove, was once the site of a small boat yard belonging to Harry Vollmers. It was here in 1901 that Captain J.C. Voss worked with Vollmers to transform a

Don't lose your head

38-foot dugout canoe into the sailing vessel, *Tilikum*, and went on—in an effort to "one-up" Joshua Slocum's achievement with *Spray*—to become the first to round the globe in so small a boat (a trip that lasted from 1901 to 1904). Look for Spotlight Studio (on the left at 20625 Porlier Pass Road), which sells paintings, hand-made sweaters, cards and dolls.

Finally, near the end of Porlier Pass Road, you'll reach Spanish Hills General Store. If it's summertime, you'll be in luck: the store will be open and you can treat yourself to a hamburger or cappuccino on the waterside deck. The store also sells groceries, navigational

charts, and fishing licences. If it's before May or after September, you'll have the view from the government dock to savour instead, and the pleasure of reading the store's outside bulletin board without being jostled by the summer crowd.

Less than a kilometre beyond the store is the North Galiano Community Hall. Here the annual July 1st Jamboree takes place, a parade and fair to which the whole Galiano community and visitors are welcomed.

The road ends at Indian Reserve land and private property. Access to Porlier Pass is now through Dionisio Point Provincial Park. From here, you have the prospect of a pleasant return trip back down the island to the ferry; the most direct route is via Porlier Pass Road to Sturdies Bay Road.

7. Mayne Island

Miners Bay and Village Bay on Mayne Island

On August 16, 1883, ships from Nanaimo, New Westminster, and Victoria brought seven hundred members of the Oddfellows to picnic at Miners Bay on Mayne Island, complete with brass bands. Early island residents, quick to recognize an opportunity, soon established several hotels and guest houses to cater to vacationers. So well did they succeed that by 1900, Mayne was one of the pre-eminent resort destinations in the Pacific Northwest. That hospitality continues today at the island's numerous accommodations and restaurants. The island is well-endowed with beaches, and it now has two parks.

Well before its charms as a holiday playground began to draw people, Mayne was already the undisputed commercial and social centre of the southern Gulf Islands. Active Pass was a major route between the islands, and in 1858 Miners Bay was a convenient stop-over point for thousands of gold miners heading from Victoria to the Fraser River and the Cariboo. Once the gold fever had passed, many of these same miners returned to settle on Mayne and the other Gulf Islands. With some of the best agricultural land of any of the islands, Mayne farmers—including many of Japanese extraction—came to be known for their fruit, daffodils, tomatoes and other produce over the years. Miners Bay grew rapidly into a busy village, its dock a regular port of call for ships loading and unloading passengers, mail and freight.

Although no longer the heart of the local domain, the island still possesses the self-assuredness of a matriarch. There's a settled feeling here, and a mellowness of lifestyle that seems to match the comfortably rounded shape of the island itself and the community spread out nicely around its curves. One comes to Mayne to visit the old buildings, stroll the many beaches or country roads, and partake of excellent food and lodgings. Long gone are the bar room carryings-on which, more than

Are they biting on your side?

90 years ago, prompted Mayne's dry neighbours to nickname it, rather peevishly, "Little Hell."

To make the most of a short trip, head straight for Miners Bay. With more time, consider following the 17-kilometre circuit suggested here. However, this recommended route is inland, and to get the best of the island you will need to take time for one or more side trips to the various bays and beach accesses, with Georgina Point as a first choice. This is an island well worth lingering over; do so and you'll discover some of the same pleasures that have enticed people here for over a century.

Village Bay to Miners Bay (2.5 km)

Disembarking at the large ferry terminal at Village Bay you can be forgiven for thinking that "village" is a reference to the relatively recent collection of homes surrounding the bay. In fact, Helen Point on the Active Pass side of Village Bay was a fishing station for First Nations more than 4,500 years ago. Not until the 1870s, though, did the Royal Navy mappers make "Village Bay" the official name of the First Nations settlement then at the head of the bay.

In 1873, Portuguese seaman John Silva and his Native wife Louisa bought 273 acres on the bay. With the drowning of two of their children in Active Pass, however, and the constant problem of sheep poachers, they sold to the Deacon family in 1883 and moved to Gabriola Island. The Deacons went on to expand their land holdings, ultimately owning 1,000 acres in the Village Bay area and the 300-acre

Hardscrabble Farm near Bennett Bay.

At the exit from the ferry terminal, carry on around the bend and up the hill. About one kilometre along, the road passes through a section of tall, dense forest. On the left is private land of the Helen Point Indian Reserve, established in

Glaucous-winged gull

Mayne Access

Ferry: From Tsawwassen twice a day (about 1.5 hours), and from Swartz Bay three to four times a day (about 45 minutes). Connections with Galiano, Pender, Saturna and Salt Spring. All ferries serve Village Bay, which is a major transfer point for ferry connections around the southern Gulf Islands. Local information, 604-539-2321.

Float plane: Hanna Air (Salt Spring) offers four return flights a day between Miners Bay

and Vancouver International Airport and downtown, 1-800-665-2359. Harbour Air provides daily return service between Miners Bay and downtown Vancouver, 1-800-665-0212.

Water taxi: By arrangement, Inter Island Launch, 604-656-8788.

Boat moorage: Government docks at Horton Bay and Miners Bay.

1877 and still occupied by members of the Cowichans. Watch for a dirt drive on the right with a sign indicating Mount Parke Regional Park, one of the few opportunities for a strenuous hike on Mayne. Another kilometre and a half along, Village Bay Road leads to the village of Miners Bay.

Miners Bay to Georgina Point (2.5 km)

From Springwater Lodge, turn right onto Georgina Point Road. The "coronation bench"

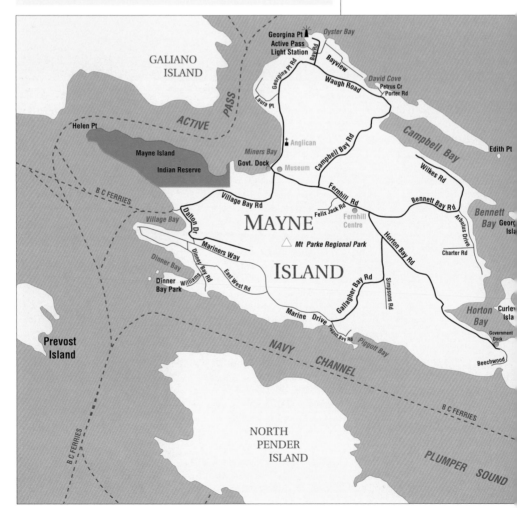

encircling the copper beech at the head of the dock was built in 1937 to commemorate the coronation of George VI.

Lining the road that runs along the bay is a wonderful collection of older homes, their verandahs and decks full of flowers. Among these is Tinkerers B&B, which sits on the site of the long-gone Mayne Island Hotel. The 80-year-old boathouse on the water side of the road is now converted into the consummate seaside cottage.

A short distance farther along the road, on a rise overlooking Miners Bay, is St. Mary Magdalene Anglican Church, consecrated in 1898. If you can, pay a visit when the church is open. In addition to the warm wood interior and red stained glass high in the west wall, the church contains a unique baptismal font, a 160-kilogram chunk of sandstone. In 1900, with much ingenuity and at least as much muscle power, Canon William Paddon and Ralph Grey of Samuel Island brought it by rowboat all the way from East

Mayne Information

Area: 21 square kilometres
Population: 743 in 1991, now over 800
Visitor Information: Write to the Mayne Island Community Chamber of Commerce, Mayne Island, BC V0N 2J0. On the island, there is a tourist information map at the start of Village Bay Road just past the exit from the ferry terminal.

Point, Saturna.

Behind the white picket

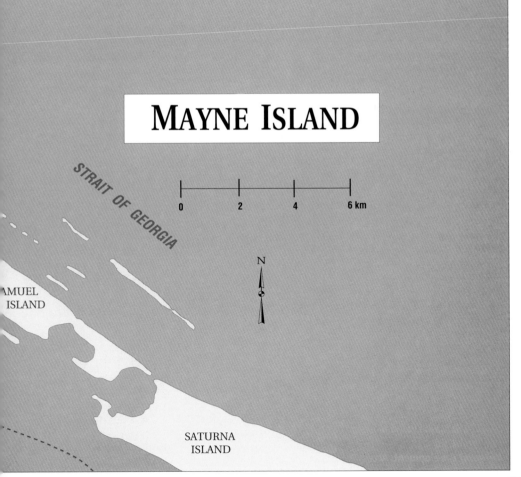

Mount Parke Regional Park

View from Mount Parke overlooking Swanson Channel

THE ONLY PUBLICLY accessible peak on Mayne, Mount Parke rises 271 metres. The hike to the top is up a gravel road, one which doubles as access for residents living on the slopes of the hill and access for service people tending to the radio communication tower at the peak. Hikers must park at the bottom of the road, well clear of the controlled-entry gate.

What the route lacks in sylvan charm it more than makes up for in the workout it provides and the views it lays on. At a steady but not too energetic pace, count on the climb taking at least 45 minutes. The ridge at the summit offers an airplane view south and west over Pender and off towards Vancouver Island and the Olympic Mountains. The land-scape below, the ferry terminal, and the activity in the waterways all assume the tidy pattern that only this kind of "big picture" perspective can give. The tower at the peak is part of the navigational radar system established to aid local shipping traffic.

A word of caution: The unfenced cliff here drops away sharply and uncompromisingly. Enjoy the view at a safe distance back from the edge, and rein in children and dogs.

Recreational Opportunities

Birding: Shores of Active Pass notable; sheltered bays good for water birds; mudflats at Horton and Village bays good for shorebirds in fall.

Cycling: For rental try some of the B&Bs, such as Blue Vista Resort (604-539-2463), Tinkerers (604-539-2280), and Wildeflower Inn B&B (604-539-2327).

Diving: Albatross Charters (604-539-2244); Viable Marine Services (604-539-3200)

Fishing charters, tackle and bait: Five currently available

Hiking: Mount Parke Regional Park

Kayaking: Mayne Island Kayak and Canoe Rentals (604-539-2667)

Museums: Mayne Island Museum, Fernhill Rd

Personal development: Access

Kayakers at Oyster Bay

to island specialists through Tinkerers Travel & Learn Network (604-539-2280)

Playgrounds: Mayne Island School (535 Fernhill Rd.)

Shopping: More than a dozen galleries, home shops and studios around the island (look for painting, pottery, fabric art including weaving and painted silk, relishes and jellies, dried flowers, knitted goods, jewelry, and hand carvings)

Swimming: Ocean dips at several bays, such as Bennett, Campbell, Dinner and Piggott

Tennis: Felix Jack Rd (off Fernhill Rd)

Some Mayne Highlights

- Active Pass Lighthouse at Georgina Point
- Beaches at Oyster Bay, Campbell Bay, Bennett Bay, Piggott Bay, and Dinner Bay
- Miners Bay village with its numerous old buildings and historical attractions
- Mount Parke Regional Park

Mayne cemetery overlooks busy Active Pass

fence of the cemetery next to the church, the names on the headstones read like a who's who of Gulf Island pioneers, among them: Bellhouse from Galiano; Spalding and Grimmer from Pender; Payne from Saturna; Aitken, Bennett, Fawkes, Maude, Paddon and Robson from Mayne.

Across the road from the cemetery, old steps lead down to a beach along Miners Bay. At the far right end of the beach, along inaccessible rocky waterfront, is painted a mark of the survey ship *H.M.S. Egeria*, 1904—one of several on the islands.

Just past the cemetery, Georgina Point Road begins to

Facilities and Services

Emergency Services
- Ambulance, Doctor, Fire, Police: 911
- Mayne Health Care Centre: 604-539-2312
- Police: 604-539-2155

Accommodation
- Inns/Resorts: Five, in different parts of the island. Well known are rural Fernhill Lodge (604-539-2544), Oceanwood Country Inn (604-539-5074), and historic Springwater Lodge in Miners Bay (604-539-5521).
- B&Bs: At least 10 spread around the island. These include: Active Pass B&B (604-539-2262) which offers fishing charters, Amigos (604-539-2524) with glass and sculpture studios on the premises, views and a hot tub at Seaview Guest House (604-539-2047), and the

Tinkerers B&B on Miners Bay, whose proprietors run the Travel & Learn Network (604-539-2280). Consult local listings, the Chamber of Commerce, or the Canadian Gulf Islands B&B Reservation Service (604-539-2930).
- Hostel: Tinkerers Mayne Hostel, (604-539-2280).
- Camping: Two private campgrounds: Fern Hollow Campground (640 Horton Bay Rd, 604-539-5253); Journey's End Farm (Simpson Rd, 604-539-2411). No trailer or RV hookups on the island

Eating Places
At least eight provide a variety of menus and prices. For low to medium price try Manna Bakery Café (604-539-2323), Perry's Place (604-539-2412), or Springwater Lodge

(604-539-5521). Fernhill (604-539-2544) and Oceanwood (604-539-5074) provide high-end gourmet dinners.

Transportation
- Taxi: Mayne Island Taxi (604-539-3439).
- Service station (repairs and gas): Active Pass Auto & Marine (604-539-5411); Active Pass Repairs (604-539-5971).
- Marine engine service: Active Pass Auto & Marine (604-539-5411).

Other
- Groceries: Four stores
- Liquor outlets: Miners Bay Trading Post
- Post office: Mayne Open Market
- Public washrooms: Ferry terminal; Dinner Bay Community Park

Miners Bay

Emery's Store and Grandview Lodge, Miners Bay, 1920s

What started out as a campground for gold rush miners is today a seaside village of homes, shops, restaurants, pubs and other businesses. Miners Bay has stayed admirably intact, its streets and many of its buildings looking much as they did back when people still rowed over from other islands to get their mail or buy supplies. Its old life is recalled every time the whistle of the passing ferries echoes through Miners Bay.

The Mayne Street Mall that you pass on the right as you enter Miners Bay from the ferry is obviously a recent addition to the village landscape. The Manna Bakery Café located here is a good place to have a latté and hot pastry while you plan your day. Across the street, The Island Cottage (604-539-2099) sells wares for island living, including clothes, giftware, decorating accessories, dried flowers and oils.

At the centre of the village—the junction of Village Bay and Fernhill roads—is the Miners Bay Trading Post. Here you'll find groceries, an agency liquor store (open during grocery store hours), fishing licences, and an eclectic range of books, magazines and newspapers.

The Mayne Island Deli, set up in an old house, is a good spot for enjoying an enchilada or pizza while watching much of Mayne pass by. Another block up the street is the Mayne Island Museum, housed in the original island jail. Across the road sits the Agricultural Hall, built in the early 1900s. As well as being the site of many community events, such as the quilter's exhibition and summer markets, the hall and its grounds host the island's annual fall fair, an event that has taken place since 1925.

Down the street from the Trading Post, presiding over the bay from its perch by the government dock, is Springwater Lodge, reputed to be the oldest continuously operating hotel in BC. Parts of the Springwater's original structure date back to 1895, when Tom and Mary Collinson built and ran the first boarding house in Miners Bay. About 1912, the Collinsons' daughter Emma and her husband Brook Naylor took over the operation, renaming it Grandview Lodge. As the success of the business grew, they eventually added another wing, including in it a bridal suite. New owners in the 1960s changed the name to Springwater Lodge. A meal or a drink out on the deck of the lodge's restaurant or pub is a delightful way to spend a summer evening. The menu is varied enough to suit most tastes, and families are welcome.

Mayne Island Museum

BY 1890, smuggling and livestock rustling was enough of a problem in the Gulf Islands that a special constable was appointed to Miners Bay. In 1896 he was proud proprietor of the first jail in the islands.

Smaller than the designer bathrooms in many a Mayne home today, the two-cell lockup was expected to house the constable as well as any charges he might have. The first prisoner was Henry Freer, arrested for larceny on Galiano Island where he'd reportedly been collecting wild plants for his hair growing and freckle removing tonics. After Henry, incarcerations were rare.

The original jail is now home to the Mayne Island Museum, open weekends in the summer. Packed into the tight space are displays of fossils dating from 70 million years ago, stone tools of the early First Nations, pieces from the wreck of the sailing ship *Zephyr* which sank off Mayne in 1872, and items from early pioneer life.

climb, leveling out after about a kilometre. It's a good workout for cyclists; the reward is the gentle descent toward the lighthouse. A worthwhile side trip en route to the lighthouse is down Laura Point Road—the first left at the top of the hill—to no. 269, the art gallery of island artist Joyce Mitchell.

Georgina Point Area

At the junction with Waugh Road, continue left on Georgina Point Road about half a kilometre to the lighthouse. Heading out again, you can turn left onto Bay Road, then right onto Bayview where you will find the Artery (508 Bayview; 604-539-2835), featuring paintings and prints by artist Frances Faminow. Just past this gallery, Bayview leads to a beach access at Oyster Bay. Facing the Strait of Georgia but protected by an offshore reef and a few scraggy islets, this little beach is especially pleasant at low tide with its sandy wading pools and wide stretch of climbing rocks.

Clowns in the Fall Fair parade

Georgina Point to Fernhill/Horton Bay Road Junction (5 km)

Oyster Bay is not the only attractive beach on Mayne, and this next leg around the island gives you ample opportunity to try several of them. Each has its own character; you decide which one suits you best.

David Cove

From Oyster Bay, return up Bayview to Georgina Point Road and turn left. At the intersection with Waugh, turn left again. About 1.2 kilometres along, a left turn onto Porter and then another onto Petrus will bring you to David Cove, with its boat launch and small beach.

David Cove is a peaceful refuge from the busier spots on the island. And a true refuge it is believed to have been in 1872 to the half-drowned crew of the sinking *Zephyr*. The 190-foot, three-

Mayne Events

July
- Canada Day Celebration Community Picnic, Dinner Bay Park, July 1
- Country Fair, St. Mary Magdalene Church
- Quilt Exhibition

August
- Springwater Salmon Derby, third weekend
- Mayne Mast Salmon Derby, third Saturday
- Mayne Island Fall Fair, third Saturday

September
- Lions Club Salmon Bake, Labour Day Sunday

November
- Christmas Craft Fair

Springwater Lodge from the government dock

masted barque, on its way to San Francisco with a cargo of stone from Newcastle Island, went down in a storm, taking the captain and a crew member with it. The others are thought to have come ashore in the cove. Several artifacts from the ship are displayed in the Mayne Island Museum.

Campbell Bay

Waugh Road bends into Campbell Bay Road a short way past Porter. About a quarter of a kilometre from the bend, watch along the left-hand side of the road for the trail that leads down to the beach at Campbell Bay. It's not well marked, but usually vehicles parked on the roadside indicate the general vicinity of the trail, a short downhill pitch to the beach.

Campbell Bay is a long, narrow inlet, embraced on its east side by the long arm of Edith Point. It is named for Dr. Samuel Campbell, the Assistant Surgeon on the survey ship *H.M.S. Plumper* in the mid-1800s. The long, pebbly beach around the head of the bay ends at the far left in great sandstone formations that invite exploration. Ocean dips are popular here and overhanging trees at the top of the beach provide welcome shade on warm days.

Campbell Bay Road leaves the shore and continues another two kilometres to Fernhill Road. Turn left to carry on around the island (or turn right to cut short your tour and head back to Miners Bay, about a kilometre away).

Along this part of Fernhill Road are the health centre and the school (with its playground). Up behind the fire hall on Felix Jack Road are the community tennis courts. Fernhill Centre, home of the Mayne Open Market and Perry's Place restaurant, lies just beyond. The Market contains the island's post office, a fax

Commander Maude of Point Comfort Hotel

Point Comfort Hotel, planned as a traditional English inn

IN 1893, the 30-room Point Comfort Hotel was built near Georgina Point, on 132 acres of land (room for a cricket ground!) overlooking Active Pass. It became a favoured watering hole of locals as well as Galiano residents, who let neither the nasty tides of the pass nor bad weather deter them from rowing over for social visits.

In 1901, Commander Eustace and Mrs. Grace Maude moved to Mayne and bought the hotel, gradually converting it into a private residence where they lived in its decaying glory until 1924. Before arriving on Mayne, Commander Maude's life had been taken up with chasing pirates in the China Sea, serving on Queen Victoria's private yacht, and living at Hampton Court. In 1926, after selling the old hotel, his adventurous spirit appealed to him again. With his wife away visiting England, Maude (aged 77) set off alone in his 22-foot sailboat bound for England via Panama. Caught in a storm off the coast of California, he suffered a crack on the head from the boom and was left temporarily unconscious and half blinded. He turned back and hoisted a distress signal, but not until he had spent nearly 100 days at sea and covered more than 6,000 kilometres was he sighted and rescued. Little the worse for wear, Maude recovered and lived for another three, full years.

The Maudes sold Point Comfort to Colonel and Lady Fawkes, who restored the home and renamed it Culzean (pronounced "culane") after the castle in Scotland where Lady Fawkes had grown up. In 1958, Culzean was torn down and today a private home stands on the site.

and photocopy service, a broad selection of choice foods, fresh produce, videos, and gifts. Pick up a Nicaraguan matrimonial hammock while you're here. The magazine rack, though modest in size, is big on substance, carrying such esoterica as *Mother Jones*, *The Utne Reader* and *The New Internationalist*. Perry's Place next door is open for breakfast, lunch, dinner, ice cream, cappuccino, and friendly rejoinders.

A kilometre past the Fernhill Centre, Fernhill Road joins Horton Bay Road on the right. The main route turns south, but you may first want to explore Bennett Bay.

Side Trip to Bennett Bay (2 km)

Continue straight along Fernhill Road, which turns into Bennett Bay Road. The fields

Log sawing contest at the Mayne Island Fall Fair

along the road were once farmed by the Deacons and Bennetts and several old homes still remain standing. Fernhill Lodge, tucked up a driveway off the main road, is on the right just past the Horton Bay junction.

The road leads directly down to the bay itself and near the junction with Wilkes Road is the Mayne Inn. This building was originally constructed by the Franco-Canadian Company to accommodate its workers at the proposed brickyard on the bay—an enterprise that never got off the ground. In 1942, the building was sold, becoming first the

The Tinkerers: Judy and Jürgen Engelhardt

JUDY AND JÜRGEN Engelhardt—who call themselves "the Tinkerers"—have created a lifestyle many people dream of. Whether at their home (serving as a B&B and hostel) or in their lives spent travelling and being guides to others, their company is at once relaxing and stimulating.

The house, with its summer cottage feel and view over Active Pass, is surrounded by a vigorous garden, its flowers spilling out through the roadside fence and its mature fruit trees sheltering a couple of hammocks. Here one comes to watch the sunflowers expand, listen to the cosmos grow and in-

Judy and Jürgen Engelhardt

hale deeply. At the same time, though, the Tinkerers' library, the guests they attract, and Judy and Jürgen themselves offer the interested visitor a link to the world beyond this seductive setting. Judy has a doctorate in holistic health sciences; Jürgen has long

run a tool-sharpening business and taught others the age-old skill.

Since the early 1970s, the two have spent half of each year running their business on Mayne and the other half on the road—in Europe, Mexico and the Pacific Northwest. This is not a lifestyle they have adopted lightly. Their interest lies in travelling, learning and teaching as a way to grow personally and, in that growth, to contribute to self-awareness and the good of the global community.

Arbutus Lodge and later the Mayne Inn.

Access to the beach is at the front of the inn, as well as down a short lane off Wilkes. With its long, clean sandy beach, expansive view of the wide bay and Georgeson Island, and proximity to the take-out counter at the Mayne Inn, Bennett Bay is one of the busiest beaches on the island.

Another public beach access is located near the end of Arbutus Drive, which runs along the bay. In the vicinity is Blue Vista Resort (604-539-2463) and Charterhouse (721 Charter Road, off Arbutus, 604-539-2028), the home stu-

dio of Heather Maxey. Stop in and see her selection of hand-woven woollens, hand-painted clothing, and quilting. From Bennett Bay, head back up Fernhill to the junction with Horton Bay Road.

Side Trip to Horton Bay (3.5 km)

At the junction of Fernhill and Horton Bay Roads, a left turn will put you back on the main route. Carry on along Horton Bay Road half a kilometre to the junction with Gallagher Bay Road. The main route turns left, but before you leave Horton Bay Road, there is the opportunity for another side

trip down to the bay itself.

Continue to the end of Horton Bay Road. At the government dock on Horton Bay, local fish and pleasure boats are frequently tied up. This is a well-protected anchorage, tucked in behind Curlew Island. On the path to the dock is a public phone booth.

The old farm visible from the dock was once that of Japanese farmer, Ei Kadonga.

On Beechwood to the right is Arbutus Bay Deer Farms, raising and selling organic fallow deer venison ("fenison") for a wide local and gourmet market. If you're interested in seeing the products, phone

Active Pass Light Station

The light shines every night

ORIGINALLY BUILT IN 1885 to keep the growing steamship traffic off the rocks at the eastern entrance to Active Pass, the Active Pass light station was first manned by Henry "Scotty" Georgeson from Galiano Island. The lighthouse and beacon at Georgina Point are ineffably picturesque, although the current buildings on the site were put up in 1940, and the 17-metre bea-

con tower only began operation in 1969. The grounds are open most afternoons; there is ample parking and no charge.

It was on this point in 1881 that Mayne pioneer Tom Collinson unearthed a 1784 English penny and the remains of a seaman's knife. Both are thought to have been left behind in the early 1790s by a shore party of Captain George Vancouver's dur-

ing his exploration of the coast.

Today the light station is one of the few that is still staffed on the West Coast, and one of the few located within easy reach of the public. In 1994, about 9,000 visitors wandered around the park-like grounds surrounding the beacon, the lighthouse keeper's home, and the outbuildings. Resting cyclists, picnicking families, and foreshore explorers are a common sight. From this vantage, the ferries entering and leaving Active Pass seem so close you'd swear you could read the cafeteria lunch specials.

Given the federal government's plans to automate the station within the next couple of years (as part of a cost-cutting measure being phased in on both coasts), local groups have raised concerns about the safety aspects and economic implications of doing away with a "live" keeper. The fate of this 110-year tradition remains unclear.

Rufous Hummingbird

first (604-539-2301). Return up Horton Bay Road to Gallagher Bay Road, and turn left.

Horton Bay Road Junction to Gallagher Bay (2.5 km)

Gallagher Bay Road winds over the rocky spine of the island to the south coast overlooking Navy Channel. Less than a kilometre along, Gallagher Bay meets Simpson Road, at the end of which lies the poignantly named Journey's End Farm (604-539-2411). The owners offer no-frill, seaside campsites on their property, at a very economical price. If you're self-sufficient and your needs are simple, this is for you.

Piggott Bay

One kilometre past Simpson, Gallagher Bay Road meets Marine Drive. Turn left and head down the hill to Piggott Bay Road. A right at the fork leads to Gallagher Bay; a left leads to Piggott Bay. The latter is the larger, more interesting of the two, with its wide sweep of sandy beach and tumbled piles of driftwood. The shallow waters make the bay a favourite spot for wading and launching small boats. (There's no boat ramp here, but it's a short walk from the roadside parking to the water's edge.) Find yourself a comfortable backrest amongst the logs and settle back. With Saturna's Mount Warburton Pike as the backdrop and often two or

three freighters at anchor in Plumper Sound, there's enough in this view to set a good imagination wandering.

Piggott Bay to Village Bay (3.5 km)

Retracing your tracks up to Marine Drive from the beach, turn left at the top of the hill and stay on Marine Drive until it reaches Mariners Way. Bear right onto Mariners and a kilometre along turn left onto East West Road. Continue to the junction with Dinner Bay Road. A left turn takes you on a side trip to Dinner Bay Community Park, while a right takes you up the hill and back to the ferry by Mariners Way and Dalton Drive.

If you've still got time before your ferry arrives, nip back to Miners Bay for a little waterfront refreshment. Shake the beach sand out of your shoes, and sit back and listen with imagination for the sounds of a 19th century crowd gathering by the Miners

Beach at Piggott Bay

Bay dock on boat day.

Side Trip to Dinner Bay Community Park (2 km)

From the junction of East West Road and Dinner Bay Road, a short dog's leg first left and then right onto Williams Road, brings you to Dinner Bay Community Park. This 11-hectare park was established in 1987. A herring saltery was situated here in 1927 and later, before the war, a Japanese family operated a small fruit orchard on the grounds.

Arbutus and cedar trees

Paradise Lost - Japanese on Mayne

A former Japanese farm on Mayne

JUST BEFORE MIDNIGHT on December 7, 1941, the Royal Canadian Mounted Police arrived at the door of Mayne Island tomato farmer, Zeiji Teremoto, and arrested him. He was led away with little time to pack or say good-bye to his terrified family. Three other Mayne Island farmers were arrested later that night. Their crime? Being of Japanese origin.

The Japanese attack on the American fleet at Pearl Harbour in Hawaii precipitated a round-up of Japanese-Canadians that eventually saw thousands displaced from the coast and their homes, businesses, farms and fishing boats confiscated. All the Gulf Islands were affected, but Mayne suffered most. By the end of 1942, one-third of the population of Mayne had been sent away to internment camps in the interior of BC and southern Alberta. With so many children gone, the island school had to close for two years.

The first Japanese families who came to Mayne at the turn of the century worked as fishermen or as farm labourers for established settlers. Many later became successful poultry farmers and, when poultry farming became uneconomic in the late 1920s, successful tomato growers. By the 1930s, Japanese growers had eight acres of greenhouses and shipped more than 50 tons of tomatoes a year to markets in Victoria and Vancouver. They were also responsible for 50% of the herring fishery on Mayne.

Before 1941, the industriousness, adaptability and neighbourliness of the Japanese made them a vital, integral part of Mayne's community. This was in stark contrast to what had been happening elsewhere in BC and other parts of Canada, where the success of the Japanese had for many years been a point of contention. More and more restrictions were imposed on them: they were not allowed to vote and they were prevented from entering such professions as law. By 1927, 60% of Japanese fishermen were forced out of the industry as a direct result of a federal government regulation. Increasingly racist and fearful rhetoric by municipal, provincial and federal politicians contributed to the growing antagonism towards Japanese-Canadians.

Pearl Harbour became the justification for the mass dislocation of these people from the coast. Such action was devastating to Mayne's community. The steamer *Princess Mary,* which at peak season had shipped tomato crops from the island twice a week, now called to take Japanese men, women, and children to internment. Most of the white residents on Mayne felt the loss of so many friends and neighbours deeply. Some looked after the Japanese greenhouses and properties in anticipation of the owners' return—until such caretaking activity was made illegal. After World War II, confiscated properties, businesses and fish boats were sold, often to war veterans. Very few of the dislocated Japanese families ever returned to the islands.

lean low over the beach, and tidal pools fill numerous pockets along the rocky foreshore. The park has many amenities, including public washrooms with sinks and running water, a covered picnic area and barbecue grills, picnic tables, a new playground for young children, a volleyball net, horseshoe pitch and a large grassy playing field. Community events and family picnics are often staged here.

At the end of Dinner Point Road, not far from the

Bird-watching at Oyster Bay

Bald Eagle

PERCHED HIGH ON trees, flapping heavily over the water, or soaring in wide circles in the sky, the Bald Eagle is one of the most spectacular birds of the Gulf Islands. The adults are easy to spot with their white heads and tails contrasting with dark bodies, but many of the birds you will see are dark brown immatures in their first three years. Eagles use a variety of feeding strategies. They can seize swimming fish in their yellow talons and, on a favourite perch, tear them apart with their hooked beaks.

In pairs they can aggressively pursue a duck or grebe, forcing it to dive until exhausted. They are also adept at forcing other birds to drop their prey, and are great carrion feeders, gathering in great numbers around a dead whale. In the Gulf Islands though, their main food is the Glaucous-winged Gull. The only time of year they are sparse on the coast is early fall, when the feeding is good at the great salmon runs on interior rivers.

National bird of the United States, the Bald Eagle has become uncommon in most parts of that country as a result of being shot, poisoned by pesticides, or driven out of its habitat. They are far more prevalent in BC, where 25% of the world's nesting population is now found. Nest trees are protected in BC by law. Each nest is a clumsy pile of sticks atop a tree. Added to year by year, some nests reach up to three metres across—until they collapse under their own weight.

Hundreds of Bald Eagles live in the Gulf Islands

Dinner Bay Park

entrance to the park, is Ocean-wood Country Inn (604-539-2262), located overlooking the waters of Navy Channel. The restaurant and accommodations of the Oceanwood have earned it a Jacuzzi-load of commendations.

Mayne Island Quilters

Leni Freed shows off a Jewish wedding canopy

THE ANNUAL QUILTING show in the community hall at Miners Bay is a testament to industry. The hall is transformed, swathed with wonderful quilts of many colours. They hang from the walls, the ceiling, and room dividers and screens, and are draped over table tops and chairs. We were surprised to learn that that the impression given of a long-standing quilting tradition was misleading, for the group had only been formally established for about three years.

Well, the long, wet winters have been filled to real effect. The quilts produced on Mayne are lovely and show a variety of styles. Some are made with traditional quilting techniques using standard patterns such as log cabin and Dresden plate. Others, like Leni Freed's work, are not strictly quilts, but use traditional techniques as the building blocks to produce magnificent modern hangings decorated with appliqué, embroidery and tapestry as well as quilting. Check the local papers for the exhibition date, probably a Saturday at the end of July.

8. Saturna Island

Sculpted sandstone at East Point

Saturna's scant 300 residents are almost obsessively protective of their privacy. The island has only one park, no camping, and little (though select) accommodation. It is the only island that is normally reached by a journey on two ferries, and the Gulf Island joke is that Saturna

islanders are the only ones who ask the ferry corporation for fewer ferries. Yet, for over 40 years, Saturna has also hosted what is probably the longest standing and most impressive annual bash anywhere on the islands, bringing in hundreds of visitors from great distances.

The isolation sets it off from its more urban, extroverted neighbours, and somewhat conceals the fact that Saturna is a recreationist and naturalist's paradise. With access to the third highest peak

in the Gulf Islands, a seaside park and long stretches of rocky shoreline from which to observe marine and bird life, the island can keep cyclists, kayakers, hikers and nature-lovers well satisfied.

The island has five peaks higher than 300 metres and long ridges of exposed rock face. There is relatively little flat land, so agriculture is little developed.

The name Saturna comes from the Spanish sailing ship *Saturnina*, which was under the command of Captain José

Maria Narvaez during his exploration of this coast in 1791. Although the island was occupied by First Nations, pioneer settlement only began in the 1870s, and for several decades much of the island belonged to Englishmen Warburton Pike and several Payne brothers. In more recent years, a substantial quarrying operation brought a flurry of activity to the island, but that closed down in the mid-60s, leaving the present quiet residential community.

Getting to and staying on

Saturna Information

Area: 31 square kilometres
Population: 271 in 1991, now around 320
Visitor Information: Tourist information map available at Saturna Point Store and Narvaez Bay Trading Company

Saturna requires some forethought. First, getting from and to either Tsawwassen or Swartz Bay is generally a two-ferry ride via Pender or Mayne. Study the ferry schedule carefully before you set off, to be sure you can make the connections. Second, although the lodges and B&Bs on the island are first rate, they are few in number and modest in capacity. Restaurants and other dining opportunities are particularly scarce, and some operate only seasonally. There are no campgrounds or marinas. Finally, among the many fine services and attractions that are on the island, you won't find a bank, bank machine, laundromat, commercial attraction or many gift shops.

Our best advice: plan on a day trip or, if you don't want any limitations set on your time, arrange accommodation before you come. We have featured the longest route, along East Point Road, as our major route. It follows the northern shore of the island, and includes a detour into Saturna's provincial marine park. Closer to the ferry terminal (where most of the services are clustered) is the drive up Mount

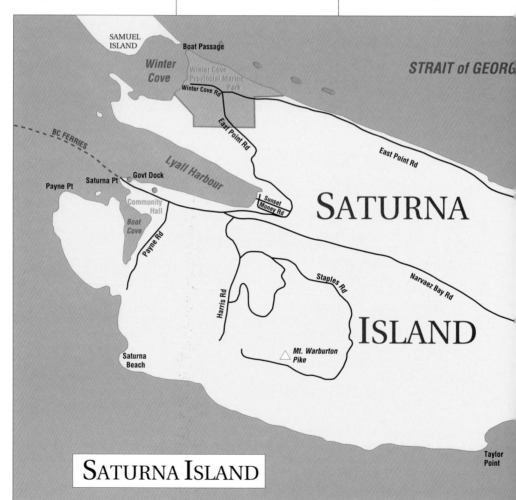

SATURNA ISLAND

Warburton Pike.

For the visitor who is looking for a simple retreat, in a setting uncluttered by any sign of urban excess, Saturna offers a huge helping of the great outdoors and a small but savoury choice of creature comforts.

Lyall Harbour Area

Although the ferry terminal is referred to as Lyall Harbour, it is actually located on Saturna Point, with Lyall Harbour on the left and Boot Cove on the

Saturna Access

Ferry: From Tsawwassen once or twice a day (1.5 to 2 hours); and from Swartz Bay at least three times a day (1.5 to 2 hours), most via Pender or Mayne. Connections with Mayne, Galiano, Pender and Salt Spring. All ferries arrive and depart from Lyall Harbour. (Local information 604-629-3215.)

Float plane: By arrangement, Hanna Air (Salt Spring) offers three to four return flights a day between Lyall Harbour and Vancouver International Airport (1-800-665-2359). Harbour Air provides a daily return service between Lyall Harbour and downtown Vancouver (1-800-665-0212).

Water taxi: By arrangement, Inter Island Launch (604-656-8788).

Boat moorage: Government dock at Lyall Harbour.

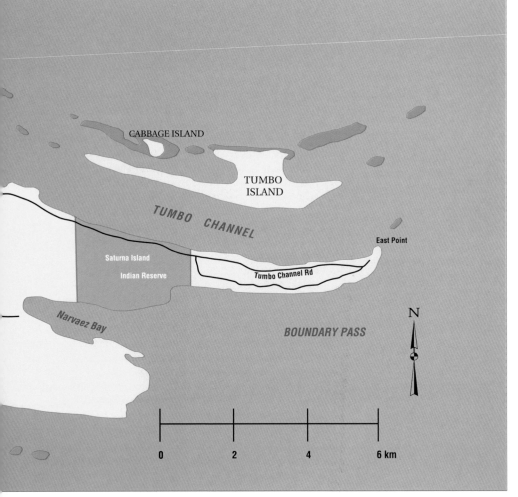

CABBAGE ISLAND

TUMBO ISLAND

TUMBO CHANNEL

East Point

Saturna Island

Indian Reserve

Tumbo Channel Rd

Narvaez Bay

BOUNDARY PASS

N

| 0 | 2 | 4 | 6 km |

Some Saturna Highlights

- Dinner at Boot Cove Lodge
- East Point
- Lamb Barbecue
- Mount Warburton Pike
- Shades of Saturna Art Gallery
- Winter Cove Provincial Marine Park

Recreational Opportunities

- **Birding:** Boot Cove, East Point, Lyall Harbour (Winter Cove)
- **Cycling:** Saturna Boat and Bike Rentals (604-539-3041)
- **Diving:** Viable Marine Services (604-539-3200)
- **Fishing:** Viable Marine Services (604-539-3200); East Point Resort (604-539-2975)
- **Hiking:** Mount Warburton Pike, Winter Cove Provincial Marine Park
- **Playgrounds:** Saturna Island School; Winter Cove Provincial Marine Park
- **Shopping:** Saturday Market at the Community Hall during the summer; Narvaez Bay Trading Company (look for books by local authors and hand-turned wooden bowls and other crafts by local craftspeople); Shades of Saturna Art Gallery (108 Payne Road)
- **Swimming:** Sea dips at East Point, Lyall Harbour, Winter Cove
- **Tennis:** Two public courts on Money Road in Lyall Harbour
- **Whale watching:** Viable Marine Services (will pick up from other islands too) (604-539-3200)

Winter Cove Provincial Marine Park

IN 1872, TWO of the first European settlers on Saturna, William and Theo Elford, established a sheep farm around Winter Cove. Other farmers followed. More recently it was the site of the BC Lightweight Aggregates Plant, an open quarry and furnace that produced stones for road-building during the 1960s.

In 1979, part of the Winter Cove area became a 91-hectare provincial marine park. With its beach, open grassy areas, forested trails, swamps, rocky east shore and large anchorage (sheltered except from northwest winds), the park is a popular destination for picnickers, nature lovers and boaters. Since 1990, it has also been the site of the annual lamb barbecue.

The park is designed for day visitors only. Efforts to incorporate camping facilities here, even walk-in sites, have been thwarted over the years by local concerns over an increase in ferry traffic and fire hazard. Facilities include outdoor toilets, drinking water, picnic tables, walking trails and a boat launch for small boats. One trail leads out to a point beside Boat Passage at the northern end of Saturna. Across this narrow gap, Samuel Island and Saturna almost touch fingertips. The tidal current through the pass can run up to seven knots at certain times of the year, and it's an impressive sight when the water of Georgia Strait "pours" into Winter Cove, or vice versa, during the change of the tide.

Facilities and Services

Emergency Services
- Ambulance, Doctor, Fire, Police: 911
- Police: 604-539-2155 (Mayne Island)
- Saturna Health Care Centre: 604-539-5435 (Tuesdays)

Accommodation
- Inns/Resorts: Boot Cove Lodge and Restaurant (604-539-2254); East Point Resort (604-539-2975); Stone House Farm Resort (604-539-2683).
- B&Bs: The few available include Breezy Bay's historic farmhouse (604-539-2937); Lyall Harbour (604-539-5577); antique-filled Poppy Hill Farm (604-539-5002); and Wild Wing (604-539-2961). For changes consult the Canadian Gulf Islands B&B Reservation Service (604-539-2930).

Eating Places
- Boot Cove Lodge and Restaurant (604-539-2254); Lighthouse Pub (604-539-5725).

Transportation
- Fuel dock: Lyall Harbour dock (604-539-5725).
- Service station (gas): Saturna Point Store and Fuel (604-539-5725), Lyall Harbour.

Other
- Groceries: Narvaez Bay Trading Company; Saturna Point Store (Lyall Harbour)
- Liquor outlet: Narvaez Bay Trading Company
- Post office: Narvaez Bay Trading Company
- Public washrooms: Ferry terminal, Winter Cove Provincial Marine Park

right as you arrive. The ferry disgorges passengers into the heart of a cluster of old homes and other buildings that include the Saturna Point Store and the Lighthouse Pub, a popular place for wrapping up a day trip to the island. The government wharf to the left of the ferry dock is a convenient spot for boaters to tie up and replenish supplies.

Up the hill leading out of Lyall Harbour is the Community Hall on the left. Built in 1933, this building continues to serve as the main venue for most island indoor events and meetings. During the summer, a market and café are held here every Saturday. A little farther along, at the corner of East Point Road and Payne Road, the mitre-shaped St. Christopher's Church stands discreetly among the firs. Carry on up East Point for an-

Tide rushes through Boat Passage

other kilometre and half until you reach a fork in the road. The Narvaez Bay Trading Company, perched commandingly at the fork where East Point Road bends left and Narvaez Bay Road begins on the right, is Saturna's commercial centre. Here are the main grocery store on the island, an

agency liquor store (which means that grocery store hours are liquor store hours) and the post office. You'll also find books, gift items, videos, garden supplies, hardware, and fresh coffee and doughnuts. The large heron mural on the south side of the building was painted by Keith

The Haggis Farmers

YOU'LL FIND THE Haggis Farm Bakery label on many Gulf Island grocery shelves, on packages of croissants, whole grain and spelt bread, cookies and granola. On Saturna, these packages are delivered to stores by vehicle from the Narvaez Bay Road bakery owned by Priscilla Ewbank and Jon Guy. Elsewhere in the Gulf Islands, they come by *White Star*, the bakery's delivery boat. By land or sea, the organic goods are fresh, tasty and sought after.

The eight-year-old wholesale business has grown steadily but slowly since it began—much the way Priscilla and Jon believe change on the island should take place. Living on Saturna since the 1970s, both are dedicated to the community. Rapid change and

Jon Guy supervises the barbecue

encroachment from the outside, Priscilla feels, are exactly what will destroy the community and the natural beauty of the island. Careful, cautious, slow growth is

the only way to go if the quality of the land and the lifestyle is to be protected.

In addition to operating the bakery, the two are involved in many community activities. Jon, for instance, is head chef at the Canada Day lamb barbecue; Priscilla is chief correspondent from Saturna for the biweekly *Island Tides* newspaper. And then there's the Saturna Island Think Tank they moderate many a Saturday night on their back deck—"a loosely organized multi-talented collective of artistic, scientific and practical thinkers" as one of its members, poet J. Douglas Porteous, describes it. But that's another story.

Warburton Pike

AN ADVENTURER, hunter, businessman, author and benefactor—handsome and moneyed to boot—Warburton Pike was an Englishman who arrived on Saturna in 1884 with Charles Payne. Before coming to the island, Oxford-educated Pike had travelled and worked in Iceland, Wyoming, California and the Canadian prairies. Even after he had established his sheep ranch on the island, he continued to go off frequently, sometimes disappearing for months at a time. His exploring took him to the Arctic, a subject on which he wrote two books, *The Barren Grounds of Northern Canada* (1892) and *Through the Subarctic Forest* (1896).

Along with his travels, Pike involved himself in numerous busi-

*Warburton Pike,
Saturna pioneer*

ness ventures such as mining and railways. It was Pike who held the mortgage on Mayne's Point Comfort Hotel until 1900. As

well, in addition to owning most of the south side of Saturna at one time, from Breezy Bay to East Point, he had properties on Mayne (pieces of which he sold for the jail and donated for the church), in Oak Bay near Victoria, and on Discovery Island off Oak Bay.

When World War I began, Pike returned to England to enlist. The rugged adventurer, the man's man, shortly fell ill and was sent to a nursing home. Utterly despondent, he took his own life. Today the memory of Pike is preserved by the hill which bears his name on Saturna, a cairn at Dease Lake in northern BC, and a plaque over the door inside Mayne's St. Mary Magdalene church.

Ancient Rivers

ROCKS EXPOSED AT East Point reveal evidence of the very different landscape that was here 70 million years ago. The soft sandstone, interlayered with conglomerate beds containing rounded gravel pebbles up to 10 centimetres across, suggest that this area was once overlain by a sandy-bottomed river channel, somewhat like those tributaries weaving through the Fraser River delta today.

At the eastern extremity of the peninsula, the geological record depicts what must, at one moment in history, have been a dramatic scene. Angular blocks of sandstone are embedded irregularly in a mix of conglomerate rock and sandstone, indicating that they once plunged haphaz-

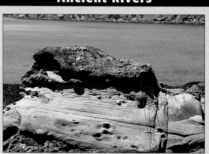

Remains of a Cretaceous delta

ardly into the sandy gravel bed of a flowing river (forming what geologists call a "collapse breccia"). Such an event would have been the result of an active river undercutting a soft sandstone cliff, thereby creating an unstable overhang which broke away so that sandstone blocks fell to the river bed. The sedimentary layering within several of the col-

lapsed blocks is bent as though the blocks had been soft at the time of their fall.

In more recent millennia, erosion has produced some spectacular rock sculptures, including honeycomb weathering in the sandstone. The erosion is exposing lime-cemented concretions (some beginning to form pillar-like hoodoos where they protect softer rock beneath). The most impressive erosion feature at East Point is the five-metre high elongated sea cave now looking much like a gallery. The cave has been carved out by centuries of high energy storms just above the high-tide mark, and is best developed near the collapse breccia.

Holmes of Galiano Island and Stan Phelps of Calgary.

East Point Road (15 km)

Soon after you leave the ferry you find yourself on East Point Road. From the Narvaez Bay Trading Company junction, keep left, staying on East Point Road. A long hill descends into the valley where several homes and the island school are nestled beside the head of Lyall Harbour. (A left onto Sunset Boulevard will lead you straight to the beach along the harbour, a pleasant place to watch the summer sun go down. Small boats can be launched from here.)

Across the little valley, the road begins to climb steeply, up and around the north side of Lyall Harbour. About two kilometres farther along, it forks. The left onto Winter Cove Road leads through the provincial park located at Winter Cove; the right is the continuation of East Point Road.

From the Winter Cove turn off, East Point Road begins the 10 kilometres out to beautiful East Point. Along this route the road passes close to the water and in several stretches the cedar and fir trees form a canopy overhead. The wide shelves of rock that lie down this northern edge, interspersed with small pocket beaches of shell and sand, are wonderful to explore, especially at low tide.

Orca

A BLACK BACK and two-metre dorsal fin rolling through the water, or a noisy exhalation from huge lungs nearby in the fog; this is how whale watchers typically encounter the Orca, the most common whale in Gulf Island waters. Luckier observers will see Orcas spy hopping (bobbing upright in the water) or breaching (leaping out of the water).

A pod of Orcas

The Orca ("Orca" being part of the scientific name) was once referred to as "Killer Whale," a misleading term whose use has gradually faded as popular perceptions have changed and knowledge improved. The Orca of the Pacific Northwest has become perhaps the best known population of any whale in the world, thanks to the efforts of professional cetologists and amateur whale watchers who have spent the last few decades documenting the animals' social behaviour, family structure and sound vocabulary.

Most Orcas live in resident pods, some of up to 50 individuals, with a rigid social structure; these Orcas feed mainly on fish. Large males sometimes reach nine metres in length and weigh nine tons; females grow only to about six metres. Many individual whales can be identified by photographs, their dorsal fins bearing characteristic marks that distinguish them one from another. Locally spotted Orcas usually belong to K pod. Other small groups of Orcas move through a wider area and have given the species its reputation for ferocity, as they will aggressively attack other marine mammals in shallow water, using their sharp teeth with devastating effect. To catch a glimpse of these magnificent animals, keep an eye on the sea and binoculars handy, or try a whale watching boat trip from one of the islands, Victoria or Nanaimo.

About six kilometres along this stretch, the road passes through Indian Reserve land and becomes Tumbo Channel Road. To the east, just across a small channel of water, lies Tumbo Island. In the early 1890s, a Canadian-Japanese company attempted to mine coal on the island. Employing 21 men at its peak, the project went under when the mine shaft filled with water. Tumbo is privately owned today, but little Cabbage Island lying northeast of it is a provincial marine park.

East Point

At East Point, the protected beach facing Tumbo Island, the fabulous rock formations, and the 300 degree views across the water make this spot the ultimate seaside heaven. One can easily spend a day here playing on the beach, climbing along the rocks, exploring the tide pools and watching the great diversity of marine life. A pod of Orcas rounding the point is not an uncommon sight.

To get to the beach, park along the end of the road. The light station property is private, but a trail to the left leads down along the fence to a sand and shell beach and, farther along to the right, all around the sandstone rocks below the light station land.

To aid ships navigating the dangerous Boundary Pass waters off East Point, the federal government first established a lighthouse here in 1888, on property purchased from Warburton Pike. The first full-time keeper stationed here was James Georgeson, brother of Scotty Georgeson, the lighthouse keeper on Mayne. After

Messing about in boats at Winter Cove

James retired in 1921, his son Peter took over the duties at the station. His departure in 1939 marked the end of the family's 52 years on the point.

To see other parts of the island, return along East Point Road to the junction with Narvaez Bay Road.

Side Trip to Mount Warburton Pike (4.5 km)

Mount Warburton Pike is a must. Turn off East Point Road up Narvaez Bay Road, and almost immediately turn right up Harris Road, across from the grocery store near the junction. The island's recycling centre and "free store" are located on the corner here. At Staples Road, turn left to begin the climb up to the 497 metre summit. The hard-packed dirt road is easily accessible for most vehicles, but you may enjoy walking up through the 131-hectare forest ecological reserve. Keep your eyes peeled for the feral goats that wander the woods up here; they've descended from domestic stock gone wild almost a century ago. At the

summit, you'll be so taken by the panoramic view that not even the tangle of utility towers, wires and buildings that occupy much of the top can detract.

As are so many Gulf Island lookouts, this one is on an unfenced ridge that drops away precipitously. Children and pets should be kept well within grasp.

Saturna Events

June
- Market and café every Saturday, Community Hall, with home produce and crafts for sale. To August.

July
- Lamb Barbecue, Winter Cove Provincial Marine Park, July 1 (See story in Chapter 5)

November
- Christmas Craft Fair, Community Hall

9. Pender Island

Spinnakers aloft in the Pender Island Race

Small but varied, busy yet quiet, Pender Island presents a great diversity of landscape, coastline and recreational opportunities. You can drive from end to end in under an hour, yet spend a lifetime exploring its corners; you can get cappuccinoed and crafty in a crowd, yet it is not difficult to laze alone on a beach, with only an otter or an eagle for company. It has a reasonable range of services and enough accommodation and eating places for all but peak periods.

Even some residents are not sure if there is one Pender Island or two. Geographically and historically it was a single island, though deeply divided by Browning and Bedwell harbours, which were linked by a short portage. Creation of a canal in 1902 physically separated the island into the parts now called North and South Pender. The two were not reconnected by a bridge until 1955, by which time some differences had developed. North Pender is now the most populated, and has most of the services and facilities, while South Pender has a smaller population and greater areas of parkland.

Ancient settlements go back more than 5,000 years, and in the late 19th century Pender became a sheepwalk and then a patchwork of small farms and orchards. There is no village on Pender, though there are greater concentrations of houses at older settlements, such as Port Washington and Hope Bay, and newer estates, notably Magic Lake. Timber extraction, quarrying and fish processing plants have played their part in its history, but now its most important industry is tourism. Concentrations of facilities are found at the Driftwood Centre on North Pender, and at the various marinas. Resorts and B&Bs are scattered across the island. Boating, fishing, and kayaking allow access to the water from numerous locations; rocky, gravel (though rarely sandy) beaches, with some fine rock pools, attract the beachcomber and naturalist. Middens and well-preserved historic buildings (virtually all still in use) attract the heritage enthusiast. Pender not only has a conventional golf course, but also the islands' only disc (frisbee) golf course. Trails and winding roads (some hilly) encourage leisurely exploration by car, cycle, or foot. Shops and studios provide shopping

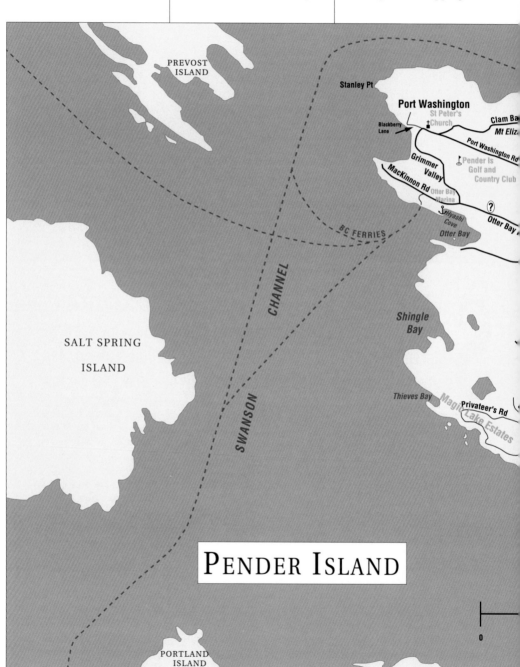

PREVOST ISLAND

Stanley Pt

Port Washington
St Peter's
Church
Blackberry
Lane
Clam Bay
Mt Eliza
Port Washington Rd
Grimmer Valley
Pender Is Golf and Country Club
MacKinnon Rd
Otter Bay
Marina
Hyashi Cove
Otter Bay
Otter Bay
BC FERRIES

SWANSON CHANNEL

SALT SPRING ISLAND

Shingle Bay

Thieves Bay
Magic Lake Estates
Privateer's Rd

PENDER ISLAND

0

PORTLAND ISLAND

opportunities, offering traditional crafts and more unusual aesthetic delights.

Pender offers many possible routes and side trips. Several beaches and a well-serviced marina are close to the ferry. For half a day, we recommend a tour of the older Port Washington-Hope Bay area, where numerous galleries and studios cluster in pastoral surroundings. Short side trips take you to Port Washington dock and Bricky Bay. For

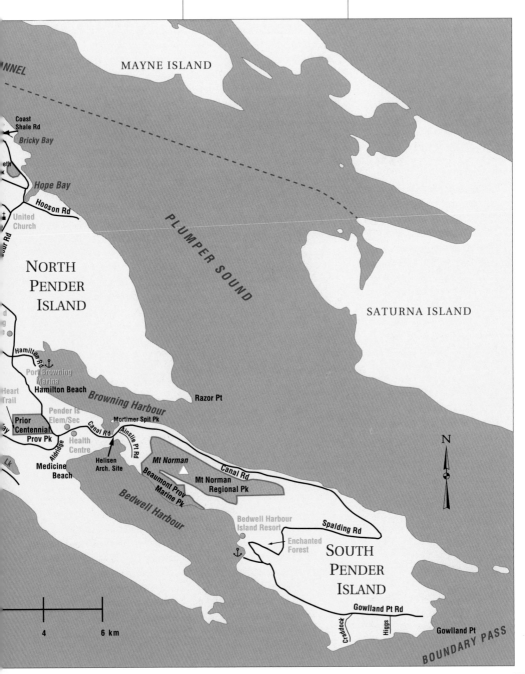

- **Birding:** Buck Lake, Canal, Gowlland Point, Hope Bay, Magic Lake, Mortimer Spit. Christmas Bird Count. Bird Check List available in stores. Pender Island Field Naturalists (604-629-3381)
- **Cycling:** Rental: Bedwell Harbour Island Resort (604-629-3212); Otter Bay Marina (604-629-3579) repair: Brett's Bicycle Base (604-629-3888)
- **Disc (frisbee) golf:** Pender Island Disc Park (free 18 pole-course)
- **Diving:** Cooper's Landing (dive charters, air fills; 604-629-6133)
- **Fishing:** Boat rental: Bedwell Harbour Island Resort (604-629-3212); Otter Bay Marina (604-629-3579) tackle and bait: Otter Bay Marina (604-629-3579)
- **Golf:** Pender Island Golf and Country Club (604-629-6659)
- **Hiking:** Mount Norman Regional Park; Heart Trail (from Prior Provincial Park to Magic Lake area); Magic Lake, Mount Elizabeth Park
- **Horse riding:** Happy Trails trail rides (604-629-3398)
- **Kayaking:** Cooper's Landing (604-629-6133); Mouat Point/Otter Bay Marina (604-629-6767)
- **Playgrounds:** Danny Martin Park, Pender Island School, Pender Island Play School, Shingle Bay, Thieves Bay
- **Scooter rental:** Sabyan Auto Marine (604-629-3240)
- **Shopping:** Driftwood Centre; Hope Bay; numerous shops and more than a dozen home studios around the island (look

for calligraphy, carvings, clothing, drums, flowers, jewelry, masks, paintings, pottery, stained glass, and weaving)
- **Swimming:** Pools: Bedwell Harbour Island Resort (604-629-3212); Otter Bay Marina (604-629-3579); Port Browning Marina (604-629-3493). Small fees apply. Lakes: Magic Lake. Sea dips (for the hardy): Beaumont Marine Park, Hamilton Beach, Mortimer Spit,

Thieves Bay.
- **Tennis:** Bedwell Harbour Island Resort (604-629-3212); Port Browning Marina (604-629-3493); Magic Lake (on Privateers at Galleon; call the number posted on the entrance for fees and key); Pender Island School.
- **Tide pools:** Good rocky beaches on North and South Pender

Fore!

AVID GOLFERS USED to 18 holes shouldn't dismiss Pender's nine-hole course; it's a challenge for the most seasoned golfers. Reports of golfers on the island go back to the 1930s and the golf club charter was eventually drawn up in 1945. The course was laid out using input from the Auchterlonie family, who originated from Scotland and were reputed to have played on the famous St. Andrews course. The nine holes have some separate tee-offs for those wanting to play 18 holes. Non-golfing visitors are welcome to drop in to the clubhouse for lunches, snacks and dinner. The golf course is open year round and the coffee shop runs daily, May through October. It generally features home cooking and the club offers a bar service. The outside veranda with its pastoral view up the valley is a pleasant lunch spot on a sunny day. Facilities include washrooms, pro shop, cart and club rentals.

visitors with more time, we guide you on the main route past the Driftwood Centre (where most services are found) and past a side trip to Hamilton Beach, to the canal between the two islands, centre of the most varied landscapes on the island. The main route continues to the end of South Pender, past Bedwell Harbour Resort and on to Gowlland Point. On the way back, a side trip to Medicine Beach and Magic Lake offers yet another aspect of the island.

Otter Bay Area

On a busy day, drivers coming off the ferry find themselves rushing up the hill with the traffic, with no place to pull off and look at a map. The immediate area of the ferry has some attractions which should not be ignored, so drivers should be prepared as they leave the ferry, if they wish to make either of the first two turns. Foot passengers and cyclists can access The Stand, a popular food outlet at the ferry dock. First left immediately past the ferry booth is MacKinnon Road, leading past historic Pender Lodge to a small beach at the end of the road. First right off Otter Bay Road leads to Otter Bay Marina at Hyashi Cove (which commemorates a turn of the century Japanese landowner, Captain Hayashi). Facilities include moorage; groceries and cappuccino bar; kayak, boat and bicycle rentals; and a swimming pool.

About one kilometre from the ferry on Otter Bay Road (past the recommended turn to Port Washington) an Infor-

Can you see the tube worms?

mation Centre provides a large map of the island, and when open can update visitors on accommodation and attractions. If you continue along Otter Bay Road, you can bypass the Port Washington-Hope Bay areas and head straight for the Driftwood Centre and the rest of the island.

Ferry Terminal to Port Washington (2.5 km)

The areas around the old settlements of Hope Bay and Port Washington are some of the most picturesque parts of the island. In early years the two were rivals, with different politics and personalities, in fierce

Pender Access

Ferry: From Tsawwassen twice a day (1.25 to 2.5 hours); from Swartz Bay five or more trips daily (35 minutes); both to Otter Bay. Connections to Galiano, Mayne, Salt Spring and Saturna. (Local information 604-629-3344.)

Float plane: Hanna Air will provide service to Vancouver International Airport or downtown three times a day on request (1-

800-665-2359). Harbour Air also provides service on request (1-800-665-0212).

Water taxi: By arrangement, Inter Island Launch (604-656-8788)

Boat moorage: Government docks at Hope Bay, Port Browning, Port Washington; marinas at Bedwell (604-629-3212), Browning (604-629-3493) and Otter Bay (604-629-3579).

Penderites celebrate Summer Solstice

January
- Polar Bear Swim, New Year's Day at Hamilton Beach

May
- Farmer's Market, from Victoria Day weekend to Thanksgiving, Saturday mornings at Driftwood Centre
- Pender Islands International Disc Tournament

June
- Summer Solstice Festival

July
- Garden Party, Anglican Women's Guild

August
- Tapestry of Words, one-day storytelling festival, Good Earth Farm (Hooson Road)
- Fall Fair, Driftwood Centre

October
- Halloween Fireworks

December
- Santa Ship, Port Washington
- Christmas Eve carol serenade to the last ferries to arrive, by informal Otter Bay Symphony Orchestra and Choral Society

competition for churches, ferry landings, post offices and schools. Port Washington is now fairly quiet, but in the last few years Hope Bay has developed a lively cultural scene and the funkiest shopping on the island.

To explore the area, turn left on Otter Bay Road, at the fire sign, just under a kilometre from the ferry. The road passes through the Pender Island Golf and Country Club, which is open to visitors.

As you bear left at the end of the golf course, look on your right for a bronze sculpture of a horse and rider by Pender sculptor Ralph Sketch. It shows pioneer Washington Grimmer riding wearily home after a hard day's work in the woods.

Continue on Otter Bay Road down the edge of what is known as the Grimmer Valley, and turn along the sea.

As you approach Port Washington Road, check out The Parlour (604-629-3785) in

Blackberry Lane for crafts and workshops. Next door, the Armstrong Gallery (604-629-6571) is one of many studio galleries on Pender. Marie and Malcolm Armstrong specialize in bird and marine paintings, and Malcolm also keeps the official weather records for the island.

The road enters Port Washington Road at an awkward angle, with poor visibility. Port Washington is worth a short detour to the left. The main road to Hope Bay continues to the right.

Side Trip to Port Washington Dock (0.5 km)

Turn left to Port Washington, and almost immediately on the right is Old Orchard Farm. The house is private, but it can be plainly seen through the heritage orchard, one of the finest surviving on Pender. At Bridges Road, turn left. Here you can park by the Port

Ralph Sketch

PENDER RESIDENT Ralph Sketch was a sculptor specializing in bronzes showing episodes of Canadian military history. His work is found across Canada and in Europe, and Pender is proud of the fact that three of his bronzes can be seen on the island: one on the golf course and two in Stanley Point Estates, an area he developed as a residential estate. Unfortunately Ralph, with his writer wife Marian Ogden Sketch, died in a house fire in 1993. His bronzes and the two books he and Marian wrote about his work are a lasting memorial to his talent.

Sculpture of Washington Grimmer by Ralph Sketch

Washington General Store (currently closed) and explore the dock. A busy centre until a few years ago, the 1910 Port Washington store at one time housed a post office, and the bustling wharf (built to save Washington Grimmer the seven-mile row to Miners Bay on Mayne for the mail) became the drop-off place for the steamers bringing in supplies. The government dock provides a sleepy little destination on one of Pender's prettiest bays. Lean carefully over the side of the floating dock and look at the white and orange tube worms attached to the pilings below. When feeding, they send out feathery fronds and look like underwa-

The water taxi gets around

ter flowers. At the right time, you may see Pender's high school students returning here by water taxi from the school on Salt Spring. Facilities at the dock include moorage and a public phone.

Facilities and Services

Emergency Services
- Ambulance, Doctor, Fire, Police: 911
- Doctor: Pender Health Centre, 604-629-3233
- Pharmacy: Driftwood Centre, 604-629-6555
- Police: 604-629-6171

Accommodation
- Motels: The Inn on Pender (604-629-3353).
- Resorts: Bedwell Harbour Resort (604-629-3212); Pender Lodge Cottages (604-629-3221).
- B&Bs: More than a dozen in all parts of the island; variety includes one-suite Arbutus Retreat (604-629-2047), lakeside Hummingbird Hollow (604-629-6392) and Cliffside Inn-on-the-Sea with hot tub and dining (604-629-6691). Some offer special features such as the art courses at Whalepointe (604-629-6155) on South Pender. B&Bs are list-

ed in a leaflet available on the ferries, or book through Canadian Gulf Islands B&B Reservation Service (604-529-2930).
- Camping: Prior Centennial Park; Beaumont Marine Park (boat access only), and at Browning and Otter Bay marinas.

Eating Places
Around eight, in various parts of the island, including snack bars, cafés, and pubs at the golf course and marinas. Lower price ranges include The Stand (604-629-3292) at the ferry (try the oysterburgers) and soup and sandwiches at Libby's Village Bakery (604-629-6453) in the Driftwood Centre. For fancier food, try Memories (604-629-3353) at the Inn on Pender, or the up-scale Bedwell Harbour Resort restaurant (604-629-3212).

Transportation
- Service: Repairs and gas at Sabyan Auto Marine

(604-629-3240).
- Marine engine service and repair: Sabyan Auto Marine (604-629-3240); Seastar Marine (604-629-3680).
- Taxi: Pender Island Taxi (604-629-9900).
- Vehicle Rental: Local Motion Rentals (604-629-3366)

Other
- Bank: Driftwood Centre (604-629-6516): no bank machine
- Groceries: Three, as well as shops at the marinas
- Laundromats: Driftwood Centre and marinas
- Liquor outlets: At Driftwood Centre (604-629-3413); cold beer and wine store at Port Browning Marina (604-629-3493)
- Post office: Driftwood Centre (604-629-3222)
- Public washrooms: Driftwood Centre, marinas and most parks

Port Washington store

Port Washington to Hope Bay (3 km)

Turn back along Port Washington Road past the junction with Otter Bay Road. On the left you will see St. Peter's Church. It was built in 1915 by volunteer labour. Outside, a ship's bell and a bench in memory of Neptune and Dorothy Grimmer both remind us that early pioneers had close ties with the sea.

Past the church on Port Washington Road is Renaissance Studio (604-629-3070). Visiting Renaissance is a little like following the White Rabbit into Wonderland: full of unexpected discoveries at every turn. In this part-studio/part-art gallery, you'll find Persian rugs, paintings, sculpture, antiques and Czech glass and other jewelry, and you can often watch expert restoration being undertaken.

Stay on Port Washington Road, which continues past Joyful Symmetry Country Crafts Studio (604-629-6476, dried flowers and a variety of crafts) and Southridge Farms Country Store (groceries, ice cream, local publications). Pass Corbett Road (along which historic Corbett House is now a pastoral B&B, 604-629-6305), and continue for another half a kilometre to Hope Bay.

Hope Bay Area

Hope Bay combines a pretty inlet with an intriguing complex of studios and craft stores. Although the mix changes from year to year, the area has developed a reputation as one of the most interesting corners of Pender. You can turn left to park by the dock, but it is then hard to decide whether to walk along the shore to look for

Old Orchard Farm

THE HOUSE WAS begun by Washington Grimmer, who came to Pender in 1882 from London via Australia. In his time, it had the island's first post office, and the Anglican community worshipped there before the church was built. In 1903 the property passed into the hands of Spencer Percival. He called it Sunny Side Ranch, enlarged the house and added to Grimmer's orchard. Social life included inter-island tennis competitions, musical evenings, and garden parties. The heritage orchard contains more than 50 varieties of apples, plums and pears, many of them now rare. The elegant farmhouse has recently been restored to its former Victorian glory, and, in season, flowers and fruit can be purchased from the stand at the gate.

Old Orchard Farm

wildlife, work your way through the shops and studios, or sit and sip a coffee or soft drink and watch the passing scene. From the dock itself, you can often see freighters from around the world sitting at anchor in Plumper Sound, awaiting their turn to proceed to Vancouver or other coastal ports.

At any state of the tide, Hope Bay is an attractive place for birds, and the waters (or mud flats) in and near the bay are likely to show cormorants, eagles, gulls, herons and kingfishers. In winter, look for a diversity of ducks, including

Common and Hooded Mergansers. Grebes and loons may be seen in the open sea nearby. In addition to the birds, you will often see seals.

The first of the Hope Bay studios is located at the end of Port Washington road, where immediately on your right is a house built by Lawrence Auchterlonie (and his son James) in the 1890s. It now houses Pender Island Pottery (604-629-6662), where you can meet Harriet and Roger Stribley in their workshop and enjoy their displays.

Down by the dock is the old Hope Bay Heritage Store, Stella Maris cooperative art gallery, and a goldsmith's workshop (604-629-6750).

Pender Information

Size: 34 square kilometres
Population: 1,646 in 1991, now about 2,000
Visitor Information: Information Centre with map off Otter Bay Road, sometimes open.

Some Pender Highlights

- Artist-run arts and crafts outlets such as Pender Pottery and Renaissance Studio
- Canal area, with Helisen archeological site
- The Driftwood Centre (especially on Saturday mornings), with its mix of shops and Farmers' Market
- Gulf Islands' only disc park in Magic Lake Estates
- Hope Bay, with its stores, galleries and events
- Mount Norman Regional Park for spectacular views
- Tide pools at Gowlland Point and other sites

Harriet and Roger Stribley

The Stribleys

WELL-ESTABLISHED Vancouver area potters, Harriet and Roger Stribley moved their wheels, kilns and other potting paraphernalia to Pender in 1990. From Harriet's fertile Swedish mind and skilful hands have sprung the many hand-built clay creations for which she has become known. Robust, nude exercising figurines, soulful cows, generously schnozzed "Herbert" pots (in which you can grow herbs), and whimsical dragons and dinosaurs are just some of her pieces. At the wheel, Roger turns out an impressive array of dinner- and cookware, as well as teapots, pitchers, vases, flower pots, and candlesticks. Much of

their work Harriet and Roger now sell directly from their home studio, though they retain a faithful clientele in the lower mainland.

Bowls and plates

Round the corner actually off the wharf is a delightful boutique called Galloping Moon Gallery (604-629-6020), where you can find Gulf Island arts and crafts, dried flowers, essential oils, jewelry, glass and table wear, clothes and hats, and musical instruments—in fact everything the well equipped Gulf Islander (or visitor) needs.

Hope Bay Heritage Store

Hope Bay, a natural gathering place

ALTHOUGH THE SIGN suggests that Hope Bay Store was built in 1905, the present building dates from 1912, when it was considered "the last word in country stores." Built by Robert Stewart Wallace Corbett, an Ontario settler who arrived on Pender in 1901, it rivaled the Port Washington store for North Island customers. Two generations of Corbetts were postmasters, so the store also contained the Hope Bay post office, and some of the original shelving can still be seen at the back of the store along with the original wooden counter. After half a century the Corbetts closed the store, and it has been reopened as an eclectic gift and book store and cappuccino bar. It retains much of its island character, especially that of a meeting place. Here residents still gather round the wood stove to exchange gossip and sometimes listen to classical or folk music by local and off-island performers (604-629-3423).

On a fine day, the boardwalk is a great place to sit in wicker chairs and watch the world and the eagles drift by while you sip a drink. The store also sells ice cream, snacks, and basic groceries. The store owners double as wharf managers and so here's where boaters using the government dock should check in for the night. On some weekends there are outdoor events to add to the fun. Gallery openings, fashion shows, and outdoor music all take place here from time to time. Facilities include moorage and public phone.

Side Trip to Bricky Bay (1 km)

This short trip takes you up the hill from Hope Bay, past a park and studio, to a beautiful beach that is also a former industrial site. From Hope Bay, head up Clam Bay Road; half a kilometre along is Mount Elizabeth Park on the left. The short trail through the woods winds through typical vegetation of a north facing slope, with extensive growth of young alders. Facilities include trail and toilet (no camping facilities or water).

Beyond the park is a drive-

Old Pender Island School Is Nu to Yu

BESIDE THE LIBRARY is an old school building with the cryptic sign "Nu to Yu". Its first floor was built in 1902, and the second was added later. It is the oldest school building surviving on the island and was used as a school until 1977.

Now it is the hub of Pender's recycling economy, and one of the best thrift shops we have seen anywhere. When islanders need a new toaster, run out of teaspoons, or fancy a new shirt, they often hit the Nu to Yu first. One discriminating visitor seized on a $2 leather coat and took it home across the Atlantic.

All the money taken in goes back into the community. Purchases made with grants from the Nu to Yu administration include a heart monitoring machine for the clinic and a wonderful selection of Canadian children's books for the playschool.

way to The Wool Shed, a home spinning and hand weaving studio run by Vi Smith of Welcome Bay Farm. The Smiths raise sheep and goats whose wool is sheared, combed, carded, spun, hand dyed, and woven on the premises.

About one kilometre from Hope Bay, turn right onto Coast Shale Road and park near the T junction with Armadale Road. To get to Bricky Bay, walk down the right-hand T of Armadale, a short, narrow lane with many orchids in spring. Almost at the end of the lane look for a narrow trail on the left which widens to steps down to the water. The bay has a pleasant stony beach strewn with barnacle-encrusted red bricks—all that remains of a thriving brick works, an industrial venture from the turn of the century. A tiny island sits in the middle of the bay and otters can often be seen at dusk swimming and fishing between the island and shore.

Return to Clam Bay Road. You can get back to Port Washington by heading right along an old-style island road. For the main route return to Hope Bay.

Hope Bay to Pender Library (1 km)

From Hope Bay dock drive inland on Bedwell Harbour Road. At the head of the bay, Hooson Road turns off to the left. It is named for the Yorkshire family who settled this area (see the story of the sinking of the *Iroquois* in chapter 3). A side trip up Hooson will take you to Kevin Oke's Photo Gallery (604-629-6786), Cres-

Hope Bay dock

cent Aviaries (604-629-6276), and (just past the llamas) Good Earth Farm (604-629-

6413) for flowers, vegetables, crafts and art works, and tarot readings (see the interview

Born at Sea

PIONEER WASHINGTON Grimmer married 16-year-old Elizabeth Auchterlonie in 1885. When she went into labour with their first child, the only midwife was on Mayne Island. They launched a rowboat and Washington started to row over—but he was not fast enough. Elizabeth delivered the baby in the middle of Navy Channel. This unusual birth place was marked by the name given to the baby—Neptune

Grimmer, with an unofficial middle name of "Navy". Elizabeth was not put off the sea; she was a friend of the Georgesons who manned the lighthouse on Prevost Island, and would row alone across the channel to visit them. The somewhat traumatic circumstances of his birth did "Nep" no harm either. He lived well into his nineties, and was a much-loved island character.

Mount Norman Regional Park

Head of Bedwell Harbour from Mount Norman, with Salt Spring beyond

ENERGETIC VISITORS CAN start their exploration of South Pender with a vigorous hike up Mount Norman. This prominent hill on South Pender is named for William Henry Norman, R.N., Paymaster on the survey vessel *H.M.S. Ganges* in 1841. The climb generally takes about 30 to 45 minutes.

Turn right onto Ainslie Point Road immediately after crossing the bridge. A small parking area is signed on the left, less than half a kilometre along. Take binoculars, camera, a picnic and perhaps a map of the Gulf Islands to help you sort out the many islands you will see from the top. Follow the well-marked trail to the summit (271 metres). The first views face north and east towards Saturna and Mayne islands and beyond to the mainland. On a clear day you'll see the Coast Range Mountains, the Tsawwassen ferry terminal, and the cities of Vancouver and Bellingham, Washington.

As you continue up the path, notice the snags and fallen debris amongst the undergrowth, signs of the logging that took place in this area. The forest of Mount Norman, scarcely touched for 6,000 years by the First Nations, was altered rapidly with the coming of new settlement to the Gulf Islands. Selective logging took place on the hillsides in the 1940s and '50s and a portion was clear-cut in 1985. The Capital Regional District acquired Mount Norman in 1988, making it the first regional park in the Gulf Islands. The interpretive theme of the park is "A park in progress" and you can see signs of the regeneration taking place. The new forest contains willow and Red Alder on the lower slopes, and gradually changes to a mix of Douglas Fir, Bigleaf Maple, Western Red Cedar, Arbutus and Western Hemlock. Sword fern and Salmonberry line the trail; Salal and Oregon Grape cover the forest floor.

At the summit a short boardwalk leads to a south-facing viewing deck where you have a bird's-eye view of the surrounding area. Bedwell Harbour is at your feet. Beyond that, sweeping from left to right, lie the San Juan Islands and snow-capped Olympic Mountains of Washington; Victoria and the Saanich Peninsula; and a multitude of Gulf Islands against the backdrop of Vancouver Island.

A new trail to Beaumont Marine Park also leads from Mount Norman. Pick it up at the main Mount Norman Park sign. Moderately challenging, it descends along huge rocky outcroppings and connects with an old coastal trail to beautiful Beaumont Park. Expect the hike to sea level to take about 45 minutes. Facilities include the trails, and pit toilets at the top of the first climb from the parking area. No camping or fires are permitted in the park.

with Karon Wallace in chapter 4).

Our main route continues on Bedwell Harbour Road straight ahead up the hill (watch out for guinea fowl wandering on the road from a nearby farm that breeds them). At the junction, take a sharp left on Bedwell Harbour Road. The United Community Church on the right was built by the Presbyterian congregation in 1906, making it the oldest church on Pender.

Shortly past the church is a small complex of community buildings, including the Pender Public Library, the Nu to Yu, and the playschool.

Past the Nu to Yu, look on the right for the old MacDonald Farm (yes, really). This her-itage farm dates from 1895, when it was built by a Scottish family, John and Jessie Mac-Donald. It is still operating (though not with the original family).

Just past the farm is the junction with Otter Bay Road. Here you can turn right and return directly to the ferry terminal (about three kilometres). Continue on Bedwell Harbour Road to see the rest of the island.

Otter Bay Road to the Driftwood Centre (2 km)

Almost immediately after Otter Bay Road you pass on the right the RCMP and fire station, and Pender cemetery where many early Pender resi-dents lie. The road winds for two kilometres through open farmlands (where Turkey Vultures may often be seen circling) and down the steep and twisty Einar's Hill to the Driftwood Centre, the island's main commercial hub.

Side Trip to Hamilton Beach (0.5 km)

Just past the Driftwood Centre, a detour left along Hamilton Road leads to Hamilton Beach, where you can beachcomb and look down Browning Harbour to the San Juans. A boat ramp provides access to the sheltered waters. Nearby is the Sh-Qu-Ala Inn and café at Port Browning Marina (other facilities include a cold beer and wine store, pool, laundry, showers, store and tennis). Return to the main route, which continues along Canal Road.

Driftwood Centre to the Canal (3 km)

About one kilometre south of the Driftwood Centre is The Inn on Pender Island, with Memories Restaurant. Prior Centennial Park offers 17 shady vehicle campsites and trails into the woods. The Heart Trail goes beyond the park and links with the Magic

---

Something You Otter Know

THE CURIOUS AND friendly otters seen around all the Gulf Islands are not sea otters but river ot-ters, despite the fact they spend much of their life on, in, or by the sea. A strong fishy smell near the shore may warn you that you are in the vicinity of an otter den or play area. Sit quietly on a beach in the evening and you may see otters fish-ing in the bays. Sea otters live in the deeper, colder wa-ters of the west coast of Vancou-ver Island, and are unlikely to frequent these waters, though

River Otters are common along Gulf Island shores

there have been a few recorded in the Victoria area.

Driftwood Centre Services

- Bakery
- Bank of British Columbia (no cash machine)
- Grocery store, bulk and video
- Laundromat, hairdresser, real estate office
- Post office, pharmacy, liquor store, gift shop
- Sabyan Auto Marine gas and service station

Lake area. About two kilometres from the Driftwood Centre, Canal Road makes a left turn which leads past the school (community centre) and Health Centre to the canal. Shortly before the bridge, a drive leads to Cooper's Landing, offering accommodation and dive and kayak charters.

Bedwell Harbour Island Resort

The docks at Bedwell Harbour Resort

BEDWELL HARBOUR Resort is the only service centre on South Pender. Parking is halfway down the hill, though the road continues to a drop-off and turnaround for those with elderly or very young passengers. The highly developed resort offers accommodation (24 units), laundry, tennis courts, pool, dining room, small boat rental, store, art gallery, and a marine pub where you can sit on the deck and refresh yourself while watching boats coming and going at the marina. Boat traffic can be heavy. The Canada Customs dock at Bedwell is a popular port of entry for many visiting American yachts, and processes more than 9,000 vessels a year. While you are on the docks at Bedwell, look on the cliff adjacent to the docks for graffiti painted in 1905 by the crew of the Royal Navy's survey vessel *H.M.S. Egeria*.

Across from the marina you may notice some boats anchored a little further around the bay on your right. These boats and their crews are visiting the 34-hectare Beaumont Marine Park which has a sheltered beach and several camp sites among Garry Oaks. It is publicly accessible from Bedwell only by boat.

Helisen Archeological Site

JUST BEFORE THE bridge, roadside plaques summarize the archeological and historical stories of the canal area. Roadside parking provides access by foot to the bridge and unsigned trails on both sides of the road.

The isthmus joining the north and south parts of Pender Island was known to First Nations as Helisen, or "lying between." When the canal was dug in 1903, work damaged a large midden—a bank of shells and other debris representing occupation by First Nations for thousands of years.

When it was realized that erosion from passing vessels was damaging the remains of the site, test excavations were made in 1957. The area was designated a provincial heritage site and, with the support of First Nations representatives, extensive excavations followed in the '80s.

Thousands of artifacts were discovered, which give evidence of occupations dating back some 5,170 years. Finds include hearths and a variety of artifacts (some of which are on display in the Pender library). These include projectile points, labrets (lip ornaments) and carved spoons. Most of the finds indicate a culture similar to that of pre-contact Coast Salish people, except that the latter are not known to have used labrets.

Although the area may be visited, camping and fires are not permitted, and excavation is illegal without a permit. The area is also a good place to look at geology (with vertically bedded rocks) and see uncommon Rocky Mountain Juniper trees.

The Canal Zone

Within half a kilometre of the canal are three attractive areas for exploration on foot. All have parking, or you can leave your vehicle at one and walk from one to another. First the Helisen archeological site on North Pender provides for intellectual and imaginative exploration. A short distance across the bridge you can enjoy a hike up Mount Norman, and follow that with a laze on the beach at Mortimer Spit.

Across the one-lane bridge you are on the less settled and somewhat less accessible South Pender.

About one third of a kilometre along Canal Road from the bridge you will find, on your left, a turn off to Mortimer Spit, a favourite spot of Pender residents. The spit was part of the Coast Salish settlement described in the previous section. Soak up some sunshine on the shell beach,

The Driftwood Centre offers many services

and watch the boat traffic enter and leave the canal. Lower parts of the spit have a growth of Glasswort (sea asparagus), uncommon on Pender where there are few salt marshes. The Glasswort here is host for a rare parasitic plant, the Salt-marsh Dodder.

The "Pender Lender"

THE PENDER ISLAND Public Library is locally known as the Pender Lender, and provides islanders with much of their reading. If you are visiting for several weeks you may register for a temporary library card.

The library was built entirely with Pender donations and labour. The lobby contains an interesting exhibit about the archeological site at the Pender Canal, and also a selection of photos of old Pender. Local publications are sometimes available for sale. Facilities include a washroom open during library hours.

Medicine Beach

LYING AT THE north end of Bedwell Harbour, Medicine Beach is the site of one of the First Nations settlements that occupied Pender for thousands of years. Evidence of that life lies in the low shell midden that remains above the beach. There is a brackish marsh area behind the midden. Plants growing in and around the marsh were used extensively for food, medicine and tools; shellfish and game provided other food.

Though it is under three hectares in size, this wetland is an exceptional example of what has become a rare and endangered habitat in the islands, and the Pender Island Conservancy Association has purchased it for future protection. Nine distinct plant communities thrive on the site. Of the many species found here, two are on the provincial

rare list: Marsh Peavine (*Lathyrus palustris*) and Marsh Hollyhock (*Sidalcea hendersonii*).

There's good birding here. Red-winged Blackbirds, grebes, mergansers, Great Blue Herons and kingfishers are plentiful. Sharp eyes may even spot a Virginia Rail, known to inhabit the marsh but more often heard than seen. Ospreys nest close by, and they may be seen making spectacular dives into the sea and emerging with a struggling fish in their talons.

The beach itself is great for strolling and offers an abundance of skipping stones. Along the east side of the beach, eroded, steeply dipping sandstones look like the long, spiny back of a great subterranean reptile.

Purple Sea Star

PEER INTO SHALLOW water on a rocky point and the most striking creature you are likely to see is a large purple or orange sea star, up to 25 centimetres across. Most remarkably, these strikingly different colours are two forms of the same species, known to scientists as *Pisaster ochraceus*. The orange form becomes more common towards the south.

Close up, you can see the coarse netlike pattern of white spines on the sea star's five broad limbs, and gently feel its rough surface. These spines remind us that sea stars (along with the sea urchins) belong to the animal group known as Echinoderms ("spiny skins"), the only group

whose bodies are typically structured in multiples of five. Among the spines are some tiny pincers which discourage other marine animals from settling on its back; if you rest your arm against it for a while the pincers may take gen-

tle hold of the hairs on your arm. If the sea star shows the underside of one of its arms, you can see the many tube feet, each ending with a little sucker, that allow it to move and catch its food.

When the tide comes in, the apparently inactive sea star becomes a busy feeder on barnacles, mussels, and limpets. Its arms embrace the shells of its prey, the suckers force it open, and it can turn part of its stomach inside out, insert it inside the shells and consume its food. Sea stars can regenerate a lost arm, and it is not uncommon to see one with a partially grown replacement.

Pender Island Disc Park

IMAGINE STANDING in a forest, surrounded by lush Arbutus and tall fir trees, rocky outcrops and mossy slopes. You have a frisbee in your hand and 33 metres between you and your target, an upright metal pole. "Par 3" notes the stone marker at the numbered tee-off position at your feet. You fix your eyes on the distant pole, take a few short sweeps for practice, let fly and then—WHAM! Who put that tree there? Wherever your frisbee ends up is the spot from which you take your next shot. It will be better, straighter, stronger than the last.

Welcome to frisbee golf. And welcome to Pender Island's 18-pole disc park (discs being to frisbees what hardballs are to softballs).

This four-hectare park was the brainchild of a few islanders

Welcome to the disc park

who, with lots of community support, laid out the course in the early 1980s. Since then it has become popular year-round with locals and visitors, hackers and competitors. Serious "golfers" use discs (which are smaller than most frisbees, heavier, faster and, in the right hands, more accurate). Really serious golfers carry shoulder bags around the course

with half a dozen discs of different sizes and weights for different shots and conditions. On the last weekend in May, the annual Pender Island Invitational Disc Tournament takes place, typically attracting close to 100 participants from Washington, Oregon, Alberta and around BC.

If you're looking for a novel way to entertain the children and the adults in the crowd, this is it. Use of the course is free; all you have to bring are your own frisbees or discs. Skill level is no obstacle to having a good time here, but just for your information, par on the front nine is 27 and par on the back nine is 29. Parking is provided beside the road. Facilities include an outdoor toilet, water fountain and picnic tables.

Mortimer Spit to Bedwell Harbour (8 km)

Continuing southward on Canal Road you will pass peaceful home sites overlooking Plumper Sound, with Saturna Island in the background. Continue right on Spalding Road, which takes you into a beautiful valley with open fields—quiet rural life at its best. As the road plunges into the trees again, the swampy area to the right is the public but undeveloped Enchanted Forest Park, accessible by informal trails. The road narrows and can become very windy at the top of the hill overlooking Bedwell Harbour on your right. At the bottom of the hill, turn right to get to Bedwell Harbour Island Resort.

Bedwell Harbour to Gowlland Point (3.5 km)

From Bedwell Resort to the southern tip of the island is a pleasant trip along Gowlland Point Road. On the way, note the sign for the Vern Simpson Gallery. Vern is a friendly artist, willing to show you his landscapes on canvases large and small. Craddock and Higgs roads provide access to interesting beaches and rocky shores. The best tide pools are along the beach at Gowlland Point. Here at low tide you can investigate the pools for sea anemones and starfish, and gaze out at the American San Juan Islands. Freighters often pass through Boundary Pass. You may see seals swimming in the kelp beds, and less frequently you may see Orcas passing the point. On a clear day you can see the distant Coast Range mountains on the mainland, including magnificent Mount Baker. Look for depressions high on the rocks which were tide pools when the sea level was

Light at Gowlland Point

higher than it is today. On a stormy day, the wind and waves can be mesmerizing.

Side Trip to Medicine Beach and Magic Lake (2.5 km)

On your way back from the canal, consider taking time to explore Medicine Beach and the Magic Lake area. Medicine Beach is an attractive natural area, while Magic Lake is one of the few accessible lakes on the island and Pender's most used swimming hole. Around the lake is Magic Lake Estates, a largely residential part of North Pender, which will give you a taste of modern suburban island living. The area is also known for attractive parks with wooded trails, bayside beaches, and the disc park.

To visit the area, begin at the junction of Canal Road and Aldridge Road, about one kilometre west of the bridge, and follow the Magic Lake road signs south onto Aldridge Road.

Make your first stop Medicine Beach, a natural area with fine beach walks, open views, and nature watching. Turn left immediately at the bottom of the Aldridge Road hill (0.3 kilometres from the Y junction) on a short unnamed road.

Return to the main road and continue west along Schooner Way. On the left, just up the hill from the beach, is P.J.'s grocery store and video rental. The outdoor bulletin board will give you a taste of island happenings. The Pender Crafts gift shop, featuring locally made jewelry, children's clothing, wooden toys, and other crafts, is located beside the store. Head up Schooner Way and follow it to the left at the Fire Hall. At the junction with Privateers Road you'll reach a small park on the left that runs along the end of Magic Lake itself. Early ref-erences call it Dead Cow Slough, and on official maps the lake is called Pender Lake, but islanders refer to it (and the surrounding residential district) as Magic Lake.

Here you can launch a ca-noe for a quiet paddle. A mix-ture of domestic and wild waterfowl is often in atten-dance. The domestic ducks and geese can be fed (they'll demand it), while several species of wild ducks, some-times sharing the water with cormorants, will tolerate the bird-watcher. The water warms up nicely in the sum-mer, but swimming is best done from the dock at the other end of the lake where the water is deep.

When you've fed the ducks, you can seek out the Gulf Is-land's most unusual recre-ational experience by heading up Privateers and turning right on Galleon Way to the disc park.

There's lots more to the Magic Lake area. Recom-mended spots include the many trails (usually marked with a WALK sign at the road-side), Thieves Bay and Shingle Bay (where a few pilings are all that is left of a once important fish processing plant; see the story in chapter 3). A roadside map board next to Fire Hall No. 2 will help you with direc-tions, but if you plan to spend much time in the labyrinth, it's a good idea to equip yourself with the detailed road map available from the real estate office at the Driftwood Centre or local stores.

The Canal

A narrow bridge spans the canal

THE CANAL BRIDGE has connect-ed the north and south parts of Pender island only since 1955. For half a century before that, contact between the two was by boat, including the steamship *Iroquois*, which tra-versed the canal and called in at Bedwell Harbour. The canal was excavated in 1903, by blasting and dredging through the narrow neck of land known as the Indian Portage. This pro-vided a short-cut for inter-island boat traffic, and now the canal serves hundreds of pleasure boats, from kayaks to large mo-tor cruisers.

A low speed limit for boats is imposed for safety and to protect the site of the remains of a First Nations settlement from further erosion.

Conglomerates

A COMMON SIGHT on Gulf Island beaches is a mass of rock con-taining large pebbles. These rocks are known as conglomer-ates, sedimentary rocks made up of rounded pebbles or boul-ders and often set in a finer-grained matrix of sand. The raw materials have been formed on beaches or in streams where rock fragments have been bat-tered and ground together by waves and currents until they become rounded. Smaller and more fragile rocks were quickly broken up and washed away, leaving tougher boulders and pebbles, often of a colourful mix of different materials.

The hard pebbles were then deposited where currents were strong enough to wash most of the finer silts away, leaving only

Conglomerate is full of pebbles of older rocks

enough to fill the gaps between the boulders. Later cementation by chemicals carried in water that moved through the sedi-ment turned the whole mass in-to a solid rock.

10. Salt Spring

Booth Inlet cuts deep into the island

"It's big, beautiful, and bursting with things to do," waxed one enthusiastic visitor to Salt Spring Island. The impression of size depends on what it's compared to, but Salt Spring is the largest and best-known of the Gulf Islands, and has the most year-round residents, highest number of visitors and certainly the most visitor facilities. It is also the easiest island to get to as it is served by three different ferries: two from Vancouver Island and one from Tsawwassen.

Other Gulf Islanders consider Salt Spring "built up" and treat a trip to Ganges the same as going to a big city—after all, they have one-way streets now, and there is talk of a traffic light. However many parts of the island are still rural or untamed, and solitude is available for those who want it.

With its abundant and wide scale accommodation, varied restaurants, and other urban facilities, Salt Spring can certainly be the simplest to visit. With more than 30 studios and 650 kilometres of road, there is plenty to see and do. Yet, because of its size and diversity, the island is harder to get to know than the smaller, less serviced islands, and it may take several visits to get a real sense of it.

Salt Spring has the Gulf Islands' highest mountain (Bruce Peak, 703 metres), and largest lake, St. Mary. Although most of its rocks are the same Cretaceous sandstones that make up the rest of the islands, the southwestern peninsula is made up of much older rocks. The salt springs in the northern area give their name to the island, but are not accessible to the public. In the early days of settlement, the island had bears, wolves and cougars, but they were wiped out as settlement advanced. Today, the island is one of the best areas to see Bald Eagles, with major concentrations at the north end in the spring, and in Fulford Harbour in the winter.

Prehistoric settlement goes back several thousand years (as documented on adjacent islands), and there is one spectacular petroglyph. First Nations populations were still present when modern settlement began, and there are eyewitness accounts of bloody battles between different

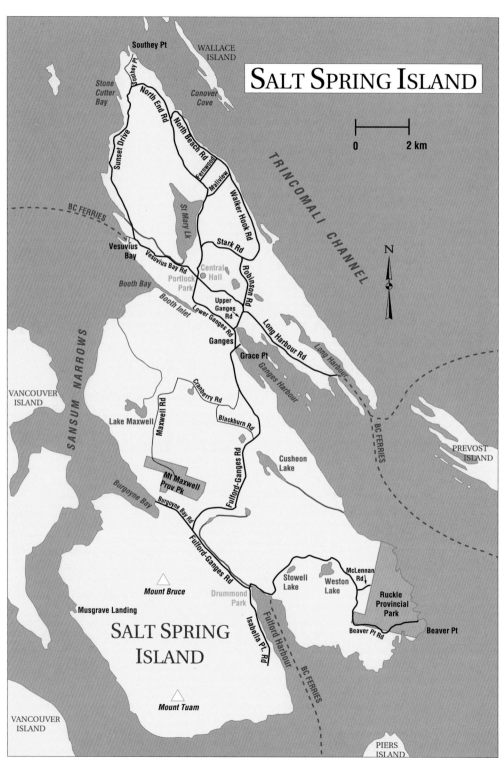

SALT SPRING ISLAND

0   2 km

Southey Pt
WALLACE ISLAND
Stone Cutter Bay
Southey Pt
North End Rd
Conover Cove
North Beach Rd
Sunset Drive
Fernwood
Mallview
Walker Hook Rd
St Mary Lk
TRINCOMALI CHANNEL
N
Vesuvius Bay
Vesuvius Bay Rd
Stark Rd
Booth Bay
Central Hall
Portlock Park
Robinson Rd
SANSUM NARROWS
Booth Inlet
Lower Ganges Rd
Upper Ganges Rd
Ganges
Long Harbour Rd
Long Harbour
Grace Pt
Ganges Harbour
Cranberry Rd
VANCOUVER ISLAND
Maxwell Rd
Lake Maxwell
Blackburn Rd
BC FERRIES
PREVOST ISLAND
Mt Maxwell Prov Pk
Fulford-Ganges Rd
Cusheon Lake
Burgoyne Bay
Burgoyne Bay Rd
Fulford-Ganges Rd
Mount Bruce
Drummond Park
Stowell Lake
Weston Lake
McLennan Rd
Ruckle Provincial Park
Musgrave Landing
SALT SPRING ISLAND
Isabella Pt. Rd
Fulford Harbour
Beaver Pt Rd
Beaver Pt
BC FERRIES
Mount Tuam
VANCOUVER ISLAND
PIERS ISLAND

groups in Ganges Harbour. New settlers came as early as 1859, and included African-Americans recently freed from slavery in the deep south of the U.S. and Kanaka sailors from the Hawaiian Islands, as well as eastern Canadians and Europeans. Settlement began around Vesuvius, Fernwood, Ganges, and St. Mary Lake, but soon spread into the Burgoyne Valley to Fulford Harbour, and by 1874 Henry Ruckle had bought land at Beaver Point, some of which is still being worked by family members.

Farming is still an important activity on Salt Spring, and its lamb is a famous delicacy. Over the years, there have been various (more or less unsuccessful) attempts to locate and develop mineral resources, but logging has been more successful and continues in some areas. As the largest island in a central position, Salt Spring also provides some services to the other islands, including the hospital and high school.

Tourism has become a major business, supporting many of the islanders directly or indirectly. Visitors have been coming for more than a century, and Salt Spring now offers a wider variety of accommodation than any of the other islands. If you like to go up scale, consider Hastings House tucked discreetly in the woods near Ganges. Several other hotels and motels, and more than 40 B&Bs offer plenty of variety. There are seaside resorts, and—only on Salt Spring—lakeside resorts. We toured a resort on St. Mary Lake and found it perfect for families, with comfortable private holiday cabins, wide grassy play areas, access to the lake shore, and canoes and

Names from the Navy

H.M.S. Ganges *was one of the warships that served on the west coast*

FIRST PEOPLES apparently knew the island as Chuan or Tuam Island, a name that survives in Mount Tuam on the southwest part of Salt Spring. The white settlers began to refer to it as Salt Spring Island as early as 1851, after the springs in the northern part of the island. However, in 1859 the British Navy surveyors decided to call it Admiral Island, to honour Rear-Admiral R.L. Baynes, then Pacific Commander. (Ironically, Baynes' flagship is remembered in the principal town, Ganges, while Baynes' other connection has been lost as the residents' usage persisted.) In 1906, the Geographic Board of Canada decided the spelling "Saltspring" should be used, but almost a century later they have not yet convinced most of the residents. We have followed their preference of "Salt Spring" Island.

Some Salt Spring Highlights

Hastings House is set in a flower garden

- The splendid Drummond Park petroglyph
- Everlasting Summer's annual garden party
- Flagstone Gallery, Gordon Wales Pottery
- Ganges: shopping, restaurants, Saturday market
- Hastings House for fine dining
- Mount Maxwell for spectacular views
- Ruckle Provincial Park
- Studio Tour

fishing gear available. Also on the island are cottages to rent, a hostel and campgrounds, or you can book yourself into a special weekend experience, such as a Yoga Retreat at the Salt Spring Centre.

The multicultural diversity brings Salt Spring a greater ethnic mix than one finds on the other islands. Nowhere is this more apparent than in the restaurants. These are only part of the attraction of Ganges, the most developed centre in all the Gulf Islands,

which is a delightfully small and exuberant village that successfully combines commerce and tourism and yet still retains a laid-back Gulf Island atmosphere. There are lots of studios in and around Ganges, and you can find the others from a tour map containing information, addresses and individual opening hours.

Salt Spring has more books and articles written about it than other islands, and has had its own guidebook for a number of years. Both its ac-

tive Chamber of Commerce and other bodies provide visitor information, much of it free. We have therefore not written as fully about Salt Spring as it undoubtedly deserves, but instead have been more selective in deciding which of its many attractions to include.

A large island with three different ferry access routes presents a multitude of choices to both visitors and guidebook writers, but (unlike some of the other islands) Salt Spring does have a clear centre in the community of Ganges. We bring the visitor in first by Fulford Harbour (the source of most incoming traffic), and initially present a side trip to Ruckle Provincial Park, which combines some of the best features of Salt Spring in a short distance. Our recommended route then takes the main road to Ganges, with some suggested side trips along the way. A walking tour of Ganges presents some of its most interesting attractions. A leisurely circuit round the northwestern part of the island takes in the old community of Vesuvius (where a ferry connects to Crofton), north to Southey Point and back via the northeast coast. The route continues to Long Harbour (where a ferry connects to other islands and Tsawwassen). Visitors arriving from ferries at Vesuvius and Long Harbour will easily be able to pick up our recommended sightseeing circuits. Particularly on this large island, absence of comment does not mean there is nothing of interest; don't hesitate to explore beyond our

Salt Spring Access

Ganges Small Boat Harbour

Ferries: From Vancouver Island, Swartz Bay to Fulford Harbour (10 trips a day, 35 minutes), and Crofton to Vesuvius (20 minutes). From the mainland, Tsawwassen to Long Harbour twice daily (1.2-3 hours). Connections to Pender, Mayne, Galiano, and Saturna. To travel from the mainland at other times, go direct to Swartz Bay and transfer to the Fulford ferry (ask for transfers when booking). Reservations and information (604-537-9921).
Float plane: By arrangement, Hanna Air (604-537-9359,

1-800-665-2359) and Harbour Air (1-800-665-0212) between Ganges, Vancouver International Airport and downtown Vancouver.
Water taxi: By arrangement, Gulf Islands Water Taxi, 604-537-2510
Boat moorage: Government docks at Burgoyne Bay, Fernwood, Fulford, Ganges, Musgrave Landing, Vesuvius. Marinas: Fulford Marina (604-653-4424); Ganges Marina (604-537-5242); Salt Spring Marina (604-537-5810).

suggested routes.

Fulford Harbour

The unobtrusive ferry dock and sleepy scatter of buildings that make up Fulford village are deceptive, as this is the busiest ferry terminal on Salt Spring. Fulford is Salt Spring's nearest harbour to Swartz Bay, and when the ferry docks, cars stream through on their way to Ganges. It is usually when leaving Fulford and waiting in the ferry line up that visitors actually explore the small stores.

The little café, Rodrigo's, is definitely worth a visit for great home-made pie. It also has a sprinkling of Mexican dishes among the BLTs and hamburgers. Colourful locals abound; on one visit, we shared a coffee and pie in Rodrigo's with writer and story-teller Ted Stone. There's also a grocery and video store, a

Salt Spring Information

Size: 180 square kilometres
Population: 8,018 in 1991, now about 9,000
Visitor Information: Write the Chamber of Commerce at P.O. Box 111, Ganges, BC V0S 1E0 (phone: 604-537-5252; fax: 604-537-4276); or stop at the Tourist Information Centre on Lower Ganges Rd

Facilities and Services

Emergency Services
- Ambulance, Fire, Police: 911
- Doctors: Mainly in Ganges; check hospital or current phone book.
- Hospital: Lady Minto in Ganges, 604-537-5545
- Pharmacy: in Ganges, 604--537-5534
- Police: 604-537-5555

Accommodation
Full information is available from the Chamber of Commerce.
- Hotels: Classy Hastings House and four more modest hotels offer a variety of accommodations.
- Motels: Arbutus Court Motel (604-537-5415).
- Resorts: A dozen resorts are found both along the sea and— unique to the islands— on several freshwater lakes. Cottage Resort is representative of several on St. Mary Lake (604-537-2214); Cusheon Lake Resort has an outdoor hot tub (604-537-9629); Salty Springs Seaside Resort (604-537-4111) is one of the seashore resorts.
- B&Bs: 46 B&Bs should offer enough diversity for everyone. Examples of the variety available include Applecroft Heritage Family Farm (604-537-5605), 300 metre high Armand Heights (604-653-9989), waterside Beach House at Fulford (604-653-2040), and Kitchener House (604-653-9879) with its delightful gardens on Booth Canal. Some offer extra facilities such as boat charters, galleries, gardens, German-speaking hosts, gourmet breakfasts, hot tubs, Jacuzzis, saunas, and spectacular views.
- Camping: Camping at Mouat and Ruckle Provincial Parks.
- Hostels: Cusheon Creek Hostel (604-537-4149)

Eating Places
More than 25 eating places, ranging from the top-of-the-line restaurants to take-out pizza. Most are in and around Ganges, but Fulford and Vesuvius have some. A wide range of food is served at such restaurants as the Kanaka Restaurant (604-537-5041) and Tides Inn (604-537-1470). Current specialties include Chinese, Greek (Bouzouki Greek Café 604-537-4181), Italian, Mediterranean, Mexican (Rodrigo's 604-653-9222), Scandinavian, and vegetarian (Crescent Moon Vegetarian Café (604-537-1960), as well as the expected fast food, seafood and "West Coast cuisine."

Transportation
- Bus: A summer shuttle bus ran in 1994, then closed down. There may be future attempts to run a bus service.
- Car rentals: Ganges Marina (604-537-5242); Heritage Car & Truck Rentals (604-537-4225, fax 604-537-4226).
- Gas: Five service stations, around the island.
- Marine engine service and repair: Several available.
- Scooter rentals: Rainbow Rentals (604-537-2877).
- Taxi: Salt Spring Taxi (604-537-9712).
- Touring: Salt Spring Tours (Azure Transport Ltd.) (604-537-4737).

Other
- Bank: Bank of Montreal, CIBC and Island Savings Credit Union (two instant teller machines)
- Groceries: Numerous stores
- Laundromat: Ganges
- Liquor outlets: Ganges
- Post office: Fulford and Ganges
- Public washrooms: Centennial Park, marinas and most parks, ferry terminals

Hanna Air

IF GETTING TO and from the islands on the ferry seems like a big chore, an alternative method of transport that makes an instant holiday experience is a trip by float plane.

Hanna Air (604-537-9359, 1-800-665-2359) is based in Ganges Harbour, and for a reasonable fee will take up to four people from Vancouver Airport's southern terminal on the Fraser River to any of the Gulf Islands. Instead of a two- or three- hour ferry trip from Tsawwassen terminal, it's a usu-

Float planes provide rapid access to the islands

ally exhilarating 20-minute flight.

Hanna will also arrange to pick people up at any one of the small government docks on other Gulf Islands for inter-island trips. On a fine day, a sight-seeing trip of this area by float plane is fabu-

lous. Orcas and seals can sometimes be seen swimming through the clear water and the low flight-path over the islands gives a wonderful view of the topography and geological features. The Hanna Air pilots are young, enthusiastic, well trained and helpful.

There are only two things to keep in mind: passengers have to be fairly lithe to clamber in and out of the plane via the float, and each person is limited to 25 pounds of luggage.

Salt Spring Centre

IF YOU WANT some quiet space where body and mind will be treated holistically, this is the place to come (phone/fax 604-537-2326). Run somewhat on the lines of a commune but without many of the drawbacks, the centre offers retreats and programs for the public, concentrating on body and spiritual awareness and self-help techniques such as yoga and tai chi. The centre also offers women's weekends and personal retreat packages, and is the home of Salt Spring's independent alternative school program that currently has 48 students from kindergarten to grade 8.

The centre is housed in a building known locally as "the Blackburn House" which may have been built about 1911 by one of the Bittancourt family. It's an elegant mansion that has retained much of its historical exterior while being renovated inside in a way that is light, airy and comfortable. The heart is a

Pamela Thornton at Salt Spring Centre

serene central space with an alcove containing a Buddha and a photo of the centre's mentor, Baba Hari Dass. This area is used not only as a meditation space, but also for concerts and special events, many open to the public.

The atmosphere is peaceful inside and pastoral outside. The centre sits on 28 hectares of meadowland and forest, and

trails and a campground are situated on the grounds. The food is vegetarian, with the produce grown by members of the community in a large garden behind the house. The food is so good that the centre has produced a best-selling cookbook, *Salt Spring Island Cooking*.

"The centre is run by a non-profit society and dedicated as a place for renewal in body, mind, and spirit," explains Pamela Thornton, one of the centre's founding community members and co-author of the cookbook. "So projects like the cookbook really help."

"We are very proud of what we have achieved here," she said as she showed us around. "And visitors are welcome to drop in and see what we have to offer." Asked about the Sanskrit letters on the rock in her photograph, she answered with a gentle smile: "I think it means 'no parking'."

Fulford Harbour from Mount Maxwell

pottery, and import clothing and gift store, and gallery lining the street (which doubles as the waiting area for the ferry). As it is wise in the summer to be in line at least 30 minutes ahead of your ferry, this gives time for a quick browse.

Fulford Harbour Marina

Not far from the ferry dock and within walking distance of Fulford Village is Fulford

Recreational Opportunities

- **Birding:** Great variety of opportunities along beaches, parks and trails. Bird checklist available from Thimble Farms, 175 Arbutus Rd, Ganges, BC, V0S 1E0. Salt Spring Trail & Nature Club, Box 998, Ganges
- **Bowling (5 pin) and pool:** Kings Lane Recreation (604-537-2054)
- **Cycling:** Bicycle rentals and repairs from Island Spoke Folk (604-537-4664), Western Cyclogical (604-537-2853, fax 604-537-4221)
- **Diving:** Three dive charter outfits
- **Golf:** Blackburn Meadows Golf course (604-537-1707); Salt Spring Golf and Country Club

(604-537-2121)
- **Fishing:** Freshwater: Larger lakes are stocked. Licences available from fishing tackle shops and government offices. Marine: Half a dozen boat charter operations for cruises and fishing
- **Hang gliding:** From the top of Mount Bruce
- **Hiking:** Along trails, especially on Mount Tuam
- **Horse riding:** Salt Spring Guided Rides (604-537-5761)
- **Kayaking:** Three rental outlets
- **Movies:** Salt Spring Cinema (604-537-4656)
- **Museums:** Ackerman's Museum (604-653-4228)
- **Personal development:** Salt

Spring has the only phone book we know with an Astrology heading in the business directory. Also Hypnotherapy, Massage Therapy, Shiatsu, and Therapeutic Touch. If you want it, it's probably here.
- **Playgrounds:** Centennial Park; Portlock Park; elementary schools
- **Shopping:** Ganges; Fulford Harbour; Vesuvius; shops and studios too numerous to list. Check Tourist Information Centre for brochures.
- **Swimming:** Outdoor pool in Portlock Park (604-537-4448)
- **Tennis:** At Fulford Marina (604-653-4424); Portlock Park (604-537-4448)

Marina, an older marina that's just had a face lift and currently has good facilities with other improvements in the works. Despite the ferry traffic, this end of the island is much quieter than the Ganges area and the whole of Fulford Harbour has the air of being a sleepy backwater. Anchorages here have a lovely view of the wide, shallow bay.

Marina facilities include: moorage, power and water hook ups (reservations recommended); fuel dock (gas and diesel); showers and washrooms; visitor information; fishing licences, bait and tackle; picnic tables; tennis courts and trails; groceries, gifts, and ice. Licensed mechanic and dive specialist available. Phone 653-9600 or 1-800-668-5526; fax 1-800-665-7977.

Side Trip to Ruckle Provincial Park (10 km)

As you leave Fulford Harbour, turn right on Beaver Point Road and follow its windings to Ruckle Provincial Park. If it's a hot day, consider a swim among the yellow waterlilies in Stowell Lake, on the right hand side of the road. This is one of the smallest island lakes, but is popular for swimming and fishing and has a couple of parking spots and toilet facilities. Further along to the right is Weston Lake, much larger, also with public access but no facilities, though it is stocked with fish. As this lake is also a reservoir, no gas motor boats are allowed.

A left turn on McLennan Road will lead you on a brief detour to Everlasting Summer (follow signs to the end of the road). Return to Beaver Point Road, turn left and continue towards Ruckle Park.

As you approach Ruckle Park you will pass Beaver Point Community Hall and the little Beaver Point School

Ted Stone: Tales from the Back Porch

TED STONE IS a professional storyteller, who travels around western Canada telling tales. He works with adults and kids, in schools, community centres, and farm groups.

"I've always been interested in stories, but I used to be more of a story listener than a story teller. I started writing, and people started asking if I would go into a school to give a journalism workshop. I gave workshops by telling stories, and sooner or later they started asking me if I would come and tell stories." Ted likes to do the old fashioned type of back-porch stories. They tend to be humorous, but not necessarily all tall tales.

Between tours, Ted is still adjusting to west coast life. "I bought my Salt Spring property from people who'd homesteaded there in 1911. Now I have what people around here call a farm—five acres—but I rent a bit of pasture from neighbours. I raise a

Ted Stone on Fulford Dock

few chickens and some Salt Spring lamb. I used to farm two quarters in Manitoba. My nearest neighbour was a mile and half away. I could see the smoke on a clear day. People coming here from the city find Salt Spring rural, but to me it's like suburbia."

After a while, Ted began writing his stories down. "I've been here six years, and everyone asks if it's inspiring to write here. Well, it's no more inspiring than a Manitoba winter."

Ted is quite clear about why he likes the Gulf Islands. "Salt Spring has the best weather in the world. I don't like it when it's too hot and I don't like it when it's too cold. If I moved back to Manitoba now I'd miss the summers out here. I lead a quiet life; I just get up in the morning and write, and wander around in my garden. I still feel like a tourist sometimes. But I'm a true islander now—you can't live in a finished house."

As we finished coffee, Ted excused himself. "I'm just finishing my ninth book, and I seem to have run out of day before I've run out of things to do."

(Ted Stone has published nine books, with such delightful titles as *It's Hardly Worth Talking If You're Going to Tell the Truth*.)

beside it. The school was built in 1885 and was used as a school until 1951. It is said to be the oldest continuously used school in BC. In 1979 it was restored, repainted in its original colour of "railroad red" and reopened as a preschool.

Pass through the gates of Ruckle Park, and stop at the farm buildings on your right.

Ruckle Provincial Park

This beautiful and unusual park was once one of the most important farms on Salt Spring. Sold to the province by the Ruckle family in 1974, some 80 hectares of the park are still farmland worked by the Ruckle family. The remains of the original farmstead are interpreted by signs and old photographs. If you're really lucky, Gwen Ruckle may be around to give one of her slide shows in the barn.

Past the farm, a short drive leads to the parking lot at the end of the road, where you can explore the many trails through the forest to the seaside headlands with wonderful views. At the water's edge, you can explore a different geology, as ancient rocks emerge from beneath the sandstones that make up most of the Gulf Islands.

It is an easy hike into the walk-in camping area, and definitely worth the trouble of hauling your gear. This is one of the most spectacular campgrounds in the Gulf Islands, with sites right on the bluffs overlooking Swanson Channel. At night, the brightly lit ferries pass close by. Highly recommended.

Facilities include trails, historic interpretation, walk-in camping, picnic tables, barbecues, water, and toilets.

When you have enjoyed your visit to the park, backtrack to Fulford Harbour, where you can return to the ferry or continue the tour by turning right on the Fulford-Ganges Road.

Fulford Harbour to Drummond Park (1 km)

The road towards Ganges first passes along the head of Fulford Harbour. On the right is a tiny white church, St. Paul's, and then, across the creek, is

Everlasting Summer

EVERLASTING SUMMER (604-653-9418) is a fabulous name for a dried flower and herb farm that nestles in the McLennan Valley and grows thousands of flowers for drying. In the summer months several hectares of blooms delight the eye and nose. To add to the attraction, owner Marcia Jeanne has developed a formal garden with thematic beds for browsing, smelling, touching and exploring the many dried herbs and flowers she has available. A nursery area grows plants for ready-made floral arrangements; wreaths, swags or posies are available at the cottage workshop. You can tour the loft and drying rooms and choose dried bunches to arrange for yourself, or, even bet-

Gardens at Everlasting Summer

ter, go almost at the end of the season when you are allowed in

the fields to pick your own blooms for a modest fee. We spent a heavenly hour wandering through the scented hay-strewn meadow, choosing an eclectic bunch of flowers and seed pods, watching the eagles and hawks soar above us and disturbing clouds of crickets at every step—a truly Mother Earth experience. Marcia also offers classes in flower arranging and the use of flowers and herbs around the home. Phone and ask to be on the mailing list for special summer events such as classes in edible flowers or garden design, the annual garden party, or an art show in the garden. Some of these may fall during your visits.

The Ruckle Family

Ruckle farmstead restored

"A MAN WHO understands farming and has a little capital will do as well or better here than any place in North America. Dairying and poultry I consider pay the best, and fruit growing is also very profitable. The chief trouble is the clearing." Thanks to direct quotations in a pamphlet promoting Salt Spring by the Rev. E.F. Wilson, we can read Henry Ruckle's opinions of his farming operation in 1894.

Ruckle was born in Ireland of German parents, and came to Salt Spring via Ontario in 1872. When he first arrived he was a bachelor and was able to pre-empt 27 acres for $1 an acre, gradually adding land over the years. About 1876 he built a large house (now preserved), perhaps in anticipation of his 1877 marriage to Ella Christensen, a Norwegian widow from the U.S., with a son, Alfred. Together, they had three more children, Ella, Agnes and Daniel Henry. Henry served his community in various ways, holding office as road foreman, school trustee, and postmaster of Beaver Point. His supplies and

produce were transported to Sidney in a rowboat and to New Westminster by a whaleboat. In 1895 a wharf at Beaver Point (now gone) made it possible to load produce on the steamship *Joan*.

By 1894, Ruckle had been farming on Salt Spring for 20 years, and had 1,000 acres, of which 40 were under cultivation. "Last autumn he thrashed 250 bushels of wheat, 100 bushels of oats, 200 bushels of peas, and put up 20 tons of hay, 60 tons of swedes and six tons of potatoes," explained the Reverend Wilson. The very profitable fruit crop came from 600 apple and other fruit trees. Ruckle died in 1895, leaving the farm in the hands of his sons Alfred and Daniel Henry. Alfred made violins, and he and his wife Helen played violin and piano for many of the island dances.

In the 1940s came big changes. Alfred sold his interest to Daniel Henry and his sons, the farm switched from dairy to beef cattle when the Salt Spring creamery closed, and the first tractor was used in the fields.

the Fulford Inn. The present building is the fourth on the site of one of the oldest inns in the Gulf Islands. Unfortunately fire was the fate of many early wooden buildings and fire struck here three times. The current pub is noted for its Christmas carol singing event that is led by the Salt Spring singer, Valdy.

The Fulford-Ganges Road swings to the right just past the inn, but if you first detour left, you will find the entrance to Drummond Park about 200 metres up Isabella Point Road.

Fulford Valley to Ganges (12 km)

Return to the Fulford-Ganges Road and drive north. About one kilometre north of the Fulford Inn, watch for a log building on the right of the road, with a thunderbird over the door. This is Bob Akerman's private museum, which is open for visitors when Bob is around.

On the left is Meg Buckley's pottery studio, displaying her functional mugs and porcelain. Continue on to the junction with Burgoyne Bay Road.

At the head of the Fulford Valley, the road turns right under the slopes of Mount Maxwell. You will pass the new Blackburn Meadows Golf course on your left, then at about eight kilometres from Fulford Inn come to the junction with Blackburn Road, also on the left. This is the turn for Salt Spring Centre, one of many alternative life style institutions that are springing up on the Gulf Islands.

Although Mount Maxwell and its associated hills dominate the landscape to the left,

Beaver Point

Fulford-Ganges Road at a sharp angle.

Side Trip to Mount Maxwell (9 km)

Drive up Cranberry Road and turn left on Mount Maxwell Road, from which the summit is reached by a narrow winding road almost nine kilometres long. At 602 metres, Baynes Peak on Mount Maxwell is one of the highest points in the southern Gulf Islands, though it is exceeded by two other Salt Spring summits. The road requires caution, and is not suitable for trailers. It goes almost to the lookout point, where there are fabulous views over Sansum Narrows to Vancouver Island, and across southern Salt Spring to the other islands. Mount Maxwell is not only an important landmark on Salt Spring, but the folks living on adjacent islands check the severity of the winter weather by looking towards Mount Maxwell to see if a coating of snow was deposited on its peak during the night.

Named after an early settler, John Maxwell, the mountain offers some old-growth forest, winding hiking trails, picnic spots and the unsurpassed views that make this a "must visit" for Salt Spring. Facilities include seven kilometres of trails, toilets, and picnic tables.

Caution: Although cliffs are fenced, there may be danger for young children.

Return by Mount Maxwell Road and Cranberry Road to the Fulford-Ganges Road, and turn left to drive north to Ganges, urban centre of Salt Spring and the islands. As you go down the hill to enter the village you will see the

you almost reach Ganges before you can find a way to get there. Eleven kilometres from Fulford Inn, turn left on Cranberry Road, which joins the

Studio Tour

SALT SPRING ISLAND is home to so many artists and artisans that they have published a couple of studio tour maps. These are available from the studios themselves, most of the accommodation places, and many stores and tourist facilities, as well as from the tourist information centre in Ganges. There are over 30 galleries and studios open to the public including those featuring glassblowing, jewelry, painting, pottery, stained glass, weaving, woodworking, and many other artistic expressions. Since it is not possible to see them all in one day, pick and choose to your own taste. Allow plenty of time, as many of the artists are happy to chat about their work and life on Salt Spring.

Salt Spring Events

January
- Polar Bear Swim (New Year's Day)

February
- Cedar Beach Resort Annual Trout Derby

May
- Sheep to Shawl Competition
- Around the Island Sailboat Race
- Mountain Bike Festival
- Open Golf Tournament
- Artists' Studio Tours (Sundays to September)
- Salt Spring Island Painters' Guild Annual May Show
- Outdoor markets (to October)

June

- SeaCapers
- Artcraft show and sale (to August)

July
- Canada Day Celebrations (1st)
- Summer Festival of the Arts

August
- Fulford Days
- Music Festival

September
- Fall Fair and Sheepdog Trials
- Terry Fox Run

November
- Christmas Craft Fair
- Studio Tours
- Light Up Parade

December
- Santa Ship

Community Centre, an imposing white building on the left, opposite the RCMP station. This building served for 40 years as the only hospital in the Gulf Islands.

Ganges

Though some of the other islands have strung-out clusters of houses and shops, Ganges is the only substantial concentrated community on the Gulf Islands. It used to be a quiet rural village, in a Gulf Island sort of way. In the last few years, however, it has been discovered by the developers, who have covered Grace Point with condos, crammed marinas into every bit of water that happened to be vacant for five minutes, and are now busy filling the once historic back-streets with neo-quaint bistros, boutiques and cappuccino bars. Despite the loss of historic character, the result (unless you are terminally nostalgic) is rather fun, and many Gulf Islanders brave the difficulty of getting to and from Salt Spring on the same day from almost anywhere so that they can get a periodic urban fix without the pain of heavy traffic and long drives.

If you have been on the small islands for too long, want a real choice of places for lunch, or drool at the thought

---

Drummond Park Petroglyph

A human face or a seal?

DRUMMOND PARK is a small recreational park between the south side of Fulford Harbour and Isabella Point Road. At low tide you can walk up the beach towards the mouth of the harbour. This stretch looks like a prime place for clam digging, but pollution and red tide make it advisable not to.

This park's main claim to fame is a beautiful petroglyph carved on a large rock that has been moved to its present site and is sheltered by a clump of Western Red Cedar trees at the park entrance. The petroglyph is described as a seal on the plaque and certainly has large magical eyes. However, the whole art of petroglyphs and their interpretation is an unlocked secret that historians and archeologists still speculate about. Other sources interpret this carving as a human face.

Despite being carved in rock, petroglyphs are delicate and easily spoiled. Please treat them with respect and as works of art. This one is difficult to photograph because of the trees, so just enjoy looking at it. If you're interested in seeing others that are more easily photographed, check out Gabriola.

Park facilities include beach access, picnic tables, barbecues, toilets and playground equipment.

Lady Minto Hospital

DR. LIONEL BEECH was a doctor on the island who initiated a community effort towards a hospital by donating land. The first hospital on the Gulf Islands was built in 1914 and named the Lady Minto Hospital after the wife of the Earl of Minto, Governor-General of Canada from 1898 to 1904. Lady Minto had started a fund to build cottage hospitals in remote districts, and she was at one time remembered in the names of more than 50 hospitals across Canada. The original building had six beds, then was enlarged to 18 beds in 1936. It was used as a hospital until 1958, when a new Lady Minto Hospital was built just off Lower Ganges Road on the other side of town.

For a while the building became a dormitory for students from other islands attending the secondary school. Later it was taken over by the Salt Spring Island Community Society, which renovated it, preserving its historical character.

of three bookshops, Ganges is for you. Celebrities tie up in the bay on glossy yachts and the star-struck hang around in Thrifty's grocery store on the off chance that they can help Barbra Streisand find the jam. (This is not just a good island rumour; we met someone who actually did.)

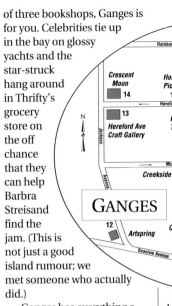

Ganges has everything a visitor (or islander) needs from an urban setting—supermarkets, banks and bank machines, post office, liquor store, hospital, galleries, boutiques, and the obligatory sprinkling of souvenir outlets. There's a variety of eating establishments in several price ranges, and it's all within easy walking distance for most people. Ganges is situated along Ganges Harbour, an attractive waterfront with government docks, marinas, and float plane and water taxi moorage, but there is no beach access.

Ganges Walking Tour (about 1 km)

The best way to enjoy Ganges is on foot, so we have provided a walking tour, starting from the tourist information centre on Lower Ganges Road. Park the car in the main parking lot behind the centre if you can, but in the summer season you may have to check the side-streets on the opposite side of

Lower Ganges Road or the car parks behind Creekside on McPhillips Avenue. Watch for a couple of one-way streets.

Follow our suggested route (see map above), or use the map of Ganges to plan your own walking tour. Just a serendipitous browse around is fun, but to help we've given our favourite highlights of either unusual shops, good food or interesting heritage buildings.

1. Tourist Information Centre (604-537-5252)

As some of the retail shops and restaurants change season to season, pick up the current edition of the Salt Spring map and studio map, and ask what island events are taking place during your visit. The volunteers will happily point out the liquor store, banks, or anything else you need.

2. Thrifty Foods (604-537-1522)

This chain has recently opened the largest supermarket in the Gulf Islands. Al-

though it has lots of standard items, it also includes some special island products such as locally made sushi.

3. Waterfront Gallery (604-537-4525)

This is our favourite downtown mid-priced gallery, with great gifts, most of them made by local artisans, such as the silk clothing by Babs O'Brian.

4. Government Wharves

Cut across to the waterfront for a view of the busy scene, with arriving and departing boats and Hanna Air's little float planes. Here you can see the wharf for the Gulf Island Water Taxi service (604-537-2510), which is available for group rentals. At early morning and mid-afternoon you may see two boats, *The Scholarship* and *The Graduate*, which are the Gulf Islands' equivalent of school buses and ferry the Outer Islands school children across to the Gulf Islands Secondary School at Ganges.

5. Mouat's Trading Company and Mall (604-537-5593)

Mouat's store was built in 1912 by Jane Mouat, an enterprising widow with 11 children, and eventually worked by two of her sons, Gilbert and William. It is a fascinating place to visit and one of several Gulf Island landmarks carrying the Mouat family name. The upper two levels of the building contain hardware and housewares, but the basement has been leased to other stores and the connecting walkways and stairwell are a gallery for interesting historical island photographs.

In this convoluted complex that goes under the name of "Mouats' Mall" you'll find a number of shops featuring local products. One is the outlet for a great local product, Salt Spring Soapworks. An excellent bookstore, Volume Two, specializes in island publications including several books edited or partially written by Sue Mouat, a family member who, with her husband Ivan, gives talks about island history. Pegasus Gallery, our local favourite, features paintings by Salt Spring residents Robert Bateman and Carol Evans, and a room full of West Coast aboriginal masks.

6. Grace Point Square
Take a waterside stroll up a path along the well-designed and landscaped condominium complex hugging a small headland. This development caused an uproar among Gulf Islanders, many of whom are worried that similar high-density development in other waterside areas will drastically change the character and landscape of the islands.

7. Bouzouki Greek Café (604-537-4181)
Imagine walking along the waterfront in the middle of summer, the sky and water so blue it's almost like being in the Mediterranean, when suddenly you smell lamb souvlaki being barbecued outside. That's exactly what happened to us. Follow your nose to 2014 Grace Point Square if you love Greek food, and don't miss Georgia and Steve Asproloupos' cooking. The savouries are homemade, tangy, full of olives, onions, and fresh herbs, while the baklava sweetly melts in your mouth. The menu includes "Alexandro's combo," an amusing tribute to a much-loved grandson ("whatever you want, you get"). If you sit outside in the sun you can look out over the marina and linger over your retsina and ouzo. Steve will probably pass by for a chat. Bouzouki's is an unexpected taste of the Greek islands.

8. Government Wharf and Small Boat Harbour
A public boat launch ramp is almost hidden behind Grace Point Square, and beyond it is another government wharf, with a harbour office on shore where you can check in to moor. Public telephones and washrooms are nearby between Centennial Park and the marina parking lot.

9. Centennial Park and Saturday Market
During the week, Centennial Park is a pleasant grass and treed area containing playground equipment, room to sit

Western Red Cedar

Western Red Cedar

TYPICALLY A TALL CONICAL tree, the western red cedar has graceful drooping branches which turn upwards at the tips. The lower branches tend to persist, hiding the vertically lined bark. Leaflets are pressed closely against the twigs in an overlapping pattern, and the cones are small. This tree is widespread along the BC coast, and is a dominant species in many Gulf Island forests, generally mixed with Douglas Fir and other species. It is able to tolerate the shade of other species and begins to dominate as faster growing trees die off. On nearby Vancouver Island, Red Cedars have been documented at 1,300 years old.

For aboriginal inhabitants, the cedar (which spread through the area some 4,000 years ago) was one of the most important species. Its loose bark was torn into shreds and used to make hats, baskets and capes; its straight-grained wood was split into planks for long houses; and whole trunks were carved into canoes and totem poles.

Later settlers found the cedar useful for lumber and shakes, and split smaller trunks to make snake fences. For such purposes, most of the large old-growth specimens on the Gulf Islands were cut down, though there are some well-grown second-growth trees to be seen.

and sun, and a quiet boardwalk that makes for an easy waterside stroll. Facilities include a playground, picnic area and seats, public washrooms and water fountain, bandstand, and sea edge board walk.

It is here that you will find a rock displaying a seat back from the Captain's galley of *H.M.S. Ganges*, after whom this village was named. The *Ganges* was the last sailing ship of the British Royal Navy to patrol these waters from 1857 to 1861.

On summer Saturdays this quiet atmosphere changes, and the brick patio in front of Centennial Park turns into a kaleidoscope of colours, textures and aromas as Salt Spring artisans and food producers display their wares market style. Crowds jostle jugglers and tarot readers, and ogle wares from musical instruments to silk scarves, folk carvings, garden produce, and aromatherapy oils. This is definitely the best market on the islands for variety.

10. Harlan's Chocolate Treats

(604-537-4434)
Across the Fulford-Ganges Road, next to Pharmasave, is Harlan's Chocolates. Handmade on Salt Spring, Harlan's chocolates have the same reputation on the Gulf Islands as Rogers' Chocolates have in Victoria. They are a "must-taste" for any self-respecting chocoholic. Don't miss the individually wrapped chocolate creams almost as big as the palm of your hand, in a wide variety of flavours. Harlan's also carries a selection of coffee beans and teas.

Bob and Molly Akerman

WANT TO TOUCH ISLAND history? Call ahead and pop in at the Akerman museum (Fulford-Ganges Rd) and talk to Bob Akerman, a vibrant and active 80-year-old who looks 60. He has collected together dreams and memories of life on Salt Spring since the early days. There's no sign to show it's a museum, but if he's home Bob will be delighted to show you around, and donations are accepted to help with heating costs. Bob's family has been in this valley since his grandparents' time, linking several of the founding families, including his Coast Salish maternal grandmother.

Joseph Akerman was an English market gardener who came to Salt Spring in 1861. His future wife, Martha Clay, arrived in Victoria on the bride ship *Robert Lowe* in 1863, and found herself only the second white woman on Salt Spring. Her first night's rest was disturbed by the howling of wolves, and years later she chased a cougar away with a broom when he came sniffing

Bob Akerman welcomes visitors to his museum

around one of her seven babies. In 1865 Joseph and Martha built a log house from which they ran a store. It became known as Traveller's Rest, because they boarded visitors, making it the first inn on the island. (The building is still standing nearby, though no longer used, and is the oldest surviving building on the Gulf Islands.) Another early settler was Irishman Mike Gyves, who married Tuwa'h'wiye, daughter of a Cowichan chief, who is remem-

bered as "Granny Gyves". These four are Bob Akerman's grandparents, and his museum contains a wealth of photographs and other memorabilia of the family, together with a remarkable collection of artifacts from his aboriginal grandmother's people, such as fishing weights and root baskets. There is even a recording of a Gulf Islands opera composed by Bob Akerman's father-in-law, the music based on West Coast aboriginal songs. Bob has acquired other island artifacts, such as a collection of driftwood sculptures made by Kanaka settler Sophie King.

When you've seen the museum, see if Bob's wife Molly will take you to see her doll collection inside the house. This is no mere hobby. A large room contains several hundred dolls, representing a diversity of periods. From Victorian dolls, Kewpies and Shirley Temples, to stylish sixties swingers in mini skirts and Barbie in her many manifestations, this collection will delight all ages.

11. Creekhouse and Creekside

This interesting complex of shops is built over a creek. Free parking behind.

12. Artspring (604-537-2125)

At the junction of Seaview and Jackson is the new multiple facility Art and Theatre Complex, due to open in 1995. Tours can be arranged; ask at the Tourist Information Centre.

13. Hereford Avenue Craft Gallery (604-537-0771)

The "new kid on the block," this is the most recent art and craft galley in Ganges. At 133 Hereford Avenue, it occupies a house built in the 1930s that was originally owned by a Miss Overend and her sister. Miss Overend was the last of the old-style telephone operators on Salt Spring. The displays fill the house from main floor to attic and the atmosphere is warm and cosy, helped by the real warmth from the fireplace you see upon entering the front door. Run by Lois Codd, one of the organizers of Artcraft, the gallery specializes in Gulf Islanders' work.

14. Crescent Moon Vegetarian Restaurant (604-537-1960)

At 134 Hereford Avenue you will find this tasty and unusual takeout or eat in. Serve yourself from the vegetarian buffet where you pay by weight. Expect some very unusual dishes from India, Morocco and the Middle East, great home-made bread and soups, and lots of fresh cilantro. Crescent Moon also runs a vegetarian cooking school from September to December.

15. House Piccolo Restaurant (604-537-1844)

At the other end of Hereford Avenue, House Piccolo offers an unusually rich and complex menu which, when we first saw it, included Russian caviar for a czar's ransom.

16. Gulf Islands Trading Company

Round to the right on Lower Ganges Road (opposite the Tourist Information Centre) is a historic store that goes back almost as far as Mouat's. This refurbished heritage building was originally built in 1912 with money invested by Henry Wright Bullock, and was set up in direct competition with Mouat's store. The story goes that Bullock, who considered himself "a true gentleman," arrived at Mouat's store in his buggy and sat outside waiting while one of the Mouat brothers helped load goods for another customer. When eventually Mouat passed his buggy, Bullock pointed out that "in England when the squire arrives, he is served immediately."

"This isn't England and you're not the squire" was the reply. Bullock drove off and instigated the start of the rival store, which was in business until 1969— when it was bought out by the Mouats.

17. Tide's Inn (604-537-1470)

This charming heritage building at 132 Lower Ganges Road contains a good mid-priced restaurant with a bar area and seven B&B rooms.

There's lots of variety on

St. Mary Lake

Canoes on St. Mary Lake

ST. MARY LAKE is 200 hectares— the largest freshwater lake not only on this island, but on any of the Southern Gulf Islands. Unfortunately it has only one public access, along North End Road (north of Central). This is a minute swimming beach that just allows for a canoe or kayak to be launched, and there is hardly any parking. Only electric power boats are permitted. If canoeing the lake, remember that foreshore rights do not apply on lakes. All the St. Mary shoreline is private property.

Several resorts surround the southern lakeshore, most with cabins and a couple with camping facilities. Their beaches have normally been improved, but there is enough wild shoreline to make interesting bird-watching. The lake is stocked with Rainbow and Cutthroat Trout, and Smallmouth Bass fishing is reported as the best BC has to offer.

the dinner menu and good-sized helpings; there's also a children's menu available. The main drawback is for non-smokers; in the one room the smoke is hard to escape. In summer, Tide's Inn regularly features live local musicians presenting folk music evenings.

18. Artcraft, in Mahon Hall

Mahon Hall was erected by the Island's Agricultural and Fruit Grower's Association in 1902, with financial help from Ross Mahon. When he was drowned while swimming in Long Harbour in 1903, the family forgave the debt on condition the hall be named in his memory. It was used as the base of the agricultural show, and for years was the island's main centre for concerts and dances.

Now in the summer months, the hall houses Art-craft, an annual arts and craft show. Artcraft sells only arts and crafts produced on the Gulf Islands and represents over 200 artisans. It's a high quality display and well worth the token entry fee. Most of the Salt Spring artists display here, so it's a good place to check several out before em-barking on the studio tour. Mahon Hall has its own park-ing lot and entrance, with ac-cess from Rainbow Road.

19. The Fishery (604-537-2457)

At the bottom of Rainbow Road, across on the water side at 151 Lower Ganges Road, is The Fishery. Unless you are in a position to meet a friendly fishing boat, this is the best place to get fresh fish on the Gulf Islands. It is fisherman owned and operated and has its own dock. Look for the catch of the day, along with fresh cod, salmon and live crab. There's also smoked fish. Just behind The Fishery is the Ganges Marina, whose facili-ties include moorage, fuel and oil, bait and ice, showers and laundry, rent-a-car, and phone.

From this point, it is an easy stroll back to your park-ing spot. If you wish, you can extend your walk along Lower Ganges Road and turn down Upper Ganges Road to other hotels and restaurants,

Sylvia Stark

Sylvia Stark at 92—with 13 years to go

A **CONSIDERABLE NUMBER** of African-Americans settlers origi-nating from the United States set-tled on Salt Spring in the 1860s. They had originally been invited to Victoria by Governor Douglas, but relocated here when they found the society there not very welcoming. Fear of First Nations raids along the coast led most of these settlers to home-stead inland.

Sylvia had been born a slave in Mis-souri, but her husband Louis was able to buy first his own freedom, then hers, and for a while they settled in California. The Starks came to Salt Spring in 1860, with two small children, and they had their third not many weeks after landing—perhaps Salt Spring's first pioneer baby. The family had a convoluted history, and some of them moved off the island for a while, leaving the el-dest son Willis who became a noted cougar hunter. Eventually Sylvia was widowed and moved back to Salt Spring, where she became known as "Aunt Silvey". She moved into a house built for her on Stark Road by Willis in 1890. The house still stands, though much changed and im-proved, and her granddaughter currently lives there.

When in her nineties, Sylvia was nursing Willis, by now an el-derly and ailing man. A neigh-bour came to visit and see how they were doing. "Well," replied Sylvia, shaking her head sadly, "I doubt I'm going to raise that boy." Willis eventually died at 86, and Sylvia died a year later at about 105.

House Piccolo is one of many appealing eating places in Ganges

including Harbour House Hotel, the Salt Spring Marina and Moby's Marine Pub, and the Gulf Islands top spot, Hastings House.

Ganges to Central (3 km)

Taking the Lower Ganges Road out of town, you soon pass the junction with Upper Ganges Road. Continue past Upper Ganges Centre, Ganges Village Market, and Foxglove Farm and Garden Supplies. At about two and a half kilometres you will pass the Salt Spring Island Golf Club on the right. The nine-hole semi-private course is open to the public, and facilities include a clubhouse, driving range and pro shop with equipment rental. It was laid out in 1960 on the site of Rev. Wilson's homestead and farm. Wilson is known for a purple prose pamphlet he wrote in 1895 extolling the island's virtues and encouraging settlement. It has been reprinted in recent years.

Past the golf club you arrive at a second junction with Upper Ganges Road known to Salt Spring Islanders purely as "Central." This area was one of the first settlements on Salt Spring. At the junction is Central Hall, built for the first agricultural fair in 1896 (replacing an earlier log building). Beside the hall was a small jail house, but it was recorded as being used only five times in nine years and has long since disappeared.

Central Hall is now Salt Spring's Cinema. For a moderate fee you get not only a current movie but also a slide show of life on Salt Spring. There's even popcorn. Get there early or you'll be stuck with the fold-out seats at the back of the hall instead of the comfortable ones at the front.

A short distance up North End Road is the Rev. Wilson's church, St. Mark's. Salt Spring's first Anglican church was built between 1889 and 1892, on land donated by the Stevens family who lived next door, and whose square white house can still be seen immediately north of the church. The church has stained glass windows in memory of Queen Victoria and of two Salt Spring

Saltspring Soapworks

IMAGINE LOUNGING in a bath back home in the city, reaching for the soap, and suddenly being reminded of the rosemary and lavender bushes from a Gulf Island garden, or the tang of the sea and seaweed from your holiday beach walk.

Saltspring Soapworks (604-537-2701) has gently captured many Gulf Island fragrances in its line of natural soaps. Lavender and oatmeal, honeysuckle, or a seaweed scrub bar are just a few of the intriguing hand-made soaps developed by Linda Quiring. Originally Linda ran the soapworks as a small cottage industry at her home. She was open for visitors who delighted in seeing soap produced. Unfortunately, success has meant she had to discontinue the open house policy as the operation became too big. However, she opened her store in Mouat's Mall, and if you are visiting Salt Spring on a Saturday morning, look for the Soapworks stall at the Farmers' Market. There you can pick up soapy seconds at a very reasonable price. Just don't pack them in your backpack next to your sandwiches: the seconds aren't plastic wrapped and we ended up with lavender-flavoured bread!

men drowned in Ganges Harbour. At the churchyard entrance, a pair of wrought iron gates were installed in 1949 in memory of Henry Wright Bullock, who attended St. Mark's every Sunday without fail.

Central to Vesuvius (3.5 km)

Turning left on Vesuvius Bay Road, you will pass Portlock Park (604-537-4448) on your left. Salt Spring's main recreation area has tennis courts (one with an all-weather bubble), facilities for soccer, baseball and softball, playground equipment, a public outdoor swimming pool open in the summer months, and toilets.

The road gives a view of the end of St. Mary Lake on the

Gordon Wales' Flagstone Gallery

FLAGSTONE GALLERY (604-537-5980), at 1340 Sunset Drive, is where Gordon Wales displays good quality pottery. If you want a full scale hand-made dinner service, this is the place to come. You are encouraged not just to pop into the gallery but to enjoy the rose garden and the views. There are arbours and terraces, a field of Salt Spring sheep and, most interesting of all, the flagstones themselves.

Flagstone Gallery is situated just above Stonecutter Bay, a historic quarry from which slabs of Gulf Island sandstone were sent around the world. Sandstone blocks and slabs from here grace not only the BC Legislative buildings, but also the San Francisco Opera House and the Legislative Buildings in Sydney, Australia.

right, and winds its leisurely way to Vesuvius Village and the ferry terminal, where hourly service is provided to Crofton on Vancouver Island.

Vesuvius

Even sleepier than Fulford (apart from an occasional flutter of activity around the ferry dock), the settlement of Vesuvius is almost conspicuous by

Hastings House

HASTINGS HOUSE is modelled after a Sussex house, and was built in 1940 for Warren Hastings, a naval architect who worked there on secret designs for the Royal Navy.

The building is now a luxury hotel (604-537-2362 or 1-800-661-9255). Its grounds and facilities are magnificent and the brochure likens it to "an English Tudor estate dropped in the Canadian Wilderness." Groomed and organized, it has a definite air of gracious country living for people who are really most comfortable with city amenities.

Hastings House has been included on so many lists of best places to stay and eat that the staff just shrug courteously when asked for details. If pressed, however, they will admit to being featured in *Gourmet Magazine*, and

Herbs are grown in the garden

will show you the world-wide list of "Relais et Chateaux" (self described as the most beautiful accommodation chain in the world) to which they belong. The menus are exciting and imaginative and often feature fresh herbs and lo-

cal produce. A sample includes white onion and apple bisque with parsley cream, followed by Fraser Valley pheasant breast with blackberry sauce, topped off with such delights as minted strawberries and plum coulis. The wine cellar is superb.

Prices for accommodation are princely. If you have better uses for a few hundred dollars, but want a special afternoon out, try the very reasonable Sunday brunch. (Reservations are a must but don't leave it until the last minute, as there is always a waiting list.) That way you can stroll the beautiful grounds, enjoy the view, and still have some cash left for the rest of your holiday. For other meals, you will be expected to fit in only when guests are not filling the spaces. A dress code is in effect.

its absence. Houses hide down winding lanes and behind sheltering hedges. Drive carefully or, since there is very little parking, walk down Langley Road to the wooden steps that access Vesuvius Beach, which north-enders say is the best sunset-watching spot on the island. (For a more invigorating experience you could drop in New Year's Day for the Polar Bear Swim.) It is possible to walk the beach and exit up a poorly marked trail at the far end, then walk around the block to your vehicle. Be sure you don't trespass; it is sometimes hard to tell the difference between some of the tiny roads and private drives.

By the ferry parking, things are a little more lively. Vesuvius Inn is a favourite gathering place, but good food is also served from The Seaside Kitchen. You can look at pottery on Mark Meredith's roadside stand and poke around in the Vesuvius Store. The most interesting place here is The Ark.

Vesuvius to Southey Point (8 km)

A little way inland from the ferry dock, turn north on Sunset Drive, one of the most beautiful pastoral roads on Salt Spring. It winds through

---

Vesuvius Inn

Flowers enliven the balcony of Vesuvius Inn

THE ORIGINAL Vesuvius Bay Hotel, built by Portuguese settler Estalon Jose Bittancourt, stood on this spot for nearly a century before being destroyed by fire in 1975. The replacement inn is a popular island watering hole that features casual dining on a large porch in the summer. In the winter it is a cosy spot to play Trivial Pursuit and darts. It's the perfect place for a quick cold beer while waiting in a hot ferry line up.

The Ark

THE ARK (604-537-9451) should be obvious, but is so tiny we missed it twice because it is almost entirely hidden from the road by the carport. Located at 782 Vesuvius Bay Rd, it is immediately adjacent to the top end of the ferry parking lot. Now The Ark is Gwen McKie's tiny home studio and gift shop where you can pass a few interesting minutes while waiting for the ferry.

Like the original Vesuvius inn, the Ark was built around 1898 by the entrepreneurial Portuguese settler, Estalon Jose Bittancourt. It was constructed as a Catholic chapel for the large Bittancourt family and its neighbours. The chapel was sold in the 1940s and deconsecrated (though the chapel bell still hangs above the glass porch). It was turned into a private residence and given its present name.

Ganges from the air

woods and a gently rolling sheep farming area, and it has a different feel from other parts of the island. There are several studios in this area that usually have a sign out on the roadside if they are open.

At the junction between Sunset Drive, Southey Point Road and North End Road, you will see a medium-sized tree in the middle of the road. This is the "North End Christmas Tree." The neighbours decorate it every Christmas—not with lights but with home-made decorations. Turn north along Southey Point Road for a trail to Southey Point.

Southey Point to Fernwood (7 km)

Return to the Christmas Tree junction and continue south along North End Road to the

St. Paul's Catholic Church

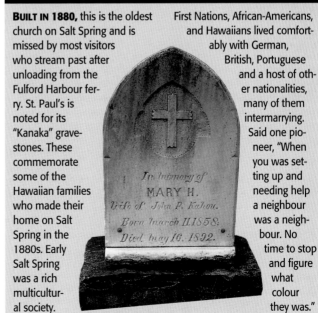

BUILT IN 1880, this is the oldest church on Salt Spring and is missed by most visitors who stream past after unloading from the Fulford Harbour ferry. St. Paul's is noted for its "Kanaka" gravestones. These commemorate some of the Hawaiian families who made their home on Salt Spring in the 1880s. Early Salt Spring was a rich multicultural society. First Nations, African-Americans, and Hawaiians lived comfortably with German, British, Portuguese and a host of other nationalities, many of them intermarrying. Said one pioneer, "When you was setting up and needing help a neighbour was a neighbour. No time to stop and figure what colour they was."

Mary Kahow lies far from her birthplace

119

junction with North Beach Road. (You can return to Ganges by continuing straight ahead at this point, past St. Mary Lake and back by Central.) To continue the tour, take a sharp left turn onto North Beach Road. You will shortly see Salty Springs Resort on the right, the only visible hint of the salt springs that gave the island its name.

North Beach Road is the only real waterside road on Salt Spring and has lovely views across Trincomali Channel to the south end of Wallace Island and across to Galiano. Unfortunately there is not a lot of public beach access here.

The community of Fernwood has beach access and a government dock rumoured to be a good spot for catching crabs. Near the junction with Fernwood Road is the Fernwood General Store, which has gas pumps.

Fernwood to Long Harbour (11 km)

Around one kilometre south of Fernwood is another beach access at the foot of Maliview Drive. It is possible to walk for a couple of kilometres along this beach from beach access to beach access, but it can be pretty hard going on the rocks.

North Beach Road continues as Walker Hook Road, then turns inland and becomes Stark Road. This is named for the Stark family, the best known of the African-Americans who moved here in 1860.

Turn off Stark Road on Robinson Road, and left again on Upper Ganges Road, which will take you back into Ganges if you wish. Another left turn will put you on Long Harbour

Salt Spring's Salt Springs

FOURTEEN SALT SPRINGS were found by early settlers, all at the north end of the island, though some have since been ploughed over or become overgrown. The largest is some 25 metres in diameter. All leave salt crystals as the water evaporates.

There is no public access to the springs, which are all on private land. The nearest you can get to them is at Salty Springs Sea Side Mineral Bath Resort on North Beach Road where they have accessed one of the springs to provide therapeutic mineral baths.

Road, which leads to the Long Harbour ferry terminal for other islands and Tsawwassen.

Henry Wright Bullock

HENRY BULLOCK CAME to Salt Spring in 1892, a bachelor of 24 who saw himself an English gentleman farmer and had an immense sense of his own importance. He thought himself, and was sometimes nicknamed, the "Squire of Salt Spring." He also had a substantial purse and bought a 220-acre property on which he had an elaborate house built, with the islands' first indoor plumbing and gasoline generator.

Bullock cared not only about his own dress and appearance, but also about that of his neighbours, and went to great lengths to influence them. He presented local women with white gloves and dangling earrings, then en-

Henry Bullock left an impression

couraged them to have their ears pierced. He bought Eton suits for the local boys to wear in church. Bullock also hosted lunch and

seven-course dinner parties, as well as balls and other functions where he insisted on a strict dress code.

Both Bullock and his farm soon became the stuff of local legend, the farm winning the reputation of producing corn 17 feet high and Bing cherries "so big they had to be individually wrapped." Bullock, despite his fads and fancies, was generous to the church, and islanders still tell stories of his eccentricities, while themselves wearing casual clothing that would make him turn in his grave.

11. Thetis

The rocky spine of Pilkey Point

Thetis Island enjoys one of the smallest populations and the least development of any Gulf Island with a regular ferry service, but is a "best bargain day trip" for the visitor. The island has a number of interesting and attractive features, but no parks or walking trails.

Accommodation is limited (at the time of writing to one B&B) and there are no campsites, so don't attempt to stay overnight unless you have booked ahead. Many visitors enjoy Thetis Island through boating, using one of Telegraph Harbour's two marinas as a base.

For most visitors the island can be an attractive day trip. Unless you really cannot survive without your car, you could leave it in Chemainus and walk on to the ferry, as most of the island facilities are within easy walking distance of the Thetis terminal. Cyclists can enjoy exploring the roads, but should be aware of the killer hill where Pilkey Point Road climbs Moore Hill. Motorists can access all the island roads, but beach accesses are tiny and hard to find, with very little parking room for cars. In short, you should be prepared to stop in likely places and explore if you want to make the most of your visit. The persistent explorer will be rewarded by small rocky beaches and other sites offering opportunities for rock, plant and bird enthusiasts. Special features include cannonball concretions and Rocky Mountain Juniper trees on the edges of the island.

Thetis and Kuper were (like Pender) once a single island until the canal was dredged in 1905. Names of both islands came from the British Navy; Captain Augustus Kuper was in command of the 36-gun frigate *Thetis* at Esquimalt from 1851 to 1853. However, the two islands have had very different histories. Thetis developed as a pioneer settlement as did many of the other Gulf Islands. Almost the whole

THETIS ISLAND

Pilkey Point

Fraser Point

North Cove

Cliff

Valdes

Fire Hall

Lawrence

N

Pioneer Rd

Cufra Canal

Pilkey Point Road

Kenwood Drive

Moore Hill

STUART CHANNEL

North Cove Road

Fuller Lake

THETIS ISLAND

Burchell Hill

Sunrise Point

Sunrise Point Rd

Leech Island

Pots by Nicé

Clam Bay Rd

Forbes Rd

Division Rd

Community Centre

Fire Hall

Mill Creek

Spinning Wheel Studio

Clam Bay

School

Pot of Gold Coffee

Forbes Rd

Thetis Is. Handcrafts

Marina Dr

Blue Heron

Canoe Pass

St. Margaret's Ln

Betty's Bed and Breakfast

This and That Cottage

St. Margaret's Cemetery

Crescent Point

Preedy Harbour

Fairview

Harbour Rd

Telegraph Harbour Marina

Telegraph

Thetis Is. Marina and Pub

Foster Pl Road

Burns

Harbour

KUPER ISLAND

Scott Island

Bellavista

Dayman Island

Foster Point

Thetis Island 30 min

Thetis Island - Kuper Island 15 min

Kuper Island - Chemainus 30 min

1 km

Hudson Island

Alarm Rock

of Kuper (the first part is pronounced "cue") is an Indian Reserve, so do not disembark there unless you are an invited guest. For a while a bridge linked the two, but since 1946 there has been no direct connection other than the ferry, which links both islands to Chemainus on Vancouver Island. The deep inlet of Telegraph Harbour, between the islands, is considered one of the safest harbours in the Gulf Islands.

Three bible camps attract student visitors from various congregations, and these seem to be the island's biggest "industry." For the average person a visit to Thetis is also something of a retreat, as there are few services for the travelling public. The facilities are largely clustered within walking distance of the ferry terminal and marinas. Most houses are unobtrusively nestled in the trees, and you can travel the island and scarcely meet a soul. Not to be missed, however, are interesting studios and a wonderful coffee roasting business.

To see the island beyond the ferry area you must be prepared to cycle or drive. There are two main routes of interest: one is along Pilkey Point Road to the far northern tip of the island and, if you have time on the way back, the other is a side trip along North Cove Road to a number of interesting spots in the northwest.

Walking Tour of the Ferry and Marina Area (3 km)

Boaters based at the marinas and day visitors arriving by ferry can explore many of the publicly oriented places on foot. Don't arrive too early; several of the island studios don't open until 11 am (and close at 4 pm), and don't expect every one to be open every day or off season. We start with the ferry terminal; if you are starting from one of the marinas, adjust your route accordingly. The farthest point on the walking tour, Spinning Wheel Studio, is approximately 1.5 kilometres from the ferry dock.

Preedy Harbour

From the ferry dock at Preedy Harbour, turn left and head up the hill on Pilkey Point Road, past Betty's Bed and Breakfast. As the ferry approached the dock, your eyes were probably drawn to a spectacular mock Tudor building that looks like a five star hotel or resort set in the centre of rolling lawns. This is the main building of Capernwray Bible Camp, which is not open to casual visitors.

Continue past the junction with North Cove Road, and you'll see a sign for Thetis Island Handcrafts. Turn left into the driveway and browse in the shop, set up in what was obviously once the garage of a private house.

Thetis Island Cannonballs

Cannonball concretions eroding out of sandstone

CONCRETIONS ARE FORMED by the movement of chemical substances through sedimentary rocks, which form a ball of rock that is harder than the surrounding material. As the surrounding rock is eroded into sand or mud, concretions often remain solid and end up lying around on a beach or riverbank. They may be more or less spherical, oval or oddly shaped, and they puzzle many people who pick them up and speculate about them being fossil bones, dinosaur eggs, artifacts of ancient peoples, or cannonballs fired from sailing ships. Although they are not usually of great importance to geologists, in some places (though not apparently on Thetis) they may have been formed around fossils, which can be revealed when the concretions are carefully split open.

Spinning Wheel Studio and Alpaca Ranch

Leola, Al and Laurie

Laurie and her partner Leola Reis-Wilcox use the soft but hardy and naturally coloured alpaca wool, along with angora and more conventional materials, to design and knit beautifully coloured sweaters. Some are adapted from patterns by American-born, British-resident designer Kaffe Fassett; others are originals which are never repeated. Most garments are knitted by Laurie and Leola, but they also carry some made to their designs by a cooperative of knitters. Wool is also sold in kits for particular garments, or you can purchase hanks of wool and yarn for spinning and weaving. Laurie and Leola also offer workshops and group tours (604-246-4695).

ON THE SHORES of Lake Titicaca in Peru, the Incas domesticated the wild Guanaco, developed a diminutive version called the alpaca, and used its exquisite wool for textiles. These intriguing animals are now the principal livestock on a small ranch run by Laurie Saul and her husband Donovan. At the time of our visit, there were seven very photogenic alpacas peering curiously through the fences. Babies appear each spring.

David Essig, Island Trustee

EXCEPT AT AN occasional concert, a casual visitor to Thetis is unlikely to be aware of David Essig, who lives with his wife Milena Campbell in a Japanese-influenced house he built himself in a quiet wooded corner of the island. However, mention David's name to a folk festival addict anywhere in Canada or the U.S., and you are likely to find he has a widespread following as a brilliant and eclectic guitarist, songwriter and performer. You might find he has the same reputation in Italy, where he performs most years and learned the country cooking he loves to indulge in at home. David is also known in Korea, where he has studied the national instrument, the

David and Milena enjoy their deck

kayagum, and he is one of the few exponents who has brought its music to the western world. David has issued more than a dozen recordings, featuring his various talents.

As an elected member of the Islands Trust, David has a public face in the islands. This governmental body exercises planning functions for the islands, with a mandate to preserve and protect their special features. "I became concerned," says David, "when I visited the Italian island of Ischia. It is about the same size as Thetis, yet it has a population of 60,000. I began to realize the same thing could happen here."

As with all trust members, David devotes a lot of time to planning and attending meetings, relating both to Thetis and the islands in general. This puts him on the firing line for the opinions of every resident, but he takes this part of the job in his stride—it is not all that much different from being out on stage with a guitar.

Telegraph Harbour Area

Continue east along Pilkey Point Road, and just beyond the junction with Marina Drive (which leads on your right to Telegraph Harbour Marina) you'll reach the Pot of Gold Coffee Roasting Company.

From Pot of Gold continue along Pilkey Point Road until you reach Blue Heron Road (third right). Head down to the end of Blue Heron to visit the Spinning Wheel Studio and Alpaca Ranch.

Retrace your steps back up Blue Heron Road and turn left on Pilkey Point Road towards the ferry, then left again down Marina Drive to Telegraph Harbour Marina.

Continue up Marina Drive, turn left on Pilkey Point Road and walk back to the ferry dock. If you have time, con-

A cruiser arrives at Telegraph Harbour Marina

tinue past the ferry onto Foster Point Road and visit Thetis Island Marina (about one more kilometre).

Side Trip on Foster Point Road

At the junction with Harbour Road you can visit This and That Cottage to see weaving, jewelry, T-shirts and children's clothing, as well as a selection of jams and baking. A further short walk down Foster Point Road will bring you to an enormous Arbutus, just before the Highways maintenance yard. This specimen is reported to be 1.6 metres in diameter, and 33.5 metres in height, and lo-

cally reputed to be the biggest Arbutus in the world.

Returning to the ferry ends the walking tour, but if you've time you may wish to turn up Harbour Road and head to Thetis Island Marina Pub for a well-deserved cold beer.

Ferry Terminal to Pilkey Point (6 km)

From the ferry, bear left and follow the windings of Pilkey Point Road, past the studios described in the walking tour. If you are cycling, be prepared for Moore Hill approximately two-thirds of the way along. It is extremely steep (15% grade) for almost a kilometre, before it descends to sea level at Pilkey Point. There is, of course, a similar climb on the way back.

Facilities and Services

Emergency Services
- No doctor but an emergency response team for "real" emergencies (911).

Accommodation
- Betty's Bed & Breakfast, and sometimes cottages and resorts are available. Get information and book before going via Chemainus Travel Infocentre, 604-246-3944.

Eating Places
- Cafés at both marinas; Telegraph Harbour Marina Pub.

Transportation
- Fuel docks: At both marinas.

Other
- Groceries: Basic supplies at marinas; no other stores
- Phones: At marinas and ferry
- Public washrooms: Ferry terminal

Thetis Access

Ferry: From Chemainus, Vancouver Is., about 10 times daily (also serves Kuper), 30 to 45 minutes; 604-629-3215.

Float plane: Hanna Air, 1-800-665-2359.

Boat moorage: Government dock at Preedy Harbour; Telegraph Harbour Marina (604-246-9511); Thetis Island Marina (604-246-3464).

Thetis Information

Size: 100 square kilometres
Population: 527 in 1991, now about 600
Visitor Information: Chemainus Travel Infocentre (604-246-3944; fax 604-246-3251)

Pilkey Point is a pretty headland between a couple of rocky beaches that include patches of white shell sand and a rock shelf with some attractive honeycomb weathering. It's a good place to see crabs, sea stars and other small marine invertebrates, and a nice specimen of Rocky Mountain Juniper clings to the craggy ridge at the point, along with Arbutus and small Garry Oaks. Birds are numerous and at low tide Black Oystercatchers are regularly seen on the rocks jutting out of the water just beyond the point. There is limited beach access, and most of the land around Pilkey Point is private property. Facilities stop at a single garbage can; camping and overnight parking are not allowed.

As you return along Pilkey Point Road, a short drive down Cliff Road (first turn on the right) will give you a nice view of the entrance to Cufra Canal.

The East Shore

On the return trip take the time to explore some of the side roads. Lawrence Road (third on the left from the point) leads to an interesting beach at low tide, with a wide rocky shelf interspersed with patches of white shell sand. Panoramic views extend to the east, showing (north to south) Valdes, Reid, Galiano, Mayne, Pender, the white beach of Kuper's Penelakut Spit, and Salt Spring. One rocky outcrop shows cannonball-sized concretions eroding out of the sandstone bedrock.

Drive back along Pilkey Point Road over Moore Hill until you see Sunrise Point Road on the left. It leads down to a level gravel beach access and a narrow stretch of water sheltered inside adjacent Leech Island. This is one of the best places on Thetis to launch a canoe or kayak.

Halfway along Sunrise Point Road is No. 134, the

St. Margaret's Cemetery

Old and new styles of grave markers

IN ST. MARGARET'S CEMETERY are many gravestones of early island settlers. Visitors in search of a little Thetis history are well served by *The Lives Behind the Headstones*, a booklet available in the marina shops, which tells the stories of some of the people remembered in this peaceful cemetery.

Connoisseurs of the unusual will appreciate the modern headstone decorated with a picture of a yellow tow truck, commemorating the island's tow truck driver who was killed in an accident. At his funeral, the cortege was formed of dozens of tow trucks that came over on the ferry to honour a fellow driver; the coffin was lowered into the grave by his own tow truck, and 100 yellow balloons were released.

At the far end of the cemetery, a trail provides a rough beach access. You can walk up the west-side beach and rock shelf for quite a way at low tide. Notice, however, the private oyster beds (denoted by warning stakes along the shore), and don't disturb them.

Some Thetis Highlights

- Pilkey Point
- Pot of Gold Coffee Roasting Co.
- Rocky shores and cannonball concretions
- Spinning Wheel Studio and Alpaca Ranch
- Telegraph Harbour

Recreational Opportunities

Birding: Try Cufra Canal, Pilkey Point and other shoreline areas
Fishing: Charters from the marinas
Playgrounds: At the marinas
Shopping: Studios in area near ferry
Swimming: Sea dips (for the hardy) in sheltered bays

home studio of Pots by Nicé. She specializes in raku and hand-built pots, and also makes painted and glazed clay masks. Nicé sells through Thetis Island Handcrafts but visitors are welcome at her home studio if they phone first (604-246-2555).

Side Trip to North Cove Road and Cufra Canal (5 km)

About half a kilometre from the ferry, leave Pilkey Point Road and turn north on North Cove Road to travel the other major road on Thetis.

After the first bend you will see the community centre and adjacent school. The centre houses the Thetis library, and it's worth checking to see if any community events are occurring during your visit. The

The ultimate honesty stand

Pot Of Gold

Nan Beals services Gertrude, the coffee roaster

ONE OF OUR favourite commercial outlets on all the Gulf Islands is run in a delightfully non-commercial way. Go up the driveway of Pot of Gold and behind the house you'll find a log building that houses Gertrude: a '50s German coffee roaster with a definite personality and a wonderful aroma. She is lovingly cared for by Gene and Nan Beals, who roast beans in her daily and ship them to customers across Canada and the U.S. and as far away as Japan.

You can drink fresh coffee, purchase 26 different varieties of roasted beans, nibble on chocolate-coated coffee beans, and (if you are in the know) line up with the locals at Gertrude's cleaning time. Gene purges Gertrude once a week by roasting peanuts in her. Apparently coffee-flavoured peanuts are a gourmet delight and deliciously addictive.

Gene and Nan never mind folks dropping in. They are a fountain of information about coffee and where and how it is grown and harvested, and they will discuss the best varieties for your taste. Then, if you insist, they will mail fresh beans to you on a regular basis—and they pay the postage. We promptly signed up and ever since have been writing this book under the beneficial influence of Pot of Gold Coffee (604-246-4944).

school is one of three remaining one-room school houses in Canada, and currently has eight students from kindergarten to grade five, and one teacher.

Cufra Canal

Almost at the end of North Cove Road, turn right onto Kenwood Drive, then left on an unmarked gravel track to the side of Cufra Canal, a fine spot for bird-watching. Descend by a muddy bank access and you can take a low tide walk along the silty beach. The canal almost dries up at low tide, creating wonderful territory for snails, clams and oysters. The silt is covered with snail shells and at every step you can see clams spouting. Do not be tempted to dig clams, however, because the area is privately leased.

Here, shellfish farmers stake out net bags of living clams often brought from ar-

The tide is out in Cufra Canal

eas with less clean water. As the tide rises, the clean water filters out any pollutants so that the clams can be sold and eaten.

Return towards the ferry by driving back along Kenwood Drive and down North Cove Road. A right turn on Forbes Road, followed by a left turn almost immediately onto St. Margaret's Lane, takes you down a wooded road to St. Margaret's Cemetery. Return to North Cove Road, then keep right until you reach the ferry.

Arbutus

"WHAT'S THAT CROOKED tree with the red bark?" The question is often asked of Gulf Islanders, who are fond of the exotic looking Arbutus. They will patiently explain that it is a broad-leaved tree that is evergreen, and that our west coast American cousins know it as the Madrona. Those who have them on their land point out proudly that the Arbutus likes sunny places, and thus that they have chosen well.

Artists and others love the leaning, contorted trunks, their beautiful sinuous branches, and the patchwork of scaly bark that peels back to reveal new smooth green and terra cotta underneath. The big leaves are shed irregular-

Arbutus is a characteristic tree of the Gulf Islands

ly, so that the tree is never bare. In spring, dense clusters of white flowers appear, with a heavy smell that attracts bees. The flowers are followed by orange berries.

12. Gabriola

Spectacular view of the southern Gulf Islands from Gabriola

Gabriola is an island, yes, but one with such a close connection to Vancouver Island that it sometimes feels as though one foot is over there. There is an hourly ferry service to the city of Nanaimo till late at night, and even the island's school children have city smarts because they attend schools in the city from grade eight.

To many Gabriolans this proximity is an added attraction; here are the delights of island living with the city in reach whenever you need it. Just don't mention the word "bridge" or you'll find yourself in the middle of a massive island brouhaha.

In fact, the easy access to the city has in many ways saved Gabriola (usually pronounced with a long "a" - GABE-riola). What is the point of condominiums and fancy restaurants when they can be found just over the water? The result is a relaxed island at-mosphere despite an aware-ness by residents that the is-land is a suburb. The regular ferries make it an easy day trip from Nanaimo, although the island also offers a variety of accommodations for those who wish to stay longer.

Gabriola is an island of beautiful beaches, sculptured shorelines, and attractive parks. Its Malaspina Galleries carved by the sea in more or less horizontal rocks were noted as a natural wonder per-haps before any other in British Columbia. The former presence of the First Nations thrusts itself upon anyone who tries to build near the shore, as aboriginal artifacts are regu-larly turned up by backhoes digging the septic field. The re-mains of one major site, the former village of Senewélets, extend over a kilometre of shoreline, and excavations have shown cultural continu-ity for at least 2,000 years. Most striking are the many mystical petroglyphs, provid-ing a keyhole carved on the rocks through which we may glimpse the dreams and fears of an ancient people.

Pioneer settlement on Gabriola began when Nanaimo coal miners began looking for places to live in the 1850s. Scots and Irish

Some Gabriola Highlights

- Fogo Folk Art
- Gabriola Sands Provincial Park
- Malaspina Galleries
- Millstones in White Hart Pub car park
- Page's Resort and Marina (arts programs)
- United Church petroglyph site

developed farms to serve the growing industry, and timber was cut for the growing city. Original settlers were joined by the Portuguese Silva family in 1883, who moved on from Mayne. Sandstone quarrying began in 1887, providing stone for the first Victoria post office and buildings in Vancouver. In the '30s, the island quarries provided millstones for wood pulping. A brickyard on the south side of the island thrived for several decades.

Specific attractions include the parks, the many sandy and rocky beaches, and the diversity of petroglyphs. There is also a vigorous cultural scene, including more than 20 craft studios, of which Fogo Folk Art is particularly notable. Literary arts are prominent as well; Gabriola has one of the Gulf Islands' few bookstores, an active group of women writers who organize an annual

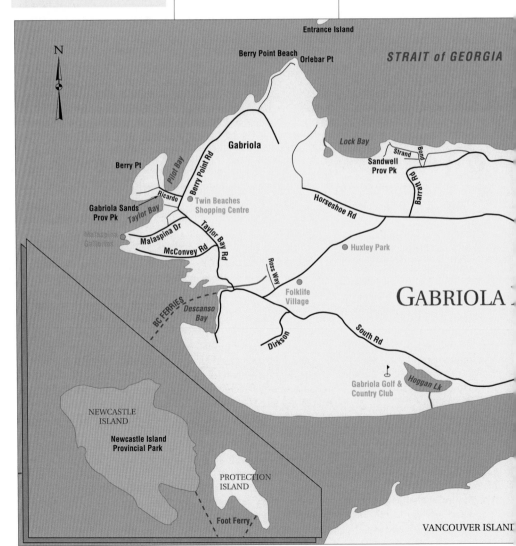

conference, performers who recently produced an original musical, *Gabriola Memories*, and one of Canada's busiest alternative publishers. The island is also headquarters of the Save Georgia Strait Alliance and site of the Gulf Islands' first custom museum building (planned for opening 1995).

The route recommended here heads around Gabriola following North Road to the southern end and returning via South Road. However, a side trip along Berry Point Road starting near the ferry dock visits many points of interest, and is a good choice for a short visit. Other brief side trips are suggested to Sandwell and Drumbeg provincial parks.

Ferry Area

Arriving at Gabriola's unobtrusive Descanso Bay dock, the

Gabriola Information

Size: 599 square kilometres
Population: 2,625 in 1991, now over 3,000
Visitor Information: Gabriola Travel Infocentre, 575 North Road, Folklife Village (phone/fax, 604-247-9332)

first thing you notice is the White Hart Pub. Mark this as a good place to while away time when waiting in the departing

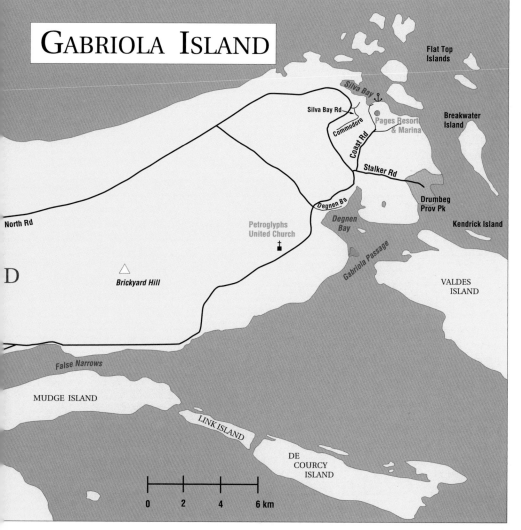

GABRIOLA ISLAND

Flat Top Islands

Silva Bay

Silva Bay Rd

Commodore

Pages Resort & Marina

Breakwater Island

Coast Rd

Stalker Rd

Drumbeg Prov Pk

North Rd

Degnen Ba

Petroglyphs United Church

Degnen Bay

Kendrick Island

D

Brickyard Hill

Gabriola Passage

VALDES ISLAND

False Narrows

MUDGE ISLAND

LINK ISLAND

DE COURCY ISLAND

0   2   4   6 km

Gabriola Access

Ferry: From Nanaimo Harbour to Descanso Bay, about 17 departures daily (30 minutes). Nanaimo ticket booth (604-753-9344).

Boat moorage: Government docks at Degnen Bay and False Narrows; Page's Resort and Marina (604-247-8931).

Eccentric Islanders?

GULF ISLANDERS HAVE a reputation for eccentricity which some of them work hard to retain, and Gabriola is not without examples of this. In 1910, phone service started, using party lines with as many as 30 subscribers. Mrs. Bennett was notorious for listening in whenever she was bored, so it became routine for islanders to say in the middle of their calls, "You can hang up now Mrs. Bennett." She would often say, "It wasn't me," but never realized that other callers could always recognize when she was on the line—her grandfather clock had such a loud tick it could always be heard.

More recently, Gabriola hit the national news when some of its residents challenged the local noise bylaw. It seems that one of the things that the bylaw mentioned was whistling. That did it. Certain islanders sat out on their porches and whistled merrily, others played whistles and sang and tapped their feet; in fact, the wording of the bylaw prompted quite a party. We didn't hear if anyone was actually charged, or whether the birds were expected to comply.

A Literary Island

THE GULF ISLANDS are known as a haven for artists of all kinds, but Gabriola seems to have more writers per capita than any of the others. Perhaps they are just more visible and vocal? Consider the evidence.

- It may have all started with Malcolm Lowry, who immortalized the island in the title of his book, *October Ferry to Gabriola* (though the protagonists never actually arrive on the island).
- There are a couple of extremely active small publishing companies, one of which (New Society) has more than 80 titles in print.
- There are no fewer than three rival newspapers: The *Flying Shingle*, *The Sounder*, and the *Gabriola Times*.
- The widely distributed alternative quarterly *New Catalyst* is published on the island.
- The island has numerous poets, playwrights, short story, novel and children's writers, and songwriters.
- The Women's Writers Group has published a collection of its writings, under the title *Undercurrents*, and hosts a women's writers conference.
- There is a Writers' Faire annually.
- Apart from Salt Spring, this is the only island with a substantial bookstore (Raspberry's), where you can find all the locals' work.

Millstones

SEVERAL LARGE sandstone millstones in the White Hart car park remind us of an unusual quarrying industry. Between 1931 and 1936, between 400 and 1,000 millstones (depending on memories of former workmen) were shipped from the island. The stones weighed about three tons each and were extracted from a neighbouring quarry nearby by means of a giant rotary saw. Quarrymen earned about $3 a day, and the noise could be heard for miles. The stones were used to smash up trees in pulp mills in Ocean Falls and Powell River on the mainland, and larger stones were sent as far away as Finland. They commanded around $500 apiece until the bottom dropped out of the business with the development of artificial stones. The stones that are still around were defective ones, which proved to contain concretions that made them uneven.

A faulty millstone got left behind

ferry line, which literally passes its door. The pub often has live entertainment in the summer.

The car park behind the pub is in the island's original sandstone quarry, where stone was cut and shipped to Victoria and elsewhere. A short distance beyond the pub, the first road on the left is Taylor Bay Road; turn left for a side trip, or continue for services and the main part of the island.

Side Trip to Malaspina Galleries (3 km)

Drive down Taylor Bay Road and turn left on Malaspina Drive. Park at the end (be sure not to obstruct the private dri-

veways) and follow the signed trail to the point. A short walk between high hedges soon brings you to a headland and beach. Follow the beach to the left, and around the corner you will suddenly find yourself in the galleries.

After your visit, return to Taylor Bay Road and turn left.

Malaspina Galleries to Berry Point (4 km)

A short distance along Taylor Bay Road is Twin Beaches Shopping Centre, on the right.

With a bank, grocery store, liquor store, restaurant, and other shops and services, this centre provides most of the visitor's necessities. A mini-golf course can keep the children amused. A flea market and craft tables are set up in summer. The most interesting outlet here is the non-profit Gabriola Artisans cooperative. Twelve local craftspeople whose work is on display take it in turn to work the sales desk. It's an interesting place to browse and the artists are ready to chat and

Malaspina Galleries

THE MALASPINA GALLERIES were once considered one of the great wonders of the western world. It is as though a giant curling wave has been turned into stone. The site has been a sacred and spiritual place for the aboriginal people who buried their dead here, and so impressed the Spanish captain Galiano that in 1792 he sketched it in his journal.

The galleries are a sea cave, 70 metres long and four to five metres high. The cave floor, a wave-eroded platform just above the high-tide mark, has probably formed since the Ice Age. The spectacular wide roof overhang is fluted and curled like a breaking storm wave. The whole cave is eroded in sandstone, of which the top few centimetres have been hardened by mineral solutions carried by ground water, while the softer lower parts have been more readily eroded. Honeycomb weathering can be seen

Malaspina Galleries, tourist attraction for two centuries

on the floor, wall and even the underside of the sandstone overhang.

Waves, especially in the winter, continue to erode the cave, so don't take any risks. Pieces of hanging rock that have already fallen litter the floor, and at the back of the present cave wall a well-formed fracture dips towards the bay, so that eventually the

whole slab may move.

Gabriolans have been very disturbed by the graffiti that have appeared on the galleries over the years, and in 1993 they spent a great deal of money and time cleaning it up. A strict watch is kept on visitors. Those who deface the site are prosecuted.

Dale Stark of Stark Rageous!

Dale Stark features red and black

IT'S A LONG WAY from teaching school in Toronto to running a second-hand clothing store on Gabriola. But maybe not so far if you are a burnt-out art teacher who decides there are better ways to spend your days.

Dale Stark's artistic training has found an unusual outlet. Stark Rageous! is no ordinary thrift store: this is second-hand clothing with flair. Each month she features a different colour scheme throughout the store. We hit the red and black clothes. What an innovation. Instead of second-hand jumble, you can mix and match coordinates, find hats, shoes, belts, and scarves to accessorize and come out with a completely coordinated outfit and change from $20.

Dale came to Gabriola with poor health and mental fatigue, two children and cat. After a year or two of hard work exercising her outrageous imagination, she is mentally and physically better than she has ever been, and she has found a new career and a peaceful place for family life. Now she needs more wonderful second-hand clothes. When did you last turn out your closet? Want to swap some clothes? Dale's ready and waiting.

Rev. George William Taylor

TAYLOR BAY IS named after Rev. William Taylor, a multi-talented eccentric Englishman who pursued two careers in his life, the church and natural history. Born in Derby in 1854, he trained as a mining engineer. Before coming to Canada in 1879 and entering the ministry. He served various parishes across Canada, while undertaking scientific research whenever he had the opportunity. His wife died while he was living in Nanaimo, and he was so discouraged he contemplated taking his four daughters back to England. Instead, however, he was offered 100 acres on Gabriola and came to live in the area that is now Gabriola Sands Provincial Park.

"Dad tried his hand at farming, but alas he was no farmer," remembered one of his daughters. He rowed to Nanaimo to get groceries, but also learned to provide meat, rake herring in the bay, catch crabs, bake, make jam, and cook raccoons.

At the same time, he continued his scientific work on insects and shells, and was the only member of the Royal Society of Canada living west of Winnipeg. He used this forum to promote the idea of a Pacific Coast biological station. When it was established in Nanaimo he moved off the island to become the station's first curator, and he continued his research there until his death in 1912.

explain each other's work.

The shopping centre is named for the beaches of Gabriola Sands Provincial Park, which may be reached by a short drive down Ricardo Road, opposite the shopping centre.

Continue east on Berry Point Road, turning left when the main road seems to leave the sea. Surf Lodge on the right is one of the largest visitor facilities on the island. The lodge has a licensed dining room that advertises "Olympic class sunset watching." It also hosts the annual Women Writers' Conference on Gabriola.

Berry Point

As you continue along Berry Point Road, there are some lovely views and several places where you can access the rocky beach. The Orlebar Point lookout at the end of the road is spectacular, and fingers of sandstone stretch out invitingly toward the water. This is a favourite picnicking area. In front of the distant (and often snow-covered) mountains of the mainland is Entrance Island, with its lighthouse, just waiting to be photographed. It was first manned by Gabriola pioneer Robert Gray for the sum of $148 per quarter. He had to supply his own boat and row himself to work. It was not always easy. On one occasion the boat capsized in a storm and his assistant was drowned. Near Degnen Bay is a road bearing Gray's name.

If you fancy some fruit, follow the road inland from the point to a spectacular hillside orchard with more than 2,300 trees: apple, pear, plum, and cherry. There's a stand where

The White Hart Pub attracts ferry traffic

Gabriola Sands Provincial Park

Sandy beach at Pilot Bay

THE PARK STRADDLES a narrow neck of land between Taylor Bay and Pilot Bay. With its beautiful beaches, this is the place to swim or sun, and the wide expanse of grass between the beaches means the kids can play frisbee, football, or a host of other games. Many of the picnic tables have lovely sea views. This is a great family spot, but in the middle of the summer come early to stake out a good site. Day use only, no fires. Facilities include washrooms, picnic tables, playground, and fresh water.

you can buy the fruit as well as vegetables and honey. To the right of the orchard along the road, Swineglass Studio (604-247-7415) sells stained glass and art photography.

Return to the junction with North Road. Turn right to re-turn to the ferry; left takes you to see the rest of the island.

North Road to Barratt Road (3 km)

About half a kilometre east of Taylor Bay Road, turn left at the junction of North and South roads. You immediately hit the North Road commercial strip, which stretches for about two kilometres. Gabriola's only garage and mechanic is to be found on the left at the junction, while on the right is

---

Recreational Opportunities

Art and antiques at Page's Marina

Birding: Drumbeg, Gabriola Sands and Sandwell parks, Degnen Bay, False Narrows. Boxing Day bird count. Field naturalists group. Checklist available from Page's Marina (604-247-8931).
Cycling: Gabriola Cycle and Kayak Ltd. (604-247-8277)
Diving: Dive Shop at Page's Marina (604-247-8443)
Fishing: Charter information at Page's Marina (604-247-8931), or check local phone book
Golf: Gabriola Golf and Country Club (604-247-8822)
Mini golf: Twin Beaches Shopping Centre
Hiking: Trail booklet published

by Page's Marina (604-247-8931)
Kayaking: Gabriola Cycle and Kayak Ltd. (604-247-8277)
Playgrounds: Elementary school
Shopping: Craft shops in malls, and several galleries and studios around the island (look for clothing, guitars, jewelry, paintings, photography, pottery, rustic furnishing, sculpture, stained glass, wool fashions, stories tailored to your specifications).
Swimming: Sea at Sandwell Park
Tennis: Courts at Huxley Park

Fogo Folk Art

"**WHAT SHALL WE** make that is silly today?" is the question that Dee and Bob Lauder ask themselves almost every morning. Formerly Saskatchewan farmers (a dried cow pie nailed to the wall proves it), their awareness of the ridiculous side of life has evolved into a flourishing folk art business and a life style they love.

Visitors start to laugh as they ring the door bell of Fogo studio, at 3065 Commodore Way. With a great rattling of chains and clanging of weighted buckets, the gate, instead of swinging open, drops to form a bridge over a pond. The chuckles continue past a ballet-dancing pig, and become guffaws as you are offered a seat on a "vult-chair"— whose arms are wings and chairback the neck and beak of the bird. By the time you are led through a workshop

The Not-So-Business-Like Business Man

containing a chorus line of stools with human legs and introduced to the "family," hysterics may start to set in.

Take, for instance, Hildegarde the Opera Singer. She's actually a drinks cupboard; pull on her bow and her tummy opens to disclose the shelves. Careful though: every time the door opens she sings at the top of her voice. Then there's the Tacky Tourist, the Not-So-Business-Like Business Man, and Mrs. McKool, a telephone answering machine with a difference. Dee and Bob are delighted to spend

Gabriola Events

August
- Salmon Barbecue

September
- Fall Fair
- Gabriola Islander Days

October
- Halloween Fireworks

December
- First Night

North End School, dating from 1927 and now the Women's Institute Hall. First left down Ross Way, you will find Sunstone Pottery with nice wood-fired stoneware displayed in a pretty cottage garden.

Highlights along this strip include Stark Rageous! Thrift Shop in a trailer at the Professional Centre, and Windecker's Restaurant with its antique store next door.

Continue east along North Road, noting Huxley Park with its tennis courts and the Rollo Seniors Centre, named after an old island family who do-

Rocky ledges at Drumbeg Park

nated the land. The recycling centre is appropriately tucked away up Tin Can Alley on the left.

At the junction with Horseshoe Road, stop at 1070 North Road and visit the honesty stand at eft (Earth, Fire and Tears) Pottery. Continue to Barratt Road, where you can turn left and take a side trip to

Sandwell Provincial Park.

Barratt Road to Silva Bay (9 km)

Continue east along North Road through shady woodlands until you reach the

Sandwell Provincial Park

SANDWELL PARK is a quiet day use park, its 12 hectares sheltered except to the northeast. To get there, follow the park signs along Bluewater Road and Bond Street. There are parking spaces at the end of Strand, then a one-kilometre trail to a lovely crescent pebble and sand beach on Lock Bay, which is sometimes warm enough for swimming. A few petroglyphs are worth a hunt along the rocks. The trail is steep in places, and is not suitable for older people or very young children. Facilities include parking, walking trail, beach, picnic area, washrooms. Camping and fires are not allowed.

Fogo Folk Art

time showing off their creations. Be warned, their sense of the ridiculous is so infectious you may never look at life the same way again. And you may wish to join the growing number of individuals and organizations that cannot resist displaying a Fogo CD cupboard, chair, or life-size figure. Just remember that if you really want a chair, you must be prepared to leave an appropriate seat impression so they can do a custom job.

Monique, the dolly on the dock

Taking the plunge at
Malaspina Galleries

settlements at the east end of the island. Look for a little log church on the right opposite Silva Bay Road. This is unusual as it is shared by both Catholics and Anglicans.

The Chapel of Our Lady of Victory and Saint Martin's Church was built in 1912 on land donated by John Silva. Note the painting over the door showing Mary protecting Gabriola with her cloak. At the time of writing, the long established Silva Bay Marina nearby was closed. Fogo Folk Art is close by on Commodore Road; they've not got around to regular studio hours, but just phone ahead (604-247-8082).

Silva Bay to Page's Marina (3 km)

While you were otherwise engaged, North Road has changed into South Road. Follow it to Coast Road, turn left, and carry on to the shore. Page's Resort and Marina is located on the edge of Silva Bay.

Mary's cloak protects Gabriola

Head back on Coast Road and shortly before you reach South Road, turn left on Stalker Road, and take a one-kilometre detour to Drumbeg Provincial Park.

Side Trip to Dr Provincial Park

At Drumbeg you can park close to the sea and picnic on the pebble beaches or stroll the extensive rock ledges at low tide. From left to right lie Breakwater Island, Kendrick Island, Valdes Island, and the narrow exit to Gabriola Passage. The tide currents

Garry Oak

CANADA'S ONLY OAK west of the Rockies, the Garry Oak occurs solely near the southern coast and in a couple of spots in the lower Fraser Valley. It becomes more abundant south of the border, where it is known as the Oregon White Oak. Its name comes from Nicholas Garry of the Hudson's Bay Company, who is also commemorated in two Fort Garrys in Manitoba. Garry probably never saw the species named after him by botanist David Douglas, who considered himself indebted for "kind assistance" he received from Garry on his travels.

The tree's scaly bark, twisted branches, and characteristic leaves make it easy to identify. The acorns are attractive to Band-tailed Pigeons and were eaten by the Salish, who cooked them to remove the bitter flavour.

Garry Oak in Drumbeg Park

Page's Resort and Marina

Ted and Phyllis in the flesh

Ted and Phyllis in the wood

THIS MARINA IS in an area sheltered and protected by the scenic Flat Top Islands, but other than that it looks a fairly standard moorage. However, the dolly hitching a ride on the dock should clue you in to a marina with a difference. This is Monique, a life-sized carved wooden figure from Fogo Folk Art.

Despite being called Page's, the marina is run by Ted and Phyllis Reeve. They've been there for seven years but kept the 50-year-old marina's historic name, and have published a booklet on its history. If by chance neither of them is around, you can try striking up a conversation with their life-size Fogo portraits just inside the door.

Initially a Japanese fish camp, the land came into the hands of the Page brothers in 1943. For years it served as a base for their fishing operations and store, but gradually the visiting boaters increased, and the Pages extended into cabins and camping. Visitors have come to the bay from far

and near, and include a trickle of the famous (Bob Hope, Prince Rainier, Prince Philip, Pierre Trudeau). They probably did not eat at the local eating spot, the Picnic Basket, which proudly advertises "the slowest fast food in the west."

Before coming to Gabriola, Ted spent 20 years as head of BC's kidney transplant program and Phyllis was a university librarian. They are now a well-respected part of the local scene, known not only for the way they run the marina, but for their knowledge of the area and their contribution to the island's cultural scene.

Ted and Phyllis brought with them a love of art, books and music, and they found that running a marina didn't have to exclude those things. In their house (part of which is the marina office) they sell books by island authors and their own pamphlets on birds, island trails and other topics. Their home doubles as the Sandstone Gallery, where you are invited to wander through and view the current show by

well-known artists from around BC. Security is provided by an extremely large Newfoundland dog, who checks visitors out on arrival. Much of the art work is hung on wooden panels behind which lies Ted and Phyllis's beloved and extensive library. The Reeves also hold public concerts in their beautiful living room. *The Islander* tells stories of harpists, classical pianists, and singers giving recitals with a "meet the artist" wine and cheese party afterwards. As we researched this book they were planning a symposium on Malcolm Lowry.

Facilities include moorage, cottages, camp sites; gas, water; basic groceries; scuba shop; art gallery and bookshop; windsurfing, and diving; fishing charter information; phone.

are often strong here; it's common to see small boats struggling through. The park offers over 18 hectares of woodland and rocky shore, and has a fine growth of Garry Oaks. Facilities include trails, rock beaches, and toilets. No camping or fires.

South Road to United Church (1 km)

Return to South Road and turn left. On your right at the next major corner is a Garry Oak, to which islanders have attached a seat and a sign, "Gossip Corner."

On the left, Degnen Bay Road provides a short detour to sheltered Degnen Bay, where there is a government wharf and one spectacular petroglyph.

About another kilometre along, turn right into the grounds of the United Church, to see one of the most accessible petroglyph sites.

United Church to Ferry Terminal (13 km)

South Road runs along relatively level ground close to the shoreline. Mudge Island can be seen across False Narrows. In this area, the remains of the ancient village Senewélets have been excavated.

From 1895 to 1952, brickyards were busy along this stretch. The Dominion Shale, Brick and Sewer Pipe Company of Vancouver started a larger scale operation in 1911. Plans were made for

Stop for a chat at Gossip Corner

production of up to 40,000 bricks a day, and both local workers and imported Chinese living in bunkhouses were

---

Facilities and Services

Emergency Services
- Ambulance: (604-758-8181)
- Police: 604-247-8333
- Fire: (604-753-2423)
- Medical clinic: (604-247-8522)
- Pharmacy: Island Apothecary (604-247-8310) fax (604-247-8313)

Accommodation
- Resorts: Haven-by-the-Sea Resort and Conference Centre (604-247-9211); Surf Lodge Resort and Conference Centre (604-247-9231).
- B&Bs: More than 10 in various parts of the island. Range includes The Captain's Cabin (604-247-8548), with one self-contained suite; Gaviota House

(604-247-9100) with an in-house watercolour exhibit; and Sunset B&B (604-247-2032) "for those who enjoy books, music and serenity." Book direct or via Travel Infocentre (604-247-9332).
- Camping: Gabriola Campground (604-247-2079); cabins and camping at Page's Resort & Marina (604-247-8931); no camping in any of the parks.

Eating Places
There are several eating places to suit different tastes and wallets. Most are on the "main drag" along North Road, for instance Windecker's Restaurant (604-247-2010). Check also the

Blue Unicorn (604-247-9448) at Twin Beaches (variety of fast foods), Olivier's Dining Room at Surf Lodge (604-247-9231), and the White Hart Pub (604-247-8588) by the ferry.

Transportation
- Service: T&T Service Station (604-247-9224).
- Taxi: Gabriola Cabs (weekend shuttle and on call) (604-247-9348).

Other
- Bank: CIBC (and cash machine) at Folklife Village (604-247-9676)
- Liquor outlet: Twin Beaches
- Public washrooms: Folklife Village, paths

employed. A drying kiln 50 metres long could hold 220,000 bricks. At first loads of bricks were pulled by horses to Descanso Bay; later, scows were loaded at the site. Before the yards closed, trucks were making deliveries using the ferry system.

After the junction with Wharf Road, the road climbs away from the water, and glimpses of Hoggan Lake can be seen on the left.

Beyond the lake is Gabriola Golf and Country Club with a beautiful nine-hole golf course. The clubhouse has a deck for summer snacking. Visitors are welcome both to play and use the clubhouse. Facilities include a lounge, snack bar, pro shop and rentals.

Close to Dirkson Road and the RCMP station is the site of the new museum, under construction in 1994 for opening in 1995. Planning has been under way for nearly a decade, and significant collections have been located in the hands of Gabriola residents. The building's entrance will be faced with Gabriola brick, as a result of a successful "brick drive" to bring together stray bricks that are in private hands. Exhibits will present stories of the Coast Salish, the Spanish explorers, pioneers and more recent history. There will also be a small art gallery.

Continue past the junction with North Road and you will soon be at the ferry.

The Magic of Petroglyphs

Petroglyphs fire the imagination

ONE OF THE MOST extensive petroglyph sites on the Gulf Islands is located behind the United Church on South Road. To explore the site, park your vehicle in the church parking lot and look for a level dirt trail that runs north from the church. Follow the trail for about five minutes to reach the bedrock panels. (The trail passes close to a barbed wire fence in places, so be careful.)

You'll know you're at the site when you emerge from the forest into a clearing with bare rock surfaces and are greeted by a mythological sea creature over 2.5 metres long. A number of other figures can be seen on this panel and similarities of style suggest that several may have been carved by the same artist. This is one of the first discoveries made on the site in the 1970s by Mary and Ted Bentley whose book, *Gabriola: Petroglyph Island*, tells the story of this and other discoveries.

There are over 50 intriguing figures in the clearing: geometric shapes, dancing human figures and a variety of animal-like mythological creatures carved into the bedrock. See how many you can find.

Though these carvings are works of art, some have been vandalized and there is talk of limiting access. When you visit, please stick to the paths. Report any vandalism to the Travel Info-centre at Folklife Village.

The Big Fire

IN THE SUMMER of 1938, the "big fire" broke out north of Hoggan Lake. It burned for three weeks within the boundaries of North and South roads and across as far as Brickyard Hill. There was no organized fire department, but volunteers worked 12-hour shifts for four days and nights in an attempt to contain the fire. More than 800 hectares of forest were destroyed. Amazingly, no lives were lost and no houses destroyed. A similar fire today on any of the islands could cause horrendous devastation.

13. Other Islands

Beachcombing on Moresby Island

Ferry travellers often gaze longingly at the multitude of enchanting islands unreachable by ferry, and wonder what they are like and if they can be visited. These little pearls are both similar to and different from their larger cousins. They share essentially the same geology, climate, flora and fauna, but each has its own unique characteristics— perhaps an unusual geographical feature or a rich past full of intriguing people. Generally, the small islands are less developed than the larger ones, giving a visitor the opportunity to experience what the larger Gulf Islands were like before development took place.

Many of the small islands are privately owned, and public access is restricted to the beaches below high tide. We have concentrated on those that can be visited by a scheduled water taxi service, such as Sidney, Portland and Newcastle islands, and a few others with particularly interesting stories. There are also a number of island marine parks that can be reached by non-scheduled water taxi service from larger Gulf islands and centres on Vancouver Island. Powerboats, sailboats and kayaks are all available for charter (though you have to know what you are doing), and some agencies offer tours of the region's waterways, such as the cruising expeditions by catamaran and kayak offered by Canadian Gulf Islands Catamaran Cruises (604-539-2930) on Galiano. Those with their own boats can, of course, explore at their leisure.

It is important to remember that, unlike the other islands described in this book, most of the small islands have no permanent population and thus no facilities or services. You will need to be self-reliant not only in what you pack, but also in your ability to deal with the wide range of emergencies that can be precipitated by health, weather, sea or equipment failure.

If you can't find the time to visit some of the small islands, you can at least enjoy the books of those who have cruised them, and learn about their colourful pasts.

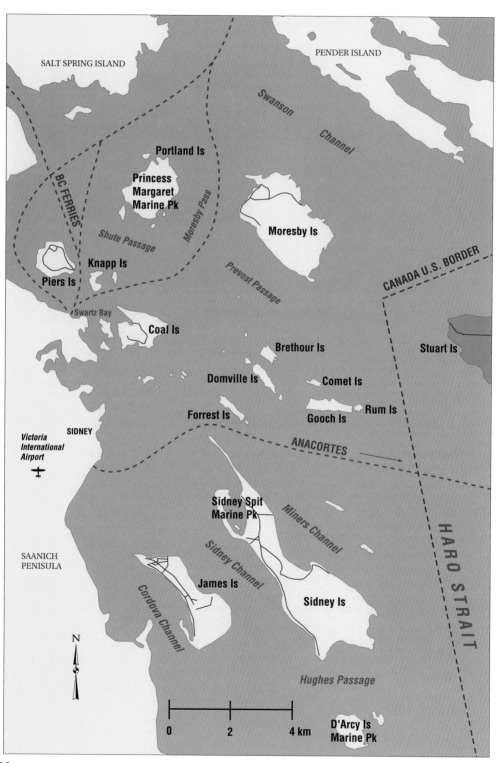

SALT SPRING ISLAND

PENDER ISLAND

Swanson Channel

Portland Is

**Princess
Margaret
Marine Pk**

Moresby Pass

Moresby Is

BC FERRIES

Shute Passage

Prevost Passage

Knapp Is

Piers Is

Swartz Bay

CANADA U.S. BORDER

Coal Is

Brethour Is

Stuart Is

Domville Is

Comet Is

Rum Is

Forrest Is

Gooch Is

Victoria
International
Airport

SIDNEY

ANACORTES

**Sidney Spit
Marine Pk**

Miners Channel

SAANICH
PENISULA

Sidney Channel

HARO STRAIT

Cordova Channel

James Is

Sidney Is

N

Hughes Passage

0   2   4 km

**D'Arcy Is
Marine Pk**

Portland Island

This little gem of an island has recently become accessible by a scheduled (summer only) water taxi, that runs from the government dock in Sidney. Hiking trails criss-cross and circle the island, known as Princess Margaret Marine Park. A walk around the island takes three to four hours. There are sandy beaches on the northwest and southwest shorelines. Beautiful rock-shelf shoreline is exposed on the southeast side at low tide. For campers, water, toilets and primitive sites are provided. Late summer and early fall visitors can enjoy apples from the many fruit trees planted long ago by early Hawaiian settlers—the Kanakas—who, in

Portland from the air

the last century, came to British Columbia on Hudson's Bay ships.

Near the reefs on the southeast corner of Portland Island lies the *G.B. Church*. This vessel was an old coastal freighter, deliberately sunk in August 1991 by the Artificial Reef Society of British Columbia. Dive boats are frequently seen in the area.

The centre of the island has a large clearing, created by flamboyant multi-millionaire, Frank "One-arm" Sutton in the 1920s. Loosing an arm when saving himself and

D'Arcy – Island of Despair

A Chinese leper on D'Arcy Island

A SMALL WINDSWEPT island, located 1.5 kilometres south of Sidney Island in Haro Strait, D'Arcy Island was a desolate, remote home for those people unfortunate to be banished there during the last century. The reason for their banishment was that they had leprosy.

The inhabitants lived in makeshift cabins. Every three months a supply ship provided the residents with their only contact with the outside world. Despair caused some of them to attempt escape in poorly constructed rafts. In 1924, the leper colony was moved to Bentinck Island, 16 kilometres south of Victoria.

Today, D'Arcy Island is a marine park accessible only by boat. On our own visits by boat to the island, we have experienced the same unsettling feeling so many other visitors there have reported. Mysteriously, our anchor has never seemed to hold properly, prompting us to push on and view the island from a respectful distance.

Fogo cowboy, Gabriola Island

comrades from a grenade tossed into his trench at Gallipoli, Sutton received the Military Cross. Having been a railroad contractor in South America before World War I, this indefatigable adventurer became a one-armed golf champion, a Siberian gold prospector, and finally served a Manchurian warlord during the Chinese civil war. Sutton retired to Victoria in 1927; it was reported that he was worth $14 million. His lavish lifestyle included many luxuries, Portland Island being one of them. Here he stocked pheasants for hunting and built a race track and racing stable for 40 horses. Alas, the "Crash of '29" brought an end to Sutton's financial well-being. He returned to China, only to be captured by the Japanese. He died a prisoner in 1945.

Sidney Spit

Sidney Spit Marine Park lies on the northern tip of Sidney Island and is served by water taxi from Sidney. The park is an extremely popular spot for visiting boaters, given its proximity to the many marinas on the Saanich Peninsula. Along the spit, visitors can find thousands of metres of sandy beach suitable for beach-combing and swimming. Twenty-seven campsites are provided, along with picnic tables, toilets and water. Hiking trails through the forested part of the park are a pleasant refuge on a hot summer's day.

Sidney Spit is truly a dynamic place. The relentless forces of strong winds and high tides, particularly during

Sidney Spit and its salt marsh

the winter months, cause ongoing erosion and deposition of materials, altering the shape of the spit and changing the location of sandbars, much to the chagrin of unwary boaters. Pilings have been placed along the narrow neck of the spit by BC Parks in a valiant effort to reduce the erosion.

Newcastle Island

Located in Nanaimo Harbour, this 336-hectare island has been a popular picnic, hiking and camping spot for over 60

years. Access is by a foot passenger ferry that leaves during the summer months from a wharf just off Front Street in downtown Nanaimo.

Interest first developed when a Native brought coal samples from the island to Victoria in 1850. Sir James Douglas immediately seized the area for the Hudson's Bay and, by 1852, loose coal was being collected by Native labourers and exported. Miners from Britain arrived in the same year and named the

S.S. Lakmé *loads with stone at Newcastle Island*

Cults, Sex-slaves and Myth

DE COURCY ISLAND lies between Vancouver Island and the southern tip of Gabriola. In 1929 it became the location of a mysterious colony, followers of the Aquarian Foundation. Its even more mysterious leader—Brother XII—became a figure about whom legends and stories abound.

Vast quantities of gold, it was said, were stashed away on De Courcy by Brother XII. During a widely reported court case in 1933, Brother XII and his wife-of-sorts—the notorious Madame Zee—were accused by some disgruntled Aquarian Foundation members of creating a "Hell on Earth" through whippings and other forms of cruelty. Other stories circulated about women being seduced into leaving husbands and families to join the

colony. Fishermen were afraid to anchor in De Courcy's coves for fear of being shot at or losing female crew members through seduction. These stories and more have been told for over 50 years.

Brother XII, whose real name was Edward Arthur Wilson, was a retired sea captain and devotee of the well-known British theophosist, Madame Blavatsky. He cultivated his early ideas for the Aquarian Foundation in Britain and, through his writings, developed a following which eventually included many wealthy and influential people. He established the Aquarian Foundation colony first on Vancouver Island and later moved it to De Courcy. His final Gulf Island refuge was on the northern tip of Valdes Island. Recent work ques-

tions many of the stories about Brother XII and reveals little or no support for most of them. In fact, Brother XII may have been just your average weird religious cult leader who, because of his own strange ideas, behaviour and reclusiveness, was a natural subject for stories that bordered on myth. It is said by people who really know, that the best Brother XII stories are told after the pubs are closed.

Today a popular marine park exists on De Courcy Island and no new stories have emerged of women being seduced into leaving visiting yachts… so far.

island after one of Britain's major coal cities. Mining developed on a large scale, and the product was shipped as far as San Francisco. In the mid-1870s, large blocks of the island's sandstone were also shipped there for use in building the San Francisco Mint—a building which has survived two major earthquakes and is now a museum. Millstone quarrying, a fish saltery and cannery, and a shipbuilding and repair shop were also part of Newcastle's busy industrial

scene.

In 1931 and for many years after, Newcastle Island was operated as a resort by the Canadian Pacific Railway, when the present dance pavilion was built and the island featured enough picnic tables for 3,500 people. Shiploads of visitors were brought from Vancouver, and were served elegant meals on engraved silverware.

In 1955 the island was purchased by the City of Nanaimo, which passed it on

to the province for a marine park in 1961. It features 18 camping sites, picnic tables, bicycle and hiking trails, swimming, and archeological sites. The historic pavilion, which is wheelchair accessible, has a seasonal concession offering meals and snacks, recreation equipment rentals, and public washrooms.

James Island, A Dynamite Place

Powder plant on James Island

THE ENTIRE 11-kilometre shoreline of James Island, located a few kilometres from the Saanich Peninsula, consists of sandy beaches — perhaps the best in all the southern Gulf Islands. These fine beaches are the result of erosion of the distinctive sand and gravel bluffs, especially on the southern end of the island, where James Spit is forming. This shallow patch of water is a hazard for inattentive yacht crews.

The 315 hectare island was not always so quiet. A Scottish

immigrant, Hugh Munro, was one of the first settlers to farm the arable land on the island, having purchased 201 acres at a dollar an acre in 1874. In 1907, Sir Richard McBride, then Premier of BC, established the exclusive James Island Club, a private hunting and horse racing venue for wealthy Victoria business people.

In 1913, the island was sold to Canadian Explosives Ltd. (now Canadian Industries Ltd.), a company whose products were booming as a result of railroad

and mining expansion. Production of the new explosive TNT, under licence from its inventor, Alfred Nobel, took place on James Island in 1915 to supply the huge demand for explosives during World War I. In 1917, it was TNT from James Island, loaded aboard the French vessel *Mont Blanc*, that exploded early one morning in Halifax Harbour, killing 1,654 people.

At peak production, 800 plant workers and their families lived in a self-contained community on the island. This town continued to function until 1962 when it was dismantled. Many of the residents barged their homes to Saturna, Thetis and the Saanich Peninsula. The plant began to wind down in the 1970s and was dismantled in 1979.

Today the island is privately owned, complete with its golf course designed by Jack Nicklaus. It was purchased by a Seattle area businessman for several million dollars—a far cry from the dollar an acre that Hugh Munro paid 120 years ago.

Wallace Islander Discovers Marilyn Monroe

View south from Wallace Island

PERHAPS THE HEADING stretches the truth, but it is fact that during World War II David Conover, later of Wallace Island, came upon a pretty girl painting wing tips in an aircraft plant in Los Angeles. He was a photographer; she dreamed of being a movie star. He photographed her and persuaded her to pursue modeling, but when he was shipped overseas he lost track of her. Later she became known as Marilyn Monroe.

David Conover had a dream, too. When he was 16, he answered a newspaper ad seeking counsellors for a boys' camp on an island in the "Canadian wilderness." Wallace Island (located between Salt Spring and Galiano) captivated his imagination. In post-war California, his time-clock punching job, mortgage payments and living the American Dream did not measure up to the lure of Wallace Island.

On a belated honeymoon trip from Los Angeles, David and his wife Jeanne learned that the island was for sale. They purchased it and returned to L.A. to prepare for an adventure friends and family thought foolhardy. The overloaded trailer they hauled behind their old car broke down a few blocks from their former house as they tried to depart. Nothing was to come too easy to these intrepid, but naive, pioneers.

Arriving in Victoria, they bought a small, open, gas-powered boat — a crucial item for living on an island. With little sea experience, David nearly died taking the boat from Victoria to Fernwood, on Salt Spring, the closest government dock. After arriving on Wallace and setting up camp, the young couple went in search of the old dug well from the boys' camp days, long since overgrown. David found it by falling into its icy depths, and was rescued by Jeanne just before exhaustion and hypothermia nearly cost him his life. Later, Jeanne

once more saved David's life when she managed to get him, sick and unconscious, from Wallace to the hospital on Salt Spring.

The first winter on the island nearly drove the young couple crazy as each new crisis hit. Ultimately, just mere survival became the goal as their stock of money, then food and finally will almost ran out. "Nothing comes easy on an island" was to become a common refrain of the Conovers. But they did eventually survive to prosper on their island kingdom. Wallace Island developed from their tent site, overlooking Conover Cove, into the Wallace Island Resort, with a comfortable home, a wharf, and cottages and boats for guests to rent. The Conovers' struggles and triumphs are recounted in David's widely read books *Once Upon an Island* and *One Man's Island*.

After 20 years in the resort business, the Conovers sold most of the island to a consortium of property owners, many of whom were former guests. The Conovers built a house on the island's Princess Bay, and retreated to a well-stocked library. Few of the other property owners completed their dreams and, in the 1980s, the province of BC obtained the bulk of the 80-hectare island as a marine park. Today it is a popular destination for cruising boats and kayakers. You can wander about and examine some of the remaining cottages, the water system, the orchards and old tractors—all vestiges of one man's dream—and one woman's patience.

Reference

Information and Reservation Services

- Discover BC travel information and accommodation reservations: 1-800-663-6000
- Tourism British Columbia, 1117 Wharf Street, Victoria, (604-387-1428), provides information on all of British Columbia and publishes useful guides on accommodation, B&Bs, camping, and other specific themes.
- Ministry of Small Business, Tourism & Culture. *British Columbia Accommodations* (comes out annually)
- Chambers of Commerce and other bodies operate Tourist Information Centres on some islands (see individual islands for information)

Bed & Breakfast

The most useful access point is the *Canadian Gulf Islands B&B Reservation Service,* which can book you into more than 100 B&Bs on the Gulf Islands. Write to them at Southwind Drive, Montague Harbour, Galiano Island, BC, V0N 1P0, or phone 604-539-5390. Tourism BC produces a separate Bed & Breakfast guide, which includes some island B&Bs. From 1995 the *British Columbia Accommodations* lists some B&Bs on the Gulf Islands. A number of books present their views on B&Bs, but these are usually selective and may be out of date.

Learning about the Gulf Islands

A few agencies offer formal courses on different aspects of the Gulf Islands. These include:

- Elderhostel - Therah Learning Centre (Galiano): 604-529-2127.
- Gulf Islands Institute for Environmental Studies (Galiano): 604-539-5390.
- Royal BC Museum (604-387-5745) is one of a number of organizations offering educational cruises through the islands.

Recommended Reading

We have listed here the major, generally less technical sources on the Gulf Islands, but not the many books that make passing references to the area, or more than a few of those that describe living and fossil plants and animals that may occur. Wherever possible, we have identified books that are in print, though some titles may only be readily obtainable on individual islands. However, some significant books no longer in print are included. These may be sought in libraries and used book stores. Publication is in BC unless otherwise indicated.

GENERAL

Sweet, Arthur Fielding, ed. *Islands in Trust.* Oolichan Books. 1988.

OUTDOOR RECREATION

Cummings, Al & Jo Bailey-Cummings. *Gunkholing in the Gulf Islands.* Edmonds, Washington: Nor'Westing Inc. 1986.

Obee, Bruce. *The Gulf Islands Explorer: The Outdoor Guide.* Whitecap Books. 1990. (2nd edition).

Pratt-Johnson, Betty. *99 Dives from the San Juan Islands in Washington to the Gulf Islands and Vancouver Island in British Columbia.* Heritage House. 1994.

Priest, Simon & Kimberley Klint. *Bicycling Vancouver Island and the Gulf Islands.* Douglas & McIntyre. 1984.

Snowden, Mary Ann. *Island Paddling: A Paddler's Guide to the Gulf Islands and Barkley Sound.* Orca. 1990.

Wolferstan, Bill. 1989. *Cruising Guide to BC. Volume I. Gulf Islands and Vancouver Island from Sooke to Courtenay. Whitecap Books.* (2nd edition).

MAPS

Canadian Cartographics. *Gulf Islands Visitor and Outdoor Recreation Guide.* Folded map. n.d. [1993].

ITMB Publishing Ltd. *Gulf Islands Recreation Map.* Folded map. 1992.

Other useful maps are available from the Geological Survey of Canada, BC Parks, and other specialized bodies. Consult your local phone directory for the appropriate source. Some of the individual islands publish their own maps.

PERIODICALS

The quarterly *Gulf Islands Guardian* (RR#1, Site K13, Bowen Island, BC, V0N 1G0) publishes articles about all the islands. Special issues on particular themes are sometimes the best summary of information available, and back issues can be obtained. There are two newspapers which range over more than one island *(Gulf Islands Driftwood,* and *Island*

Tides), and most of the islands publish a monthly news magazine of some sort, which can be picked up in local stores or obtained by subscription. Articles on the islands are occasionally published in many other magazines, as well as in specialized scientific and historical periodicals.

EARTH SCIENCES

Eis, S & D. Craigdallie. *Gulf Islands of British Columbia. A Landscape Analysis.* Environment Canada, Forestry Service. 1980.

Ludvigsen, Rolf & Graham Beard. *West Coast Fossils. A Guide to the Ancient Life of Vancouver Island.* Whitecap Books. 1994.

Thomson, Richard E. *Oceanography of the British Columbia Coast.* Ottawa: Dept. of Fisheries & Oceans. 1981.

LIFE SCIENCE

Yates, Steve. *Orcas, Eagles & Kings. A Popular Natural History of Georgia Strait & Puget Sound.* Seattle: Primavera Press. 1992.

Plants

Pojar, Jim & Andy McKinnon, comp & ed. *Plants of Coastal British Columbia.* Lone Pine. 1994. 526 p.

Birds

Campbell, Elaine C., R. Wayne Campbell & Ronald T. McLaughlin. *Waterbirds of the Strait of Georgia.* British Columbia Waterfowl Society. n.d.

Campbell, R. Wayne et al. *The Birds of British Columbia.* Royal British Columbia Museum. 1990. (two volumes so far).

Mammels

McAskie, Ian. *British Columbia Marine Mammal Directory.* West Coast Whale Research Foundation. 1992/3.

ARCHEOLOGY

Bentley, Mary & Ted. *Gabriola: Petroglyph Island.* Sono Nis Press. 1981.

Burley, David V. *Senewélets. Culture History of the Nanaimo Coast Salish and the False Narrows Midden.* Royal British Columbia Museum, Memoir No. 2. 1989.

Carlson, Roy L. & Philip M. Hobler. "The Pender Canal Excavations and the Development of Coast Salish Culture." *BC Studies* 99: 25-52. 1993.

Hill, Beth & Ray. *Indian Petroglyphs of the Pacific Northwest.* Hancock House Publishers. 1974.

HISTORY

Claxton, Captain & Mrs., ed. & comp. *A Gulf Islands Patchwork. Some Early Events on the Islands of Galiano, Mayne, Saturna, North and South Pender.* Gulf Islands Branch, BC Historical Association. 1961.

Gibson, Andrew, ed. Island Heritage. *Gulf Islands Guardian* 4(3) theme issue. 1995.

Graham, Donald. *Lights of the Inside Passage. A History of British Columbia's Lighthouses and Their Keepers.* Harbour Publishing. 1986.

Harker, Douglas, ed. *More Tales from the Gulf Islands. An Anthology of Memories and Anecdotes.* Gulf Islands Branch of the British Columbia Historical Federation. 1993.

Hill, Beth. *Seven Knot Summers.* Horsdal & Shubert.

Handy Numbers for Visitors

BRITISH COLUMBIA'S telephone area code is 604, which is now required for all in-province calls out of the local area.

- Canada Customs: Visitors coming from out of country should check in advance with Customs offices. If travelling by boat and intending to touch land, you must check with one of the Customs entry points, such as Bedwell Harbour (Pender Island), or Sidney or Victoria on Vancouver Island. There are restrictions on a number of items that may be brought in, including fireworks and weapons, and some pets and food items.
- Emergency: Call 911 for ambulance, fire or police on most islands. There is usually a vol-unteer fire department, but not all islands have resident doctors or police.
- Ferries: Information and reservation in Vancouver (604-669-1211), and Victoria (604-386-3431). Local numbers have been listed with the individual islands.
- Hospitals: The Lady Minto Hospital on Salt Spring is the only island hospital. Depending which island you are on, there may be nearer hospitals on Vancouver Island.
- Weather forecasts are available from 604-656-3978, marine forecasts from 604-656-2714.

    For other information, consult the appropriate sections of the guide, or local residents.

1994.

Murray, Peter. *Homesteads and Snug Harbours. The Gulf Islands.* Horsdal & Schubart. 1991.

Ovanin, Thomas K. *Island Heritage Buildings.* Islands Trust. 1987.

Reimer, Derek. *The Gulf Islanders.* Sound Heritage Vol. V (4). 1976.

BIOGRAPHY (See also specific islands)

Conover, David. *Once Upon an Island.* Don Mills, Ontario: Paperjacks. 1967.

—— *One Man's Island.* Don Mills, Ontario: Paperjacks. 1972.

—— *Sitting on a Salt Spring.* Don Mills, Ontario: Paperjacks. 1978.

Garner, Joe. *Never Fly Over an Eagle's Nest.* Oolichan Books. 1980.

Parker, Marion & Robert Tyrrell. *Rumrunner. The Life and Times of Johnny Schnarr.* Orca. 1988.

Stevens, Peter. 1992. *Dorothy Livesay. Patterns in a Poetic Life.* Toronto: ECW Press.

COOKING

Kynaston, Jo. *Cooking in the Gulf Islands.* Sidney, British Columbia: Mermaid Publishing. 1983.

Montgomery, Georgina & Andrea Spalding. *The Pender Palate.* Loon Books. 1992.

Polden, Rodney & Pamela Thornley. *Salt Spring Island Cooking. Vegetarian Recipes from the Salt Spring Centre.* Toronto: Macmillan Canada. 1993.

The Gulf Island Quilt

THE MAYNE QUILTING SHOW is one of the places to view the locally famous "Gulf Islands Quilt." This quilt was made in the late 1950s as a raffle prize to raise money for the publication of a Gulf Islands history book, and actually gave its name to the collection of pioneer stories—*A Gulf Islands Patchwork.* A portion of the quilt is on its cover.

Squares were allotted to craftswomen on all the islands, and each embroidered her favourite scene. The Pender Island Women's Institute did the quilting and the quilt batting was made with pure wool from island sheep. The finished quilt was duly raffled and won by Dr. Adam Beatty. And that was the last heard of it for over 30 years.

After Dr. Beatty's death in the 1980s, his daughter found the quilt among her father's possessions, recognized its historical value, and donated it back to the Gulf Islands Branch of the BC Historical Society. Now it is displayed with pride and delight at many island functions.

FERRIES

Spalding, David and Andrea, Lawrence, P.H.. *BC Ferries and the West Coast.*Altitude Publishing Canada. 1995.

LITERATURE

There are many writers resident on the islands, but most of their published work reflects their diverse interests beyond the islands. We have listed here just a sample of books, mainly by island writers, about specifically island stories. The examples are fiction, as island non-fiction is generally listed in its appropri-

Island Books for Children

Taking your kids for a holiday on the Gulf Islands? You might want to find them some reading about the area. Here are some suggestions:

Alderson, Sue Ann. *A Ride for Martha.* Douglas & McIntyre. 1993. (Salt Spring)

Crook, Marion. *Island Feud.* Toronto: Stoddart Publishing Company. 1991.

Gaetz, Dayle Campbell. *A Sea Lion Called Salena.* Pacific Educational Press. 1994. (Salt Spring)

McFarlane, Sheryl. *Waiting for the Whales.* Orca. 1991.

—*Jessie's Island.* Orca. 1992.

Russell, Ginny. *Voices on the Bay.* Beach Holme Publishers. 1993. (Mayne, Salt Spring)

Scott, Victoria & Ernest Jones. *Sylvia Stark: A Pioneer.* Seattle: Open Hand Publishing Inc. 1991. (Salt Spring)

Woodson, Marion. *The Amazon Influence.* Orca. 1994. (Gabriola)

ate place above in "Recommended Reading." Look also for fiction, non-fiction and poetry by many other island writers, including James Barber, Marlene Cookshaw, Bill Deverell, Sandy Frances Duncan, Joe Garner, Bob Harlow, Beth Hill, Jean Howarth, Stephen Hume, Michael Kenyon, Dorothy Livesay, Daphne Marlatt, Susan Mayse, Andrea Spalding, David Spalding, Ted Stone, Phyllis Webb, and Jack Webster.

Richardson, Bill. *Bachelor Brothers' Bed & Breakfast.* Douglas & McIntyre. 1993.

Rule, Jane. *After the Fire.* London: Pandora Press. 1989.

Thomas, Audrey. *The Wild Blue Yonder.* Toronto: Penguin. 1990.

PLACE NAMES

Walbran, John T. *British Columbia Coast Names 1592-1906.* Douglas & McIntyre. 1971.

VISUAL ARTS

Ainslie, Patricia. *A Lifelong Journey. The Art and Teaching of H.G. Glyde.* Calgary: Glenbow Museum. 1987.

Sketch, Ralph. *Equestrian Sculpture.* Toronto: New Canada Publications. 1986.

Sketch, Marion Ogden. *Ten Moments in Canadian History.* Campbell's Publishing. 1980.

DE COURCY

MacIsaac, Ron, Don Clark & Charles Lillard. *The Devil of De Courcy Island The Brother XII.* Porcépic Books. 1989.

Oliphant, John. *Brother Twelve. The Incredible*

Island News

WHEN ON THE Gulf Islands, only the local papers make sense of the local scene. Where else can you read about the fire at the Miners Bay dock, of the latest 100th birthday among the long-lived Gulf Island residents, of the Island Trust wrangles and of all the current events, from fishing derbies to art shows. Many islands have their own periodical news magazines, like the *Mayneliner,* the *Pender Post,* or *Thetis Island Quarterly.* These are always worth picking up at the grocery stores to take the pulse of the local scene. For a weekly paper, pick up the *Gulf Islands Driftwood* if you want mainly Salt Spring news, or *Island Tides* for news of the outer Gulf Islands.

The advertisements alone are worth the read. Rental equipment, real estate, loggers, and carpet cleaners are cheek by jowl with tarot readers, naturopaths and shiatsu massage therapists (massage therapists on the islands are the real thing and *not* a seedy city cover up). Other adverts offer tantalizing glimpses of enterprising Gulf Island cottage industries. Our favourites include a pottery studio "open sometimes" and a cottage that offers "Sheep Skin Hearthrugs and Farmgate Sales of Island Lamb." The most enigmatic is one that is "Formerly 'the Fish and Chip truck' home delivery" but neglects to specify what it delivers now, probably because everyone on the island already knows!

Story of Canada's False Prophet. Toronto: McLelland & Stewart. 1991.

GABRIOLA
Lewis-Harrison, June. *The People of Gabriola: A History of Our Pioneers.* Friesen. 1982.

GALIANO
Steward, Elizabeth. *Galiano Houses and People: Looking Back to 1930.* Published by the author. 1994.

JAMES
Bond, Bea. *Looking Back on James Island.* Porthole Press. 1991.

MAYNE
Elliott, Marie. *Mayne Island & The Outer Gulf Islands. A History.* Gulf Islands Press. 1984.

PENDER
See Cooking, History and Visual Arts for titles related to Pender.

SALT SPRING
Hamilton, Bea. *Salt Spring Island.* Mitchell Press Ltd. 1969.

Hill, Beth et al. *Times Past. Salt Spring Island Houses and History before the turn of the century.* Published by the author. 1983.

Smart, Anne. *All About Salt Spring Island. A Visitor's Guide.* Published by the author. 1994.

Toynbee, Richard Mouat. *Snapshots of Early Salt Spring and Other Favoured Islands.* Mouat's Trading Co. Ltd. 1978.

Wilson, Rev. E.F. *Salt Spring Island British Columbia.* 1895, reprint n.d.

SATURNA
Howarth, Jean. 1984. *Treasure Island.* Toronto: Penguin.

Murray, Peter. *Home from the Hill. Three Gentlemen Adventurers.* Horsdal & Schubart. 1994.

THETIS
Kelsey, Sheila, comp & ed. *The Lives Behind the Headstones: Glimpses into the History of Thetis Island Through the Lives of the People Buried in St. Margaret's Cemetery.* Green Gecko Electronic Publishing. 1993.

Waiting for the ferry, Lyall Harbour, Saturna Island

Index

A

accommodation, 9-10, 38-39
  Gabriola Island, 141
  Galiano Island, 44, 45-46
  Mayne Island, 63
  Pender Island, 87
  Salt Spring Island, 103
  Saturna Island, 76
  Thetis Island, 125
Active Pass, 48, 68
agriculture
  Mayne Island, 58
Akerman Museum, 113
alpaca ranching, 124
animals, 14, 17, 23-24
Aquarian Foundation, 148
arbutus trees, 125, 128
Ark, The, 118
Artcraft, 115
artists, 34, 38, 50

B

bald eagles, 71, 99
B&Bs, 9
beaches, 17, 20, 21
Bedwell Harbour Island
  Resort, 94
Beech, Dr. Lionel, 110
Bellhouse Provincial Park, 48
Bennett Bay, 67-68
Berry Point, 135-36
bible camps, 123
birds, 18-19, 22, 89, 95
Bittancourt family, 118
Blackburn House, 104
Black-tailed Deer, 24
Bluffs Park, 48-49
Bodega Ridge Trail, 55
Bossin, Bob, 34
Bricky Bay, 90-91
Brother XII, 148
Bullock, Henry Wright, 114,
  117, 120
bumper stickers, 36

C

Campbell Bay, 66-67
camping, 39
canal area
  Pender Island, 93-95, 97, 98

cemeteries
  Galiano Island, 51
  Mayne Island, 63
Centennial Park, 112-13
Central, 116-17
Chapel of Our Lady of
  Victory, 139
climate, 16-17
coal mining, 147, 149
coffee roasting, 127
Collinson family, 64
Collinson Reef, 51
concretions, 123
conglomerates, 98
Conover, David, 150
conservation, 24-25
Corbett, Robert Stewart
  Wallace, 90
Coulthard, Jean, 34
credit cards, 10
Cruikshank, Mr., 41
cuestas, 14
Cufra Canal, 128
cycling, 38

D

D'Arcy Island, 145
David Cove, 65-66
De Courcy Island, 148
Deacon family, 59
Dinner Bay Community
  Park, 70-72
Dionisio Point Provincial Park,
  49, 55, 56
Driftwood Centre, 93, 95
Drumbeg Provincial Park,
  139, 141
Drummond Park, 109, 110

E

East Point Road, 77, 79-80
ecological reserves, 24
economy, 32-33
emergency services
  Gabriola Island, 141
  Galiano Island, 44
  Mayne Island, 63
  Pender Island, 87
  Salt Spring Island, 103
  Saturna Island, 76

  Thetis Island, 125
Enchanted Forest Park, 97
Engelhardt, Judy and
  Jürgen, 67
Enke, Max, 49
erratics, 15-16
Essig, David, 124
events, 40, 42
  Gabriola Island, 137
  Galiano Island, 48
  Mayne Island, 65
  Pender Island, 86
  Salt Spring Island, 109
  Saturna Island, 80
Everlasting Summer, 107
Ewband, Priscilla, 77

F

famous people, 34
farming, 35
Fawkes, Colonel and Lady, 66
Fernhill Road, 66-67
Fernwood, 120
ferries, 7, 8-9
fires, 24, 142
First Nations people, 14, 32,
  99-100, 129
fish plants, 33
Flagstone Gallery, 117
float planes, 104
Fogo Folk Art, 136-37, 139, 140
forests, 22-23, 92
frisbee golf, 96
fruit, 33, 35
Fulford Harbour, 103,
  105-106, 107-108

G

Gabriola Island, 129-42
Gabriola Sands Provincial
  Park, 135
Galiano Festival, 54
Galiano Island, 43-57
Gallagher Bay Road, 69
Ganges, 109-116
gardening, 37
Garry oaks, 139
gas stations, 10
geology, 14-16, 26
  Mayne Island, 78

Georgeson Bay Road, 51
Georgeson family, 53, 91
Georgina Point Road, 60-61,
   63, 65
gold miners, 58
golfing, 39
   Gabriola Island, 142
   Galiano Island, 51
   Pender Island, 84
   Salt Spring Island, 116
Good Earth Farm, 34
Gowlland Point, 97
Gray, Robert, 135
Grimmer, Dorothy, 88, 91
Grimmer, Neptune, 88, 91
Grimmer, Washington, 86, 87,
   88, 91
guest houses, 38-39, 52
Guy, Jon, 41, 77

H
Haggis Farm Bakery, 77
Hamilton Beach, 93
Hanna Air, 104
Hastings House, 101, 117
Helisen Archeological Site, 94
Hennessy, Tom and Ann, 52
heritage
   protection of, 7-8, 37-38
history, 26-31
H.M.S Ganges, 101
honesty stands, 35
honeycomb weathering, 16
Hooson, Fanny, 28
Hooson Road, 91
Hope Bay, 85-86, 88-91, 89-91
Horton Bay, 68-69
Howarth, Jean, 34
Hummingbird Pub, 50-51

I
"island time," 31
Islands Trust, 38

J
Jackson family, 52
James Island, 149
Japanese people
   on Mayne Island, 70
Jeanne, Marcia, 107

K
Kanakas (people), 145

Karon Wallace, 34
Kuper Island, 6, 121, 123

L
Lady Minto Hospital, 110
lakes, 22
lamb barbecue
   on Saturna Island, 41, 77
Lauder, Dee and Bob, 136-37
libraries, 95
lifestyles, 35-38
light stations, 68
lighthouses, 33
literature, 34
Lowry, Malcolm, 34, 132
lumber industry, 33, 35
Lyall Harbour, 75, 77, 79

M
madrona trees, 128
Magic Lake, 97-98
Magic Lake Estates, 30
Mahon Hall, 115
Malaspina Galleries, 133
marshes, 22
Maude, Commander
   Eustace, 66
Mayne Inn, 67-68
Mayne Island, 58-72
Medicine Beach, 95, 97
millstones, 132
Miners Bay, 58, 59, 60-61, 63,
   64, 69-70
Minto, Lady, 110
money, 10
Montague Harbour, 53, 54
Moore Hill, 125
Mouat family, 111
Mount Baker, 15
Mount Elizabeth Park, 90
Mount Galiano, 53
Mount Maxwell, 109
Mount Norman Regional
   Park, 92
Mount Parke Regional Park, 62
Mount Warburton Pike, 80
mountain ranges, 15
Murcheson family, 50
museums
   Gabriola Island, 142
   Mayne Island, 64
   Salt Spring Island, 105

music, 34

N
Nanaimo Sedimentary
   Basin, 15
natural history, 13-14
Newcastle Island, 147-149
newspapers, 132
Nu to You, 90

O
Old Orchard Farm, 33, 86, 88
orcas, 79
orchards, 33, 35, 135-36
Orlebar Point, 135
Otter Bay, 85
otters, 93
Overend, Miss, 114

P
Page brothers, 140
parks, 24. See also names
   of parks
Paterson, Thomas W., 28
Pender Island, 81-98
Pender Island Disc Park, 96
Pender Island Public
   Library, 95
people, 35, 37
Percival, Spencer, 88
petroglyphs, 27
   Gabriola Island, 129, 142
   Salt Spring Island, 110
Piggott Bay, 69
Pike, Warburton, 78
Pilkey Point, 126
Poetry Festival, 54
Point Comfort Hotel, 66
politics, 38
Porlier Pass Road, 55, 57
Port Washington, 85-87
Portland Island, 145, 147
Pot of Gold, 127
pottery stands, 35
prehistory, human, 26
produce stands, 35
protected areas, 25
publishing companies, 132

Q
quilting, 72
Quiring, Linda, 116

R

recreation, 39
Gabriola Island, 136
Galiano Island, 47
Mayne Island, 62
Pender Island, 84
Salt Spring Island, 105
Saturna Island, 76
Thetis Island, 126
red tide, 21
Reeve, Ted and Phyllis, 140
Reis-Wilcox, Leola, 124
reserves, Indian, 32
restaurants, 10
Gabriola Island, 141
Galiano Island, 44
Mayne Island, 63
Pender Island, 87
Salt Spring Island, 103
Saturna Island, 76
Thetis Island, 125
Retreat Cove, 55
Richardson, Bill, 34
rocks, 14-15
Ruckle, Henry, 101
Ruckle family, 107, 108
Ruckle Provincial
Park, 106-107

S

Salt Spring Centre, 104
Salt Spring Island, 99-120
salt springs, 120
Saltspring Soapworks, 116
sandstones, 33
Sandwell Provincial Park, 137
Saturna Island, 73-80
Saul, Laurie, 124
Schoenfeld, Matthew, 48
sea stars, 96
seals, harbour, 54
Senewélets village, 129
Shell Beach, 53
shellfish, 21
Shingle Bay Fish Plant, 33
shopping
Galiano Island, 44, 46, 47
Mayne Island, 62
Salt Spring Island, 105
Sidney Spit Marine Park, 147
Silva family, 59
Sketch, Ralph, 86

sports. See recreation
S.S. Iroquois, 28
St. Margaret's Cemetery, 126
St. Mark's Church, 116-17
St. Martin's Church, 139
St. Mary Lake, 114
St. Mary Magdalene Anglican
Church, 61
St. Paul's Catholic Church, 119
Stark, Dale, 134
Stark, Sylvia, 115
Stark family, 120
Stone, Ted, 106
Strait of Georgia, 7, 13
Stribley, Harriet and Roger, 88
studios, art, 109
Sturdies Bay, 46-47
Sunset Drive, 118-19
Sutil Lodge, 52
Sutton, Frank, 145, 147

T

Taylor, Rev. George
William, 134
Telegraph Harbour, 125
Thetis Island, 121-28
Thomas, Audrey, 34
Thornton, Pamela, 104
tide pools, 17, 20, 97
tides, 17, 20
time, 31
Tinkerers, the, 67
tourism, 7, 38-39
Mayne Island, 58
Salt Spring Island, 101-102
Saturna Island, 75
transportation, 10-11
Gabriola Island, 132, 141
Galiano Island, 44, 45
Mayne Island, 60, 63
Pender Island, 85, 87
Salt Spring Island, 102, 103
Saturna Island, 75
trees, 22-23
Tumbo Island, 80

U

United Community
Church, 93

V

Vesuvius, 117-18
Village Bay, 59

vocabulary, 36

W

Wales, Gordon, 117
Wallace Island, 150
water conservation, 8
weather, 16-17
Western red cedar, 112
wetlands, 21-22
whaling, 32-33
Winter Cove Provincial Marine
Park, 76
Women's Writers Group, 132
Wood, Paul, 38
writers, 132

Photographic Credits

HISTORICAL IMAGES

British Columbia Archives and Records Services: 26 (C3811), 28 (F5242), 29 (A4588), 30A (B7180), 35B (C7655), 50A (B7915), 64 (B3269), 66 (E7867), 78A (B2557), 101A (A6662), 115 (A1726), 120 (G11), 133B (E1846), 134B (A1855), 145B (F5162), 148 (A337), 149 (G5036)

CONTEMPORARY IMAGES

Chris Cheadle: 18/19, 57A, 58, 59B, 79, 81, 105, 119A, 128B, 138, 145A, 147, back cover top
Janice Cheadle: 85
Georgina Montgomery & Associates: 11A, 15, 17, 23A, 38, 42, 43, 46, 47, 48A&B, 49, 50B, 51, 52, 53, 55A, 56A, 56C, 57B, 59A, 62A&B, 63, 65A&B, 67A&B, 68, 71A, 73, 77A, 78B, 86A, 89A&B, 91, 92, 94, 97, 143, 150, 155
Esther Schmidt: 71B
Dennis Schmidt: 22, 54, 69A, 93, back cover bottom
Andrea Spalding: 121, 124A, 127B
David Spalding: 2, 6, 7, 8, 9, 10, 11B, 12, 13, 14A&B, 16A&B, 20, 21A&B, 23B, 24, 25, 30B, 31, 32, 33A&B, 34, 35A, 37, 39, 40, 41, 55B, 56B, 69B, 70, 72A&B, 77B, 80, 84, 86B, 87, 88A&B, 90, 95, 96A&B, 98A&B, 99, 101B, 102, 104A&B, 106, 107, 108, 109, 110, 112, 113, 114, 116, 117, 118, 119B, 123,124B, 125, 126A&B, 127A, 128A, 129, 132, 134A, 135A&B, 136A&B, 137A&B, 139A&B, 140A&B, 141, 142, 146, 153, front cover and inset

Acknowledgements

Our appreciation goes first to those without whose help we would not have discovered the Gulf Islands and could not have gathered the data for this book: Ed Andrusiak and Sherry O'Hare, David Essig and Milena Campbell, Vic and Phyllis Fafard, Tom and Ann Hennessy, Ellie Thorburn, Pat and Angela Verriour.

Second, we thank the many other islanders—too many of them to list individually— who have gone out of their way to help us. Some are featured in the book, but many others have also cheerfully left aside their urgent concerns to take us to interesting places and give us information we otherwise would not have been able to obtain.

We have also had help in and outside the islands from many agencies, including the BC and Victoria Archives, Pender Library, Victoria Public Library, the Islands Trust, and many Vancouver and Victoria bookstores. Behind all these people are the many Gulf Islanders and others who have collected, photographed, recorded, written, and published data of great importance to the history and natural history of the islands.

A manuscript does not become a book without hard work by many others, and we would like to express our appreciation to Stephen Hutchings and his staff at Altitude for their unfailing enthusiasm.

The Authors

The four principal authors all live on Pender Island, and wrote the Pender chapter in tandem. Andrea, David and Lawrence are also co-authors of Altitude's SuperGuide to the BC Ferries.

Andrea and David Spalding write together and individually. Andrea has written several books for children, two

David and Andrea Spalding

Lawrence Pitt and Georgina Montgomery

cookbooks, and a biography. David's book *Dinosaur Hunters* is the most substantial of his writings in the natural sciences. They also operate Arbutus Retreat Bed & Breakfast, and are folk musicians and storytellers, well-known as Brandywine. Andrea led the work on Gabriola, Salt Spring and Thetis, and David, as well as coordinating the project, has led the work on introductory and reference sections.

Georgina Montgomery and Lawrence Pitt moved to Pender in 1990 after several years of cruising Gulf Island waters. Georgina has written several articles and co-wrote *The Pender Palate* with Andrea. Lawrence's papers in plasma physics ably prepared him for this, his first popular writing project. Together they have led the work on Galiano, Mayne and Saturna, and Lawrence on the other islands.

Ed Andrusiak has contributed the petroglyph sections, and John Godfrey several geological stories.